TURNING **HIGH-POVERTY** SCHOOLS INTO **HIGH-PERFORMING** SCHOOLS

William H. Parrett
Kathleen M. Budge

TURNING HIGH-POVERTY SCHOOLS INTO HIGH-PERFORMING SCHOOLS

ASCD

Alexandria, Virginia USA

ASCD®

1703 N. Beauregard St. • Alexandria, VA 22311-1714 USA
Phone: 800-933-2723 or 703-578-9600 • Fax: 703-575-5400
Website: www.ascd.org • E-mail: member@ascd.org
Author guidelines: www.ascd.org/write

Gene R. Carter, *Executive Director;* Judy Zimny, *Chief Program Development Officer,* Gayle Owens, *Managing Director, Content Acquisitions and Development,* Scott Willis, *Director, Book Acquisitions & Development;* Genny Ostertag, *Acquisitions Editor;* Julie Houtz, *Director, Book Editing & Production;* Darcie Russell, *Senior Associate Editor;* Greer Wymond, *Senior Graphic Designer;* Lindsey Smith, *Graphic Designer;* Mike Kalyan, *Production Manager;* Valerie Younkin, *Desktop Publishing Specialist;* Kyle Steichen, *Production Specialist*

Printed in the United States of America. Cover art © 2012 by ASCD. ASCD publications present a variety of viewpoints. The views expressed or implied in this book should not be interpreted as official positions of the Association.

All web links in this book are correct as of the publication date below but may have become inactive or otherwise modified since that time. If you notice a deactivated or changed link, please e-mail books@ascd.org with the words "Link Update" in the subject line. In your message, please specify the web link, the book title, and the page number on which the link appears.

PAPERBACK ISBN: 978-1-4166-1313-8   ASCD product #109003   n01/12

Also available as an e-book (see Books in Print for the ISBNs).

Quantity discounts for the paperback edition only: 10–49 copies, 10%; 50+ copies, 15%; for 1,000 or more copies, call 800-933-2723, ext. 5634, or 703-575-5634. For desk copies: member@ascd.org.

Library of Congress Cataloging-in-Publication Data
Parrett, William.
    Turning high-poverty schools into high-performing schools / William H. Parrett, Kathleen M. Budge.
        p. cm.
    Includes bibliographical references and index.
    ISBN 978-1-4166-1313-8 (pbk. : alk. paper)   1. Poor children—Education—United States. 2. Children with social disabilities—Education—United States.   3. School improvement programs—United States.   4. Academic achievement—United States.   I. Budge, Kathleen M. II. Title.
    LC4091.P36 2011
    371.2'07—dc23

                                                                                2011028954

20 19 18 17 16 15 14 13   2 3 4 5 6 7 8 9 10 11 12

To our children: Mia, Jonathan, Katrina, Nathaniel, and Ashley; and our parents: Carey, Jan, Oscar, and Carlene.

We love you.

TURNING HIGH-POVERTY SCHOOLS INTO HIGH-PERFORMING SCHOOLS

Part III | Working Together: Continuing the Commitment to Lead Underachieving Students in Poverty to Success

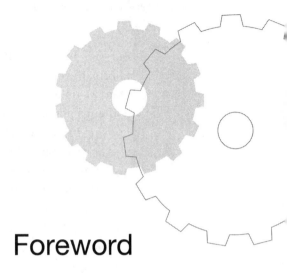

Foreword

Early in my career as a school administrator, I was standing in front of the faculty in an after-school staff meeting to present data about the achievement of our students. I was working the room to engender a dialogue about what we were going to do about the gaps in the numbers. The numbers, frankly, suggested we weren't serving many of our students very well. This was the late 1980s and the education field was embarking on the era of standards, just post–*Nation at Risk*, and beginning to incorporate data on student performance in conversations about improvement. Our school, while facing circumstances nowhere near as difficult as many of the schools chronicled in this volume, worked with a student population that was among the poorest and most racially and linguistically diverse in our small city district.

As I stood at the overhead projector and began to present the data on student achievement, some hands started to go up in the back of the meeting room. The questions went something like this (and I'm paraphrasing to condense the commentary): "I know many of our kids struggle, but they come to school way behind other kids. How can you expect us to teach those kids to the same level as kids who have two parents, get breakfast every morning, and have adequate support to get their homework done every night? We just can't do it all!" While I'm sparing you a lengthier diatribe, this was the tenor of many comments from a concentrated group of faculty members. This group, despite stating mainly good intentions for trying to do the right thing for our students, just couldn't get past the difficult circumstances and learning needs our kids brought with them to school every day. Unfortunately, despite my efforts, the conversation deteriorated into blaming the kids and their circumstances instead of talking about owning the problems that we saw in our data and engaging in efforts to shift practice that could be powerful for the kids. Looking back, it was a failure of my early leadership for sure, but the episode was an example of how our beliefs about what is possible for children's learning hamper our efforts to teach all kids.

The confused wisdom of *some* (not all, let me emphasize) of my educational elders in the room that day, regrettably, was that what we needed to be most effective in ensuring adequate learning growth in our students was *better students.* By "better students," this group was implying that we needed kids raised in more affluent socioeconomic circumstances; kids from two-parent, traditional, nuclear families, who benefited from a "Leave It to Beaver" home environment where dad was the breadwinner and mom stayed home to tend the children. The idea was that we needed kids with many of the privileges afforded to those called the "haves" and fewer of those kids who hailed from families who are characterized as "have-nots." Latent in the dialogue among a *few* (again I emphasize) of our mostly white, mostly middle-class teachers was that we would do a lot better if we only had fewer of "those" minority kids, many from immigrant families from Southeast Asia who came to school without English as a first or second language and who had begun populating the apartment complexes in our immediate neighborhood. And if those few teachers could just have the pleasure of teaching a batch of kids from better circumstances, who looked and talked more like they did, by golly, they'd do a heck of a job of educating them.

I want to believe that the profession has traveled far from that late 1980s faculty meeting conversation. Certainly, the book you are about to read is predicated on an argument that absolutely and completely refutes the claims I heard from some of my faculty that day. Building on long-standing work done by organizations like the Education Trust and scholars studying how schools manage to teach virtually all children well, what Bill Parrett and Kathleen Budge have rendered is an analysis and an accompanying tool kit for understanding how schools all over the United States manage to realize outstanding student achievement results among high-poverty, high-minority populations.

What this volume reinforces for the field are foundational ideas that compose a sort of recipe for success in serving all children's learning needs. The argument goes something like this: (1) experience from the high-poverty, high-performing (HP/HP) schools that Bill and Kathleen chronicle tells us that all children *can* learn at high levels, regardless of their race, socioeconomic background, language, family situation, or (pick your descriptor);

(2) for children from a diverse spectrum to learn at high levels, they need to be taught by people in schools who believe they can learn, who approach teaching with the idea that students will learn if taught well, and who take seriously an ongoing effort to improve their practice in line with best thinking and examples in the field; and finally, (3) for teaching of this kind to be realized across a whole school (or system), leadership at the school and district needs to be squarely focused on supporting the improvement of teaching in an ongoing, routine way.

A simple recipe, but complex to implement, yet powerfully rendered here. Much of my work in education has been dedicated to teaching and to the research that supports ways to make these simple ideas come to life in practice. Bill and Kathleen synthesize learning from research and practice that specifically highlights the moves that leaders take in schools and systems that have realized significant growth in learning for all kids, regardless of their race, language, or socioeconomic status.

I wish I had this book in my hands to give to my faculty that day back in the late 1980s. For all educators and practitioners reading these ideas now, take them to heart and put them into practice.

—Michael Copland
Associate Professor and Chair of Educational Leadership and
Policy Studies, College of Education, University of Washington

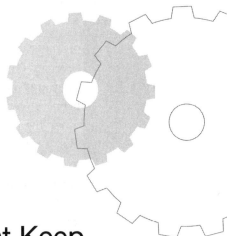

Introduction: We Must Keep Asking the Questions

The work of improving schools is about thinking... and asking questions.

—*Andres Alonso, chief executive officer,*
Baltimore City Public Schools

As a nation, are we content that 70 percent of our entering 9th graders read below grade level? Is it acceptable that one out of every three minority students attends a high school where 40 percent of the students drop out? Are we willing to continue spending $2.6 billion a year replacing teachers, half of whom choose to leave the profession before they begin their sixth year in a classroom? Can we excuse the fact that kids are twice as likely to be assigned to inexperienced or uncertified teachers in schools with large enrollments of poor and minority students? As a country and as a profession, we have not systematically asked these questions, let alone answered them. The Alliance for Excellent Education (2010) and many others would say public education is in crisis, and we agree.

Overcoming the Crisis

Yet our crisis is one that is being successfully countered in hundreds of public schools across the United States. These schools enroll high proportions of underachieving children and adolescents who live in poverty but have reversed long-standing traditions of low achievement and high dropout rates. They are "models of the possible," where the mind-set of "it's impossible" has been proven wrong. They provide blueprints for improvement from which other high-poverty schools can learn. More important, these schools are places where students who live in poverty experience success, which leads to optimism, hope, and self-efficacy. In these schools, the crisis *has* been overcome, because the educators sought to control what they could, held high expectations for student learning, and supported their students in surmounting the debilitating effects of poverty on learning.

Still, what of the thousands of other underachieving students living in poverty and failing in schools that have yet to transform? The plight of these children and adolescents *should* surely capture our attention. Their plight *should* become a priority of policymakers, parents, taxpayers, and other stakeholders. And it *must* capture the attention of educators, whose profession is arguably paramount to preserving our democracy. As a profession, we are poised to significantly improve all of our schools; we know enough and possess the capacity to do so. The question of whether we do is not one of knowledge and skill, but of will.

Improving schools alone can make a significant difference in reducing poverty. Yet systemically eliminating poverty is a *both/and* proposition, because transformation must occur in *both* the broader society *and* in schools. Educators must *both* become knowledgeable about issues related to poverty in the broader society *and* take action where they can have the most influence—in their own schools and school systems. As a profession, the question we must consider is not "Can schools solve all of society's perpetual problems, chief among them high rates of poverty?" Rather, the question is "Are we doing our part?" Must we, as a society, address poverty before we can improve schools? High-performing, high-poverty (HP/HP) schools demonstrate that successfully educating students who live in poverty significantly counters many barriers posed by poverty and improves children's life chances. Isn't that proof enough to compel us to act?

How to Use This Book:
Learn Together, Lead Together

High-poverty schools do not become high performing by tinkering their way to success. As Harold Ott, former superintendent in Lapwai, Idaho, described his elementary school's journey: "We could not continue to do what we knew would at best only minimally raise student achievement... and for only some of the kids. We simply had to fundamentally change the way we did business."

We have written this book to support schools in "doing business differently." Those in high-poverty schools can benefit from the information provided in this book, as can anyone working in a school where an achievement gap exists between students who live in poverty and their more advantaged peers. For your school to become high performing and to close the achievement gap, all of the theory, research, and practical ideas in this book must be applied to your unique context. Learning to do business differently in your school entails applying the information provided here to your situation. Throughout the book we have provided tools to help you do so.

The book is organized in three parts. Part I, Learning Together: Getting Ready to Lead Underachieving Students in Poverty to Success (Chapters 1 through 4), lays the groundwork for informed conversations among colleagues and future action planning. Although an individual can gain valuable knowledge, we encourage school stakeholders to learn together. These chapters provide information about poverty and the optimistic message that schools can and do make a difference.

In Part II, Leading Together: Taking Action to Lead Underachieving Students in Poverty to Success (Chapters 5 through 10), we provide specific examples of the actions that leaders in HP/HP schools have taken to build leadership capacity, foster the necessary learning environment, and improve learning. Integrated throughout these chapters is the manner in which these actions appear to influence the school's culture (values, beliefs, and norms). For each arena of action, we provide a chapter related to what leaders *stopped* doing or eliminated and a chapter focused on what they *started* doing or improved. Each of the six chapters includes a self-assessment rubric that can be used to assess your school's current situation, as well as to guide your reading and discussion. Additionally, a planning template is provided at the conclusion of each chapter to help you determine your next steps.

Throughout the six chapters of Part II, a number of inserts highlight the practical applications of strategies used in HP/HP schools. These highlights include Uncommon Sense (novel approaches to problem solving), School Culture Alerts (strategies for improving the culture of a school), and District "Ad-vantage Points" (successful supportive practices that a district could initiate to assist low-performing, high-poverty schools). In addition, end-of-chapter lists of recommended actions appear as Action Advice.

Uncommon Sense

As noted earlier, there is an extensive knowledge base from which we as educational leaders can gain insight into our own school improvement work, *and* there is no silver bullet. Leaders in the schools we studied consistently considered the research base in the context of their own schools. They also used strategies that were uncommon but made sense in the school context. We call this out-of-the-box thinking "uncommon sense." In the following chapters, we share specific examples of leaders using uncommon sense, which may prompt others to think creatively about how they might apply the Framework for Action described in this chapter to their unique setting. For example, the principal at Lapwai Elementary School used uncommon sense by hiring a local school bus driver to tutor students in reading.

School Culture Alerts

Because changes in a school's culture are inextricably linked with changes in action—and because culture is difficult to see—we use School Culture Alerts in Chapters 6, 8, and 10 to highlight actions taken by leaders in HP/HP schools that seem to lead to change. These alerts may provide insight into the opportunities other leaders have to improve their school's culture.

The District's "Ad-vantage Point"

Although research has begun to provide needed insight into the district's role in supporting high performance systemwide (Knapp et al., 2003; McFadden, 2009), the vast majority of our information regarding what works for educating students who live in poverty continues to originate from the school level. The Framework for Action takes an "inside out" look at effective practices at the school level that have implications for leadership needed at other levels of the system (district, state, regional, national). These implications are especially important for those education leaders who serve at the district level.

In many instances, school-level leaders have the authority to create the structures and processes needed to build leadership capacity within their school. Then again, in many other schools, school-level leaders report that district personnel, as well as district policies and procedures, place limitations on their authority, pose unintended barriers, or create inefficiencies. As one principal in an urban, high-poverty school described the problem in her context, district-level leaders continued to send pallets of workbooks linked to the district-adopted curriculum although the school had adopted a comprehensive school reform model with an altogether different set of curricular materials. Several pallets of shrink-wrapped, unused workbooks were stored in the school's basement. The principal explained, "It was less trouble to store the workbooks in our basement than to fight the system and send them back to the central office." Throughout Chapters 6 through 10, we have inserted ideas, talking points, tips, and considerations for those who lead from the vantage point of the district office. Such a vantage point, as we see it, is an "advantage" that district-level leaders could use to support site-based leaders.

In Part III, Working Together: Continuing the Commitment to Lead Underachieving Students in Poverty to Success, we briefly reiterate the interactive, dynamic nature of the components of the Framework for Action and challenge all of us—educators and other stakeholders—to confront the reasons we have not yet ensured that every high-poverty school is high performing. Finally, we foreshadow the current research focused on moving beyond improvement in individual schools to improvement of entire systems at the district, regional, state, and national levels.

Begin by Taking Stock: What's Your School's Story?

Allow time to reflect on your unique situation as a school, department, grade-level team, collegial cluster, or individual by completing the self-assessments, Assessing Our Ability to Take Action, that appears in Figure I.1 and Assessing Our Willingness to Take Action in Figure I.2. The self-assessments are based on what we know about how leaders facilitate organizational change. We hope the assessments will provide support in two ways—first, by generating data related to your school's readiness to undertake an improvement effort, and second, by guiding your use of the resources and information provided in this book.

A school's readiness to benefit from a change initiative refers to how committed people are to the change and how capable or efficacious they believe themselves to be. In other words, the current state of a school's readiness to benefit from any change effort can be examined by assessing two factors: ability and willingness. There are many ways to evaluate both. The assessments elicit beliefs about an individual's *ability and willingness* to work with students who live in poverty, together with his beliefs about his colleagues' *abilities and willingness* to do so. It is a tool that provides leaders with information about the gap, if any, between an individual's beliefs about himself and beliefs about his colleagues. It also gauges stakeholders' beliefs about specific topics and issues presented and discussed in this book.

Although the questions in the assessment are designed to help you assess your school's readiness to benefit from change, this does not mean

FIGURE I.1	Assessing Our Ability to Take Action

Please rate each statement from highly unlikely (-3) to highly likely (3).

1	I have a good understanding of what is meant by "living in poverty" in the United States and in my local school. -3 -2 -1 0 1 2 3	My colleagues have a good understanding of what is meant by "living in poverty" in the United States and in my local school. -3 -2 -1 0 1 2 3
2	I know the percentage of students in my school who live in poverty and who, of those students, are underachieving. -3 -2 -1 0 1 2 3	My colleagues know the percentage of students in our school who live in poverty and who, of those students, are underachieving. -3 -2 -1 0 1 2 3
3	I know how poverty affects lives and learning. -3 -2 -1 0 1 2 3	My colleagues know how poverty affects lives and learning. -3 -2 -1 0 1 2 3
4	I can provide a research-based answer to the question "How do schools make a difference in the lives of students who live in poverty?" -3 -2 -1 0 1 2 3	My colleagues can provide a research-based answer to the question "How can schools make a difference in the lives of students who live in poverty?" -3 -2 -1 0 1 2 3
5	I know how high-performing, high-poverty schools develop the leadership infrastructure necessary for improvement. -3 -2 -1 0 1 2 3	My colleagues know how high-performing, high-poverty schools develop the leadership infrastructure necessary for improvement. -3 -2 -1 0 1 2 3
6	I know how high-performing, high-poverty schools develop a safe, healthy, and supportive learning environment for students and adults. -3 -2 -1 0 1 2 3	My colleagues know how high-performing, high-poverty schools develop a safe, healthy, and supportive learning environment for students and adults. -3 -2 -1 0 1 2 3
7	I know how high-performing, high-poverty schools improve student learning, support adult learning, and "work smarter" as a system. -3 -2 -1 0 1 2 3	My colleagues know how high-performing, high-poverty schools improve student learning, support adult learning, and "work smarter" as a system. -3 -2 -1 0 1 2 3
8	I know which mind-sets, practices, policies, and structures perpetuate underachievement and how high-performing, high-poverty schools eliminate them. -3 -2 -1 0 1 2 3	My colleagues know which mind-sets, practices, policies, and structures perpetuate underachievement and how high-performing, high-poverty schools eliminate them. -3 -2 -1 0 1 2 3
9	I can describe the beliefs, values, and norms that constitute a school culture conducive to the success of students who live in poverty. -3 -2 -1 0 1 2 3	My colleagues can describe the beliefs, values, and norms that constitute a school culture conducive to the success of students who live in poverty. -3 -2 -1 0 1 2 3

FIGURE I.2	Assessing Our Willingness to Take Action

Please rate each statement from highly unlikely (-3) to highly likely (3).

1	I believe I make a difference in the lives of my students, despite the challenges some of them face. -3 -2 -1 0 1 2 3	My colleagues believe, as teachers, they make a difference in the lives of students, despite the challenges some of those students face. -3 -2 -1 0 1 2 3
2	I believe I am professionally responsible for learning and all students can meet high academic standards in my classroom, despite the challenges some of them face. -3 -2 -1 0 1 2 3	My colleagues believe they are professionally responsible for learning and all students, despite challenges, can meet high academic standards in their classrooms. -3 -2 -1 0 1 2 3
3	I believe redistributing resources schoolwide would help us better meet the needs of students who live in poverty. -3 -2 -1 0 1 2 3	My colleagues believe redistributing resources schoolwide would help us better meet the needs of students who live in poverty. -3 -2 -1 0 1 2 3
4	I believe learning more about how poverty influences life and learning would help us better meet the needs of students who live in poverty and are underachieving. -3 -2 -1 0 1 2 3	My colleagues believe learning more about how poverty influences life and learning would help us better meet the needs of students who live in poverty and are underachieving. -3 -2 -1 0 1 2 3
5	I believe working more collaboratively would help us better meet the needs of students who live in poverty and are underachieving. -3 -2 -1 0 1 2 3	My colleagues believe working more collaboratively would help us better meet the needs of students who live in poverty and are underachieving. -3 -2 -1 0 1 2 3
6	I believe our school has an organizational climate that encourages innovation, risk taking, and professional learning. -3 -2 -1 0 1 2 3	My colleagues believe our school has an organizational climate that encourages innovation, risk taking, and professional learning. -3 -2 -1 0 1 2 3
7	I believe our school staff is open to new ideas and willing to make changes, even changes of significant magnitude. -3 -2 -1 0 1 2 3	My colleagues believe our school staff is open to new ideas and willing to make changes, even changes of significant magnitude. -3 -2 -1 0 1 2 3
8	I believe in our ability, as a school, to succeed in making changes, even changes of a significant magnitude. -3 -2 -1 0 1 2 3	My colleagues are confident in our ability, as a school, to succeed in making changes, even changes of a significant magnitude. -3 -2 -1 0 1 2 3
9	I believe our school staff feels a sense of urgency about meeting the needs of all our students, particularly those who live in poverty. -3 -2 -1 0 1 2 3	My colleagues believe our school staff feels a sense of urgency about meeting the needs of all our students, particularly those who live in poverty. -3 -2 -1 0 1 2 3

that if a school isn't ready to change, it should do nothing. Rather, assessing readiness helps leaders tailor their actions to the needs of those whom they lead. For example, if school stakeholders score more positively in terms of their willingness than their ability, leaders may want to initiate conversations and professional development to build knowledge and skills. If the opposite is true, leaders will likely need to address the factors that are influencing a low level of willingness to step up to the challenge of successfully educating their students who live in poverty.

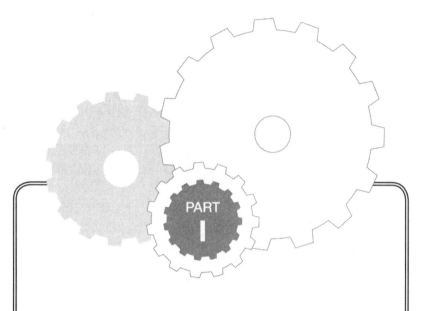

Learning Together:

Getting Ready to Lead
Underachieving Students in Poverty
to Success

Any High-Poverty School Can Become High Performing

William and his four siblings had been homeless for an entire year until they found stable housing. He had a tough transition when he came to our school,... but as he spent more time with his teachers, his achievement steadily improved and the year ended really well; he moved on to the middle school. I was blown away when he came into my office to apologize [for his behavior the previous year]. He told me, "I know that was wrong and that's not the way I want you to remember me." He knows his short time here turned him around, and not just academically. This tough kid now cares how he will be remembered. He knows we cared about him. It's great to be reminded that what we're doing here makes a difference. Every school could be doing this.

—*Andrew Collins, former principal,*
Dayton's Bluff Achievement Plus Elementary School

The kids at Dayton's Bluff Achievement Plus Elementary, a Minnesota school where most of the students' families live in poverty, believe in their school. Once a place where low achievement prevailed, the school now is a model of respect, achievement, and optimism. Getting there wasn't easy. The school embarked on a goal-driven course to counter a host of long-standing obstacles to high achievement, and it succeeded. Indeed, high achievement at Dayton's Bluff Elementary and hundreds of other high-poverty schools across the United States with a similar sense of mission has become what is expected. Yet in many schools, particularly those where a large percentage of the students live in poverty, low achievement continues to be the norm.

A Crisis That Can Be Overcome

Most students who drop out—more than a million a year—leave school between the ages of 14 and 16 after enduring years of schooling in which minimal achievement, frustration, embarrassment, and failure were daily realities. Many simply lose hope, seeing little reason to stay in school. Of the roughly 70 percent who do make it to graduation, it is estimated that only one-third of that group (23 percent of the total) graduate prepared for the demands of the workplace or higher education. Graduation rates for Hispanic (56 percent), African American (54 percent), and Native American (51 percent) students are even more dismal. These rates reflect the failure of public schooling to work for a significant number of our children—our most precious resource (Alliance for Excellent Education, 2010).

Dwarfing the number of students who leave early is the number of kids who remain in school and graduate woefully underprepared for postsecondary education or the workplace. More than two decades ago, Lizbeth and Daniel Schorr (1989) spoke eloquently to this crisis within a crisis, calling for schools to address the critical needs of the adolescents for whom this is true. A parade of national reports, along with countless CEOs and other business leaders, continue to echo this concern today. Combined, the number of students who drop out and the number who are unprepared for life beyond graduation illustrate the crisis that continues to plague the United States.

Not all students who drop out or who underachieve live in poverty, but many do. Despite recent modest progress in student achievement at the elementary and middle school levels, most of our high schools continue to demonstrate little success in closing long-standing achievement gaps between low-income and more advantaged students. Why are so many ambivalent about recognizing, let alone addressing, this crisis? Are the daily needs of underachieving children who live in poverty too immense for most of us to grasp? Are their lives too distant from our own for us to see? Are we too embedded in an unspoken reality of classism and racism, as many argue? What will it take to educate the "whole child" if that child lives in poverty?

Are We Asking the Right Questions?

Our children are the victims of this legacy. They suffer the consequences of a widespread unwillingness on the part of policymakers and education leaders to ask three key questions:

- Why are some high-poverty schools high performing and others not?
- What do we need to do to significantly improve our lowest-performing schools?
- What can we learn from high-performing, high-poverty (HP/HP) schools that can help underachieving students who live in poverty, regardless of where they go to school?

Asking and answering these questions could result in improved educational outcomes for virtually every underachieving child living in poverty. Although federal policy calls for all students to meet their state's established learning standards by 2014 and policymakers in all 50 states have defined proficiency through the use of mandated tests, far too little has been done to create the conditions that research has demonstrated are necessary to ensure that most, if not all, students will meet these standards. Thus our crisis continues, and the questions remain unasked and unanswered.

Solutions Are Out There

Kati Haycock, president of the Education Trust, and her colleagues have observed and studied enough schools like Dayton's Bluff to know that any school, regardless of its condition, has the capacity to reverse long-embedded trends of low achievement. For more than a decade, Haycock has traveled the United States on a mission to help others understand this new reality. As she puts it,

> It is hugely important for both educators and the general public to know how powerful schools can be. And indeed, the stories of schools that serve very poor children, yet produce very high results, provide exactly the tonic of hope and inspiration that help restore the luster of a public education system that has lost considerable public confidence over the last two decades. (Haycock, 2007, p. xix)

Ron Edmonds, Asa Hilliard, Sam Stringfield, Charles Teddlie, and others first wrote and spoke passionately about the same possibility 20 to 30 years ago. Today, joining Haycock, noted scholars Richard Elmore, Daniel Duke, Michael Fullan, Rick Stiggins, and others fervently urge educators to study the successes of high-performing, high-poverty schools to gain authentic insight and guidance regarding their sustained accomplishments.

Learning About the Critical Importance of Leadership

In 2007, Robert Barr and William Parrett synthesized the emerging work of many regarding how low-performing, high-poverty schools become high performing. Their synthesis identified eight strategies that were common to the high-performing, high-poverty schools studied. Of the eight strategies, *ensuring effective school and district leadership* was central to the successful execution of the other seven. (See Chapter 2 for more on the other strategies.)

Building on the contributions of Barr and Parrett, the continuing work of the Education Trust, and that of other scholars, we began a study to develop a greater understanding of the impact, influence, and inner workings of leadership in HP/HP schools. Drawing from the research base, we developed a framework to capture conceptually the function of leadership in these schools. We then selected a small, diverse group of schools against which we could "test"—or in research terms, "member check"—our framework. Each of the schools selected demonstrated significant and sustained gains in academic achievement for at least three years; enrolled 40 percent or more students who qualified for the free and reduced-price meals program; reflected racial, ethnic, organizational, and geographic diversity; and were willing to work with us. In addition, the Education Trust, the U.S. Department of Education, and individual state departments of education have recognized these schools for their significant gap-closing improvement.

Schools selected were Dayton's Bluff Achievement Plus Elementary in St. Paul, Minnesota; Lapwai Elementary in Lapwai, Idaho; Molalla High School in Molalla, Oregon; Osmond A. Church School (K–8), in Queens, New York; Port Chester Middle School in Port Chester, New York; Tekoa High School (7–12) in Tekoa, Washington; and William H. Taft Elementary in Boise, Idaho.

A Framework for Action in High-Poverty Schools

The leaders we interviewed confirmed what the growing research base on HP/HP schools had identified and what was reflected in our framework: Leadership—collaborative and distributed—served as the linchpin of success. This included the critical role that the principal and often a small group of teacher-leaders played in *developing systemic, shared leadership capacity* throughout the school, which was a catalyst for the creation of a *healthy, safe, and supportive learning environment* and an *intentional focus on improving learning*. Leaders' actions in each of these areas also led to changes in the school's culture. Leaders further noted that beyond influencing the classroom and the school at large, they *developed relationships and formed partnerships* with the district office, students' families, and the broader neighborhood and community to reach their goals.

In our Framework for Action (Figure 1.1), we have attempted to illustrate the complex interactions between the three arenas in which leaders take action, the nature of the culture found in HP/HP schools, and various spheres through which leaders influence the lives of students in poverty. In Chapter 2 we describe the schools we visited and our conclusions in greater detail. The Framework for Action is elaborated in Chapter 4.

It's Complex, but Doable!

Schools can disrupt the cycle of poverty, in both the long term and short term. An effective school can rescue a child from a future of illiteracy; it can save hundreds of students from the grim reality awaiting those who exit school unprepared. An effective school can directly impact and improve our society, but to do so, it must have leaders who are oriented toward social justice. Such leaders ask questions that cause themselves and others to assess and critique the current conditions in their schools. They identify whose interests are being served by the current conditions and whose are not. Although the administrators, teachers, school trustees, and other leaders whom we interviewed did not use the words "social justice" to describe their mission or purpose, their professional practice was consistent with what others have identified as "social justice leadership" (Dantley & Tillman, 2006; Scheurich & Skrla, 2003; Theoharis, 2009). Their vision for the school and their professional practice centered on students who, for whatever reason, were not succeeding, and focused on inclusive practices ensuring that all students had equal opportunities for powerful instruction. They confronted structures, policies, practices, and mind-sets that perpetuated inequities and thus created more equitable schools where expectations were high, academic achievement improved overall, and achievement gaps were closing.

Excellence, Equality, and Equity: Compatible Goals

These leaders and those in other HP/HP schools aim for three ideals: excellence, equality, and equity. What do we mean by this? First, these leaders understand the distinction among the three words and the possible

FIGURE 1.1 A Framework for Action:
Leading High-Poverty Schools to High Performance

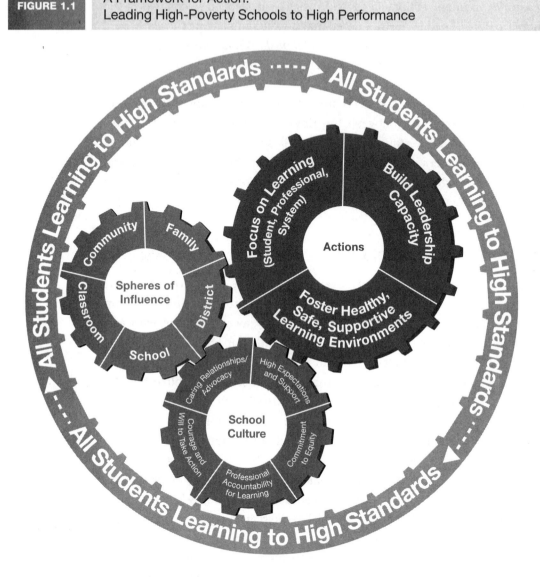

tension among them. Excellence *is* the expectation in HP/HP schools, and it is not sacrificed to attain the other two goals of equality or equity. These schools are not places where curriculum is watered down, standards are lowered, or the pace of instruction is slowed to ensure equality in outcomes (for example, everyone gets an *A*). Rather, these schools strive for equality in outcomes (for example, all students meet high standards; all students graduate ready for college) by committing to equitable opportunity for learning.

In the case of underachieving students who live in poverty, providing such opportunity often necessitates *equitable*, in contrast to *equal*, distribution of resources (time, money, people). In HP/HP schools, all students do not get the same thing—all students get what they need to succeed.

Academic Achievement: A Key Element in Social Justice

Although many high-poverty schools are criticized for focusing too much on standardized testing, which has been perceived as narrowing the curriculum and emphasizing the "wrong" things, this was not the case in the schools we visited. They focused on multiple indicators of high performance, including (but not limited to) increased attendance, improved graduation rates, fewer discipline violations, increased parent and community involvement, improved pedagogy, and improved climate.

At the end of the day, however, there can be no social justice without addressing academic achievement. These schools both increased academic achievement overall and closed achievement gaps, but as the framework in Figure 1.1 is intended to indicate, they did so by doing much more than simply focusing on raising standardized test scores. Our approach in writing this book is one of understanding how schools transform to better meet the needs of children and adolescents who live in poverty, in contrast to "fixing" these students so that they can better "fit" in the current system of schooling.

Poverty's Intersection with Race, Gender, Immigration, and Family Structure

In the United States, any discussion of poverty must acknowledge the inextricable link between poverty and race, gender, immigration status, and family structure. African American and Hispanic children are three times more likely to be poor than are their white and Asian counterparts (Danziger & Danziger, 2008). Additionally, children of single-parent households and first-generation immigrant parents have a greater chance of living in poverty than do children living in two-parent households and those living with native-born parents (U.S. Census Bureau, 2010).

When student outcomes are considered, these intersecting factors are often at play. Strategies such as book studies and other forms of professional learning related to multiculturalism and cultural relevancy, as well as critical conversations related to racial-identity development, white privilege, and institutional marginalization of those considered "different," have been central to social justice leadership in other studies (Theoharis, 2009). Although leaders in the schools we studied did not note specific strategies used to confront racism or marginalization, in each case they knew their students, families, and communities well. This knowledge allowed them to form relationships of mutual respect, identify needs appropriately, and build on assets to create conditions in which students thrived.

Social Justice Leadership: The Importance of Place-Consciousness

Scholars who have studied the effect of poverty on students and schools assert, "When school leaders subscribe to conceptions of poverty that divorce individual instances from local and historical contexts, they risk employing prescriptive efforts that overlook individual and collective responses to poverty that can benefit learners" (Rodriguez & Fabionar, 2010, p. 67). By contrast, when they understand the broader history of the community, school leaders "are more likely to recognize community strategies that are used to cope with and counteract the conditions that maintain poverty" (p. 69).

Poverty looks different in every community. In a rural community where the formerly vibrant agriculture-based economy has struggled and the population is predominantly white, poverty will manifest itself differently than it will in a suburban community that is, for the most part, working-class but also serves as a refugee relocation site, or in an urban setting with a racially diverse population and opportunities for employment that have been severely compromised for decades.

Leaders in the HP/HP schools that we studied were in tune with the neighborhoods and communities they served. Their leadership was informed by knowing the answers to questions such as these: What has happened in our community that has shaped collective experience? How have the demographics of the community changed over the years? What is the community's social and political response to poverty? What support is available? How are wealth and income distributed in the community—who are the "haves" and the "have-nots"? Is there a "wrong side of the tracks"? If so, who lives there? Where is the school located? Where do our families come from? How long have they been in the community? What are the traditional places of employment? What is the economic structure of the community? Who are the major employers? What are the hopes and dreams of our families for their children's futures? How are educators viewed? What does our community believe to be the purpose of school?

Research can support or hinder leaders' efforts to meet the needs of students in poverty. To be of benefit, research and the practical strategies it implies must be considered in light of unique factors found in the local context. Our intention is to present the lessons learned from HP/HP schools in a manner that supports what scholars refer to as "user generalizability" (Merriam, 1998). Although the schools we studied, and many others like them, had in common the foundational elements represented in the Framework for Action, there was no single silver bullet approach to success. These elements interact and play out differently in every school.

Learning from High-Performing, High-Poverty Schools

We have much more to learn from studying high-poverty schools that are on the path to improvement than we do from studying nominally high-performing schools that are producing a significant portion of their performance through social class rather than instruction.

—*Richard F. Elmore* (2006, p. 943)

Until early in the new millennium, little was known about how chronically underperforming schools with high populations of impoverished children could systematically improve. Efforts of the past two decades to improve schools yielded a smattering of recommendations, including examples of successful schools, correlates of effective schools, elements of comprehensive school reform, and a wide variety of curricular and instructional research and analysis on effective classroom practices. But the specifics about how all the pieces fit together were, for the most part, unavailable.

The Education Trust Breaks New Ground

By the late 1990s, significant improvements in the technology used to keep and report state and district data began to sharply improve the availability of comparative data, making it easier to systematically identify schools whose achievement gains were showing steep trajectories. At that time, the

Education Trust (Ed Trust) took one of the initial comparative looks at state-based achievement data on high-poverty schools. By disaggregating factors of free and reduced-price meal eligibility, ethnicity, exceptionality, and achievement, Trust researchers verified that in many schools, poor children and students of color were significantly outperforming their more advantaged peers.

Ed Trust presented this analysis in the 1999 report *Dispelling the Myth*, which identified 366 schools across the United States in which 50 percent or more of the students lived in poverty or were students of color, and were outperforming two-thirds of their more advantaged peers in their respective states (Barth et al., 1999). This analysis spurred numerous efforts geared toward learning how schools with high populations of poor and minority students could indeed dramatically improve.

Ed Trust continued its work, producing two more reports, *Dispelling the Myth Revisited* (Jerald, 2001) and *Dispelling the Myth...Over Time* (Education Trust, 2002), which expanded the original analysis by identifying more than 3,500 high-performing, high-poverty schools in 47 states that demonstrated performance in the top one-third of their respective states' required achievement testing. To better understand the leadership implications, Ed Trust also interviewed principals of these HP/HP schools and found that the following seven practices were central to their schools' improvement:

- Extensive use of state and local standards to design curriculum and instruction, assess student work, and evaluate teachers;
- Increased instruction time for reading and mathematics;
- Substantial investment in professional development for teachers that focused on instructional practices to help students meet academic standards;
- Comprehensive systems to monitor individual student performance and to provide help to struggling students before they fall behind;
- Parental involvement in efforts to get students to meet standards;
- State or district accountability systems with real consequences for adults in schools; and
- Use of assessments to help guide instruction and resources and to serve as a healthy part of everyday teaching and learning. (Jerald, 2001, p. 3)

These seven areas continue to be recognized as central tenets of improvement in virtually every subsequent study, data analysis, or evaluation of HP/HP schools. As of 2011, the Education Trust continues its pioneering work through various efforts related to understanding the learning needs of students who live in poverty; analyzing data aimed at identifying and assessing Dispelling the Myth schools; and providing tools that support practitioner analysis of local, state, and national comparative data.

An Emerging Confluence of Understanding About Effective Practice

In the early 2000s, a number of organizations, along with multiple universities, foundations, and individual scholars, began undertaking similar efforts to identify how to improve low-performing, high-poverty schools. These organizations included Just for the Kids and the National Center for Educational Accountability, national and regional educational labs and technical assistance centers, the National School Boards Association, the National Staff Development Council, the U.S. Department of Education, the Consortium on Policy Research in Education, and state departments of education.

As noted in Chapter 1, Barr and Parrett (2007) attempted to synthesize many of these efforts. This synthesis was described by Ed Trust President Kati Haycock as the first time anyone had attempted to look "across all of the many studies [and] to distill the major findings" (p. xi). Conclusions and recommendations of 18 disparate studies, evaluations, and data analyses conducted over a 20-year period were synthesized to identify practices used to significantly improve a low-performing, high-poverty school. Similar to those identified in 2002 by Ed Trust, these key practices focused on eight specific dimensions of improvement:

- Ensure effective district and school leadership;
- Engage parents, communities, and schools to work as partners;
- Understand and hold high expectations for poor and culturally diverse students;
- Target low-performing students and schools, starting with reading;
- Align, monitor, and manage the curriculum;
- Create a culture of data and assessment literacy;
- Build and sustain instructional capacity; and
- Reorganize time, space, and transitions.

Barr and Parrett further concluded that *effective leadership* linked to successful use of the other seven practices from the Ed Trust report. In fact, 16 of the 18 other studies synthesized concluded that leadership, often collaborative and distributed, was essential to improve school practices or to receive the district-level support necessary for high-poverty schools to become high performing.

Taking a Closer Look at Leadership

While virtually all studies of HP/HP schools identify effective leadership as essential to success, exactly what effective leadership looks like across those schools has yet to be clarified. To address this need, we considered the emerging knowledge base, and many examples from successful practitioners, to begin conceptualizing how various leadership roles and functions influenced sustained improvements in student achievement and school success. Our intent was to test—or "member check"—the Framework for Action that we had created to provide better understanding, guidance, and support to education leaders working from various vantage points within school districts, but particularly at the school level (principals and teacher-leaders).

We identified and visited each of the seven HP/HP schools introduced in Chapter 1. These schools had demonstrated significant gains on multiple measures of student success (such as achievement tests, graduation rates, attendance, behavior, parent engagement and satisfaction, and post-school success). They have sustained their high level of performance over time and have been recognized for their success by national and state entities. Geographic, demographic, and organizational diversity characterize the seven schools. Located in urban, rural, or suburban settings, some are large schools and others are small. They include three elementary schools, one middle school (6–8), one high school (9–12), one K–8 school, and one school that serves grades 7 through 12. A brief description of each of the seven schools, together with a snapshot of their achievement gains, follows.

Dayton's Bluff Achievement Plus Elementary School

In 1999, Dayton's Bluff Elementary School was one of the lowest-performing schools in the district of St. Paul (which has nearly 40,000 students) and the entire state of Minnesota; fewer than 10 percent of its students were meeting state standards. Located in an aging inner-city neighborhood, with more than 90 percent of its students qualifying for free and reduced-price meals, the school was deep in a downward spiral. Rampant student mobility, staff turnover, and the absence of a culture of safety and learning plagued the school. Yet another principal, Von Sheppard, began his tenure in 2001. Raising expectations and creating a safe environment for the school of more than 80 percent African American, Hmong, and Latino students characterized Principal Sheppard's approach. The adoption of a Comprehensive School Reform model, America's Choice; the support of a local foundation's "Achievement Plus" funding for high-poverty schools; and a significant amount of staff turnover combined to create a new, positive environment for the students, staff, and community. By 2005, math achievement at Dayton's Bluff Achievement Plus Elementary School had soared, and reading scores were well on their way to high performance (see Figure 2.1). That year Principal Sheppard moved to a central office position, and one of the teacher-leaders, Andrew Collins, took over. Also that year, Ed Trust bestowed its Dispelling the Myth Award on the vastly improved school. Little did anyone know, the school was just beginning its trajectory to remarkable levels of high performance.

FIGURE 2.1 Data for Dayton's Bluff Achievement Plus Elementary School

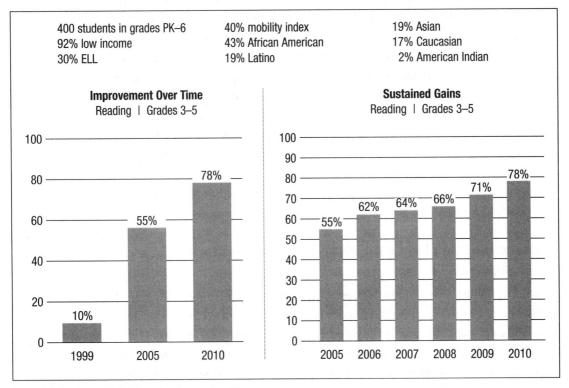

Source: Data from Minnesota State Department of Education, 2010

Sustaining all gains, Principal Collins and the staff continued their tireless work. Dayton's Bluff has continued to be recognized as one of Minnesota's highest-performing high-poverty schools. Collins believes that "all personal breakthroughs come with a change in beliefs." This phrase captures the spirit of possibility for their school and for any school like Dayton's Bluff.

Lapwai Elementary School

Situated in the rolling hills of northern Idaho, Lapwai Elementary School serves Lapwai School District No. 341, which has a total enrollment of just over 500 students. Among students at the elementary school, more than 80 percent are Native American, and 80 percent are eligible for free and reduced-price meals. In 1999, less than 20 percent of the school's 3rd graders were scoring at the state's proficiency levels in reading and math. Unwilling to settle for a continued trend of chronic underachievement, a team of teachers and leaders committed to doing whatever it took to reverse the unfortunate history of low achievement. Led by Teri Wagner, formerly the district's middle school principal and curriculum director and presently the principal at Lapwai Elementary, the group studied student data, created a plan, and implemented a variety of structural improvements and needs-based interventions to turn around their school. By 2005, achievement means had reached the 75th percentile, attendance had risen to the mid-90s, and a culture of high expectations and student success had been established (see Figure 2.2). The Ed Trust, based on the school's dramatic achievement gains and gap closing,

| FIGURE 2.2 | Data for Lapwai Elementary School |

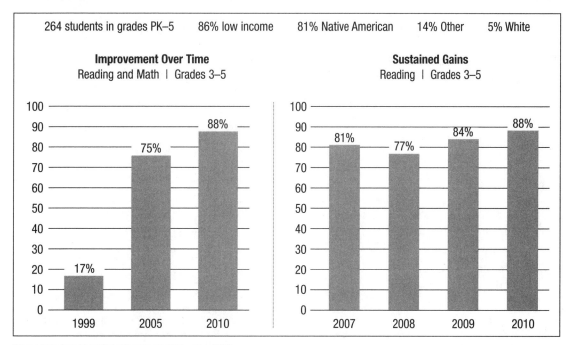

Source: Data from Idaho State Department of Education, 2010

awarded its 2004 Dispelling the Myth Award to the school. Lapwai's gains have been sustained over the years that followed; yet as Principal Wagner explains, "Every year brings a new set of challenges… we're never done… that's the work."

Molalla High School

Located about an hour southwest of Portland, Oregon, near the terminus of the Oregon Trail, Molalla High School's doors have been open to the adolescents of the rural Molalla prairie since 1906. Taking its name from the original inhabitants of the area, the Molalla Indians, the school serves the Molalla River School District of 2,600 students. The school continues to honor the tribe as its mascot. The percentage of students who are eligible for free and reduced-price meals is 41 percent.

When Kevin Ricker was hired as principal in 2005, math and reading scores for the school were topping out in the 35 to 53 percent range. In response to the school's focused efforts to improve, achievement climbed significantly (see Figure 2.3), earning Molalla the Oregon Department of Education's 2010

FIGURE 2.3   Data for Molalla High School

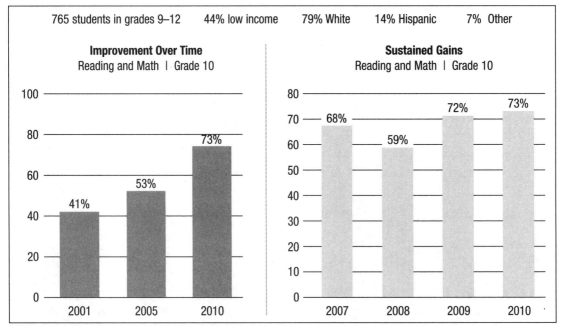

Source: Data from Oregon State Department of Education, 2010

Celebrating Student Success Champion award for closing achievement gaps and making it the only high school in Oregon to be so recognized. Principal Ricker, who recently moved on to a larger high school in the Portland area, attributes the dramatic change to a dedicated staff that aligned their instruction to state standards, targeted interventions on underachieving students, reduced daily student absences and tardies, and developed a culture of high expectations and collaborative leadership. The new principal, Randy Dalton, has assumed the reins of what he describes as "a school on an upward trajectory that's ready to go to the next level." He describes the Molalla staff as cohesive and committed to establishing a "Nordstrom's" type of culture that places meeting the needs of the students first.

Osmond A. Church P.S./M.S. 124 K–8 School

The roar of planes taking off from JFK International Airport in Queens, New York, often deadens the normal sounds of 1,200 students entering and leaving their school (94 percent low income and 97 percent African American, Asian, and Latino) for another day. Osmond Church's District No. 27 is part of Queens County District, along with 6 other districts, with a total 2010 enrollment of 258,908. In 1999, the school's K–8 students were mired in a tradition of low achievement. New principal Elain Thompson, working with new assistant principal Valarie Lewis and other staff, successfully acquired a Core Knowledge Comprehensive School Reform grant to initiate an aligned, focused curriculum. The school moved to an approach that focused on high expectations for all kids, working together as a staff to plan instruction and better connect with families, as well as targeting individual students' learning and life needs. Slowly, the school became a cohesive community.

By 2006, 83 percent of the students in grades 3 through 8 met or exceeded state standards in English language arts, and math results were even better (see Figure 2.4, p. 28). Principal Thompson retired in 2005. As is often (but unfortunately not always) the case in HP/HP schools, an able assistant principal stepped up as the new principal, ensuring a smooth transition and continued success. Two years later, in 2007, Osmond A. Church garnered Education Trust's Dispelling the Myth Award for its substantial achievement gains and closing of gaps. As of 2010, the gains were sustained, and the success continues. According to Principal Lewis, "Building our community means everything... it's allowed us to get where we are, but if we ever think we've arrived, it's time to leave." Translation: the work is never done.

FIGURE 2.4 Data for Osmond A. Church P.S./M.S. 124

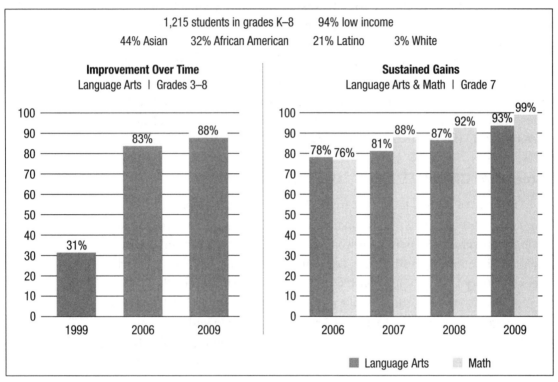

1,215 students in grades K–8   94% low income

44% Asian   32% African American   21% Latino   3% White

Source: Data from New York State Department of Education, 2010

Port Chester Middle School

Port Chester–Rye Union Free School District has an enrollment of 4,057 students. Within that district, and about 30 minutes north of New York City in Westchester County, Port Chester Middle School and the community of Port Chester is a working-class island surrounded by the largely affluent towns and neighborhoods. For years, the middle school (serving grades 6–8) struggled with an array of academic and behavioral challenges, the most critical of which was safety. When Principal Carmen Macchia arrived in the early 1990s, he described behavior in the school as "out of control." His first priority: establish law and order. With that goal accomplished over the next five years, the school and its staff embarked on an ambitious course of getting their students, more than 70 percent of whom qualify for free and reduced-price meals, to proficiency on the rigorous New York State tests. With an enrollment demographic of mostly Latino students and significant underachievement in reading, the staff chose to focus on English language arts (ELA) as the core of all instruction throughout the school.

The staff became highly competent at analyzing data, aligning instruction to standards, and creating effective interventions based on the needs of their students, all with a core focus on building student capacity in ELA. A set of 24 bundled ELA skills became a common practice in all classes. The approach paid off, as mean performance levels in the 30th percentiles in ELA and math in 1999 climbed to the high 60s in math and the 80s in ELA by 2005 (see Figure 2.5). Based on these significant gap-closing and achievement gains, Port Chester was awarded a National Blue Ribbon Award by the U.S. Department of Education that year, followed by a 2006 Dispelling the Myth Award from Ed Trust.

Principal Pat Swift, who joined the school in 2000 as an assistant principal, worked closely with Principal Macchia to collaboratively lead and sustain the years of improvement through Macchia's retirement in 2009. Swift's transition to the principal role has been seamless, as the district chose to "stay the course of success." As of 2010, Port Chester students continue to outperform their state peers. Principal Swift reflected on the journey: "We make

---

FIGURE 2.5 | Data for Port Chester Middle School

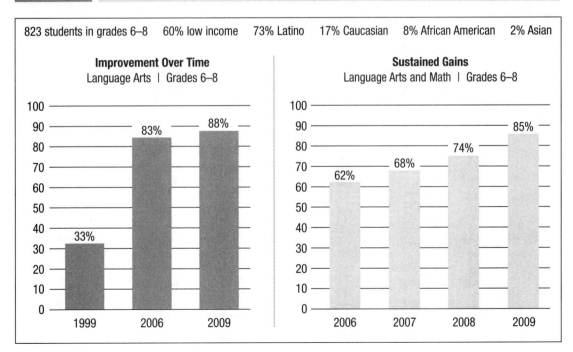

823 students in grades 6–8   60% low income   73% Latino   17% Caucasian   8% African American   2% Asian

Improvement Over Time
Language Arts | Grades 6–8

1999: 33%
2006: 83%
2009: 88%

Sustained Gains
Language Arts and Math | Grades 6–8

2006: 62%
2007: 68%
2008: 74%
2009: 85%

Source: Data from New York State Department of Education, 2010

this a big family… we're their bridge between elementary and high school. It's worked so far, but we have to constantly keep improving if we're going to serve all of our students."

Tekoa High School

Nestled in the farmland of eastern Washington palouse is the small rural community of Tekoa in Tekoa School District with 205 students, whose schools have served the population for more than 100 years. Known as the home of the Nighthawks, Tekoa High School, a 7–12 school enrolling 110 kids (more than half of whom qualify for free and reduced-price meals), had achievement means in the 35 to 40 percent range in 2002. That year a new superintendent brought a renewed commitment to improvement, which included the appointment a few years later of Principal Wayne Roellich.

Leading the small group of teachers on their collaborative journey to connect personally with the students and their lives, meet their needs regardless of the challenges presented, and close achievement gaps, Principal Roellich brought a new cohesiveness to the school. In the spring of 2010, following steady and sustained academic success (see Figure 2.6), Tekoa High School

 FIGURE 2.6   Data for Tekoa High School

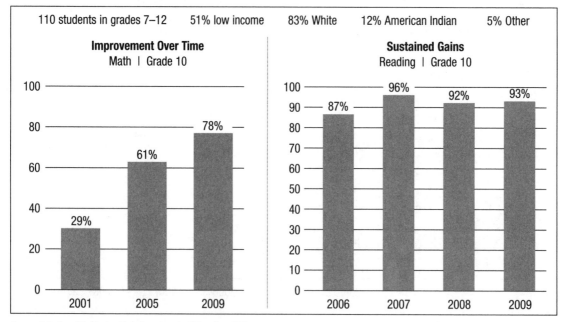

Source: Data from Washington State Department of Education, 2010

became the State of Washington's sole high school to be recognized as a Blue Ribbon School by the U.S. Department of Education. That same year, Tekoa's 18 graduating seniors earned $300,000 in postsecondary scholarships and grants. Principal Roellich gives all credit for the school's accomplishments to his staff, the superintendent, the Tekoa Elementary School, and kids who believe in their school and work hard. Conversely, when asked how the school does so well, staff members explain, "Every day, Mr. Roellich's leadership makes it all work here."

William H. Taft Elementary School

William Howard Taft Elementary School, located in Boise, Idaho, is the home of the Tigers. Surrounded by neighborhoods of modest homes, low-income housing, and pockets of commercial and industrial development, Taft is one of the older schools in the Boise Independent School District (which serves about 25,500 students). Historically, it is one of the lowest-performing elementary schools in the district and state. More than 75 percent of the students are eligible for free and reduced-price meals, and nearly a fourth are English language learners or refugees.

When Principal Susan Williamson arrived at Taft in 1998, test scores were low, morale was dismal, and student behavior was what she termed "unacceptable." Then the school embarked on its journey of improvement. Providing a warm and stimulating learning environment was the first priority, along with creating a place of safety, high expectations, and academic excellence. Following five years of hard work, Taft was awarded a U.S. Department of Education Blue Ribbon Award in 2003 and has continued to be recognized with other honors and awards as its academic achievement remains strong (see Figure 2.7, p. 32).

Principal Williamson describes Taft's continued success: "In a short span of time, teachers, parents, and students have woven the fabric of a culture that is inviting, encouraging, and consistently striving for excellence. We've developed a cadre of leaders who daily endeavor to empower each and every individual."

A Framework for Leading High-Poverty Schools to High Performance

During visits to the schools, we listened as leaders (administrators, teachers, school trustees, and other personnel) described the actions they believed had resulted in their school's improvements, and we looked for evidence that confirmed or refuted the leadership concepts represented in our framework.

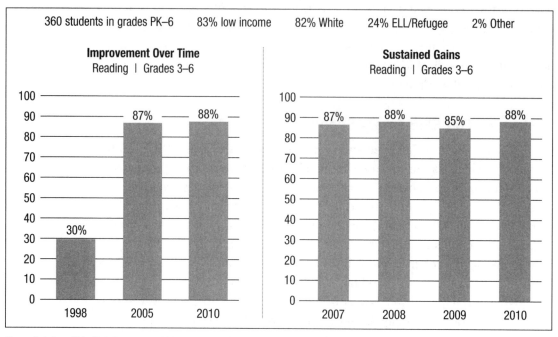

FIGURE 2.7 Data for William H. Taft Elementary School

Source: Data from Idaho State Department of Education, 2010

We reviewed data from school improvement plans, district and state report cards, state and district websites, and school evaluations. We also conducted informal observations and discussions with individuals familiar with the schools.

Our exploration into the function of leadership in the seven schools allowed us to verify our framework. The framework elements of building leadership capacity; fostering a healthy, safe, and supportive learning environment; and focusing on student, professional, and system learning indeed appeared vital to success. Our analysis focused not only on leaders' explicit statements of actions taken and the apparent results, but also on their perceptions of changes in the culture of the school (norms, beliefs, values). It was in the area of school culture that our visits to these schools most informed our emerging framework.

In our initial conceptualization of the role of leadership in shaping the culture in HP/HP schools, we included the value they placed on relationships, the beliefs they held that students in poverty could be held to high expectations, and their courage and will to take action. As a result of our visits to these schools, we added three characteristics that we had previously neglected to include, although they too were represented in the research. They are (1) the importance of advocacy, (2) an unwavering commitment to equity, and (3) an unyielding sense of professional accountability for learning. Each of these three characteristics was prominent in each school.

To further verify the accuracy of the framework, we considered the conclusions drawn from eight additional studies of HP/HP schools that were conducted after Barr and Parrett's (2007) synthesis was developed or were not included in their analysis. In the Appendix we provide a brief description of each of the recent studies, together with the conclusions drawn in relationship to the framework.

These eight studies contribute significantly to the knowledge base on high-performing, high-poverty schools. Just as the schools have matured over time, so have the investigations of their actions, resulting in a better illumination of how these schools succeed. The studies also serve to further validate the earlier work of the Ed Trust and other organizations, Barr and Parrett's synthesis, and the work of a host of other scholars and practitioners who have endeavored since the late 1990s to understand why some schools with high concentrations of students who live in poverty and underachieve are able to significantly reverse historic trends of underachievement and failure, and sustain this success.

At the Heart of Improvement—Leadership

Although the answers are complex and challenging to distill, one feature stands out from the understandings gained from the hundreds of HP/HP schools studied: significant student gains will not be sustained without effective leaders who serve as catalysts for the specific actions that in turn drive the success of these schools—actions that build further leadership capacity; focus on student, professional, and system learning; and foster safe, healthy, and supportive learning environments.

Schools like those we visited, others involved in the eight recent studies, and many more have unequivocally demonstrated that the barriers posed by poverty to learning and achievement can be overcome. Yet poverty presents a daunting set of circumstances that can overwhelm even the best-intentioned educators in their efforts to teach kids who live within its influence. High-performing, high-poverty schools begin their efforts by gaining an understanding of the unique needs of their students who live in poverty and those of their families.

Chapter 3 provides insight into poverty and its complex influence on children, adolescents, and learning. High-performing, high-poverty schools make a practice of knowing their kids and families in their efforts to counter the challenging effects of poverty.

Poverty and
Our Moral Responsibility

Teacher-leaders at Lapwai Elementary, located on the Nez Perce reservation in northern Idaho, say, "Working here, where almost everyone is poor, requires more of you. We knew our kids were as smart as any other kids, but we also knew we weren't reaching them. We had to do things differently." Doing things differently meant understanding how poverty influences lives and learning. At Lapwai one can now witness effective classroom instruction; elders teaching Nez Perce language and culture; home visits to connect with the most vulnerable families; extra time and support via tutoring programs; and on cold winter days, mittens distributed to anyone who needs them.

Many of us grew up hearing admonitions from parents that we should clean our plates "because there are children starving in India" (or China, or Africa). It was not clear how eating everything on our plates would help hungry children, but what *was* clear was that hunger was a terrible thing that happened to other people in faraway places. In the United States, we have been reluctant to acknowledge class distinctions, often viewing ourselves as a society composed of one big middle class. Yet in one of the wealthiest countries in the world, the number of children forced to live in poverty is unconscionable. Before you continue reading, we urge you to use the survey in Figure 3.1 to reflect upon what you know and believe about poverty.

| FIGURE 3.1 | What Do You Know and Believe About Poverty? |

Respond to the statements with T/F or rate from highly unlikely (-3) to highly likely (3).

1	Childhood poverty rates are higher in the United States than in any other industrialized nation.	T/F
2	Childhood poverty rates are rising in the United States.	T/F
3	We are living in an era of increasing inequity between the wealthiest and the poorest.	T/F
4	One in five school-age children lives in poverty.	T/F
5	The formula for establishing the "poverty threshold" is based on the "thrifty food plan formula" established in the early 1960s.	T/F
6	The U.S. Census Bureau has proposed 12 alternative methods for determining the poverty rate in the United States, all but one of which result in a greater rate of poverty than the current formula.	T/F

7	Poverty is caused by poor character and poor choices an individual makes. -3 -2 -1 0 1 2 3
8	People in poverty do not work, or they have a poor work ethic. -3 -2 -1 0 1 2 3
9	Education, as a way out of poverty, is readily accessible to everyone. -3 -2 -1 0 1 2 3
10	Parents of students who live in poverty are uninvolved in their children's education because they do not value it. -3 -2 -1 0 1 2 3
11	The bias and assumptions we hold about poverty can pose barriers to effective problem solving and change. -3 -2 -1 0 1 2 3
12	Schools can have only a limited effect on students who live in poverty. -3 -2 -1 0 1 2 3
13	Schools are only part of the solution to the problem in poverty. -3 -2 -1 0 1 2 3
14	Schools are holding up their end of the deal in eliminating poverty in the United States. -3 -2 -1 0 1 2 3

The Scope of the Poverty Problem

Childhood poverty rates are higher in the United States than in any other industrialized country, and this rate is on the rise. As of 2010, 36 percent of all people who live in poverty were children—more than 15.3 million, or 21 percent of all children in the United States. Another 16 million (22 percent) reside in low-income families. Between 2000 and 2009, the number of children living in poverty increased from 11.5 million to 15.3 million, or by a factor of 33 percent (Chau, Thampi & Wight, 2009). The number of people in poverty in 2009 climbed to 46.3 million—one in seven Americans—the largest number since poverty rates have been published (U.S. Census Bureau, 2010). Equally startling, a recent study indicated that between 60 and 75 percent of Americans will live below or near the poverty line for at least one year of their lives (Neuman, 2008).

Increasing Inequality

Whether or not one personally experiences poverty, if unabated, its effects are likely to touch everyone in this country. The past quarter century has been an era of rising inequality. Income in the poorest one-fifth of the U.S. population rose 7 percent, while it increased for the wealthiest one-fifth by 63.5 percent (Danziger & Danziger, 2008). In the last decade alone, the wealthiest 20 percent of the population earned one-half of the income in America (West Coast Poverty Center, 2010). Such inequality weakens the fabric of a democracy.

Since the early 1970s, the minimum wage relative to the average wage has both fallen and not kept up with inflation. During the same period, wages fell for workers with the least education, while wages for professionals far outpaced inflation. Males with a high school diploma or less lost the most ground. Real income levels (adjusted for inflation) for male high school dropouts were 23 percent lower in 2002 than in 1975 and 13 percent lower for high school graduates (Danziger & Danziger, 2008).

A broader picture of income and wealth inequality is witnessed at the intersection between poverty and other factors, including race, gender, immigration status, and family structure. Whites make up 79 percent of the general population, whereas 67 percent of all low-income people are white. On the other hand, although blacks and Hispanics make up 12 and 13 percent of the population, respectively, each group makes up about 25 percent of the low-income population (U.S. Census Bureau, 2009). Likewise, 68.9 percent of all families are married-couple families, but this family structure represents only 31 percent of families living in poverty. Furthermore, whereas single-female-parent families make up 24.5 percent of all families, they represent 61 percent of families in poverty (West Coast Poverty Center, 2010). Nearly one in every four children (23 percent) is born to an immigrant parent, and nearly 20 percent of immigrants live in poverty (U.S. Census Bureau, 2009).

Combined, these data present a grim portrait of the bleak landscape of poverty that confronts so many U.S. children. Living in this condition, one in five of our children heads to school.

What Educators Need to Understand About Poverty

> Solutions to poverty are like pieces of a puzzle. Those pieces include education, housing, health and nutrition, employment, child care, and community support services to name a few.... Education is the glue that can help keep the other pieces in place.
>
> —*Jacquelyn C. Jackson,*
> *in the Foreword to* Educating the Other America (Neuman, 2008)

Children who live in poverty are as worthy of attending good schools as their more affluent counterparts, and much is known about what it takes to transform schools into places that better meet their needs. Improving such schools begins with leaders who are unequivocally committed to equity. This commitment starts with a better understanding of the meaning and influence of poverty in the lives of the students they serve.

Poverty in America is not easily defined, nor can its causes be simplistically explained. It can be experienced by anyone—male and female, as well as people of all ages, racial or ethnic groups, and immigration status. Given the complex nature of poverty, in this chapter we focus on what we believe to be most important for educators and other professionals to understand in the context of their efforts to improve academic achievement and other measures of school-related success. We begin by describing how poverty is defined by the federal government and the limitations of such a definition, after which we address how poverty is often defined and discussed in schools. These definitions are important because they are linked to the support and services provided to people who live in poverty, not only in schools, but also in the broader community.

How Is Poverty Defined?

In the United States, the federal government defines poverty as a certain level of income relative to family size. For example, in 2009, the poverty threshold ranged from $10,830 for a single person to $22,050 for a family of four. Originally coined the "thrifty food plan," the formula used to establish the poverty line was created by federal statisticians who based it upon what was determined to be three times the annual cost of food for a family of three in 1963. Although the basic formula for defining who lives in poverty is viewed as excessively conservative and controversial, it continues to be used as the official measure. In 2007, the U.S. Census Bureau released 12 alternatives to the current formula, all but one of which set the official poverty rate at a higher level (Neuman, 2008). According to Sarah Fass (2009) with the National Center for Children in Poverty (NCCP), the current income threshold is inadequate for even the bare necessities, and in some areas of the country it is grossly inadequate. For instance, Fass estimates a family of four living in a lower-cost region of the country needs between $37,000 and $41,000 to meet its basic needs; in locations where the cost of living is higher, the same family needs $52,000 to $67,000.

What Do We Mean by Poverty in the Context of Schools?

It is important to be aware of the ways in which we, as educators, define and discuss poverty in schools. When we define poverty in schools, we primarily mean the percentage of students who are eligible for the free and reduced-price meal program. For the 2009–10 school year, income eligibility for reduced-price meals was 185 percent of the federal poverty line and 130 percent for free meals. In less complex terms, a family of four with a gross income of $40,793 was eligible for reduced-price meals; and if they earned less than $28,665, they could receive free meals. Although schools are sometimes criticized for using this criterion for describing the percentage of students living in poverty, clearly these income levels fall at or far below the needed income level estimated by the NCCP for basic necessities. These families face significant challenges, and the schools that serve them do as well.

How Do We Talk About Poverty in Schools?

In practice, educators use many terms or labels to discuss children and families who live in poverty. Gloria Rodriguez and James Fabionar (2010) assert that the many terms we use should serve "as a reminder of how often we are called on in education to talk about—but not necessarily to"—our students and their families who live with low incomes (p. 64). They claim these terms are not uniformly understood and reveal varying understandings of poverty in the context of school that are largely influenced by thinking about children and families who live in poverty as a "deficit." They identify the following commonly used terms or labels, together with their purposes in schools:

- Low Income—Typically describes a family-level measure indexed against a certain average or range. It can be assigned to students and their families by determining their eligibility for specially funded programs that rely on a particular income cutoff to select program participants.
- Free or Reduced-Price Lunch Eligible—Using the poverty threshold established by the U.S. government for low-income students, eligibility is determined for meal programs offered by the U.S. Department of Agriculture based on income.
- Title I Eligible—Individual eligibility is based on a combined consideration of academic performance and income eligibility using similar guidelines as those used to determine eligibility for free or reduced-price meals.
- Economically Disadvantaged—Lower economic status creates a disadvantage in securing full educational benefits that in turn might guarantee certain economic benefits. Accountability systems that require disaggregation of data by certain student subgroups typically include the category of "economically disadvantaged" students. Application of this label can vary, but it is often equated with eligibility for free or reduced-price meals.
- Low Socioeconomic Status (Low SES)—The term identifies students who are low income and identified according to certain social background characteristics that are believed to operate in tandem with economic status to facilitate or impede social mobility. Within schools, "low SES" is often used as shorthand for many status definitions or social processes. (Adapted from Rodriguez & Fabionar, 2010, p. 65)

As children we may have been taught that "sticks and stones can break our bones, but names can never hurt us." Unfortunately, that is simply not true. Children who live in poverty, like all children, deserve to be treated with respect and in a manner that preserves their dignity. The words we use to describe and label children do matter. Educators must reflect upon the many labels used to describe children (and their families) who live in poverty, and critique their own use of such terms, to become attuned to the many ways that schools unwittingly limit students' self-determination.

Poverty shapes one's view of self and others. Living in poverty affects many of the basic necessities that people of middle- and upper-income levels tend to take for granted, such as personal appearance, condition and size of home (if one is not homeless), availability and quality of food, health and well-being, and even the value of one's work. In *See Poverty… Be the Difference!*, Donna Beegle (2006), who grew up in poverty, describes the shame that she and others felt because of their families' economic condition. All of the participants in Beegle's study (college graduates who had lived in poverty throughout their childhoods) reported that they and other members of their families felt a great deal of shame and humiliation because of their economic condition, which resulted in a sense of hopelessness. They related stories of smelling bad because they lived in their cars and had limited access to showers; of being embarrassed by the condition or style of their clothing; and "snickering" by others about members of their family, the content of their lunches, or the nature of their parents' work. In many cases, living conditions entailed a perpetual state of hunger and exposure to chronic health conditions. For most, not having money contributed to their sense of hopelessness. Their lives were "a series of reactionary battles for survival with little, if any, opportunity to shape or choose their futures. For too many this comes with a strong feeling that something is personally wrong with them, and that there is nothing they can do to change it" (Beegle, 2006, p. 53).

As educators, we must be sensitive to the effects of poverty on our students' state of mind and ensure we separate their developing sense of self from their living conditions. As a starting point, we must be extremely careful how we talk about children who live in poverty. For example, describing these students as living in homes *with* a low income or *with* low SES (socioeconomic status) is very different, and more accurate, than calling them "low-income students," "low-SES students," or "high-poverty kids." This distinction may seem like splitting hairs, but it is important.

Why Does Poverty Exist?

There is a widespread lack of understanding about poverty and the people whose lives are so severely circumscribed by it. Its causes have been explained from both a structural-institutional and a personal-individual perspective. From a structural-institutional perspective, scholars and policymakers have argued that our economic system (capitalism) inherently results in an uneven distribution of wealth; that factors such as racism have caused persistent disadvantage for specific groups of people; and that social institutions, including schools, confer unequal relationships in terms of power and privilege based on income level, race, and ethnicity. Personal-individual explanations for poverty often focus on the values and behaviors of individuals who live in poverty. In other words, from a personal-individual perspective, poverty can be explained by the character of poor people and the choices they make.

How educators think about poverty is important, because it influences how we respond to students and their families. One barrier that is likely to prevent educators from being as successful as they might be otherwise is the prevalence of "deficit model thinking" (Rodriguez & Fabionar, 2010). Deficit theory (Valencia, 1997) explains the cause of poverty as located within students and families, rather than viewing the problem of underachievement as lack of school responsiveness to the unique needs of these students. Deficit thinking reinforces the idea that there is a universal norm (usually white, middle class, male) against which all students should be assessed and to which all students should aspire.

Rodriguez and Fabionar (2010) suggest that some well-intentioned school practices seek to intervene in the lives of children living in poverty by asking them to replace the cultural norms, beliefs, and language of their families with school-defined notions of success. They state, "Good intentions notwithstanding, by not interrogating deeply our operating assumptions about the nature of poverty, including the deficiencies we ascribe to poor children and their families, we run the risk of carrying out educational leadership practices that do more damage than good" (pp. 57–58).

We can begin this process of introspection by examining the research base, which in turn can support us in making more informed decisions and taking more informed action. A critical element of developing an understanding of why poverty exists is to understand what poverty *isn't*.

Confronting Common Myths

> We should never, under any circumstance, make an assumption about a student or parent—about their values or culture or mindset—based on a single dimension of their identity... the "culture of poverty" is a myth. What does exist is a culture of classism, a culture most devastating to our most underserved students. And *this* is a culture worth changing.
>
> —*Paul Gorski,* Teaching Tolerance, *Spring 2007*

In Chapter 8 we elaborate on how poverty shapes life conditions and affects learning. This information is critical for success with students who live in poverty; however, to best serve the needs of these students, we are also obliged to develop the "will and skill" to challenge common myths and stereotypes about people living in poverty, which means we must confront our own bias and stereotypes.

Myth: Poverty is an issue that solely affects people of color. Poverty cuts across all racial categories. As previously discussed, blacks and Hispanics are overrepresented among people living in poverty; however, nearly 56 percent of all people living in poverty are white (U.S. Census Bureau, 2010). Nonetheless, when considering student outcomes, class and race are inter- secting factors; and racism, as well as classism, is often at play. For example, long-term poverty rates are higher and long-term income rates are lower for African Americans. Even when African American children and white children are raised in similar economic conditions, African American children are less likely than whites to be upwardly mobile (Corcoran, 2008).

Myth: With government assistance, people can get out of poverty. Donna Beegle's (2006) personal experience with government assistance pro- vides insight into the complex nature of poverty-related policy and the barri- ers it can pose. Receiving a welfare check of $408 per month, with rent at $395, Beegle had $13 left for basic necessities such as transportation, laundry, utili- ties, and other needs. When she didn't pay her rent and she and her children were evicted, her welfare counselor suggested that she needed to take money management classes. She describes how current welfare policies create barri- ers to getting out of poverty:

> When I was presented with the opportunity to go to school, I was notified that the state welfare policies dictated that in order to qualify for welfare I needed to be available for any minimum wage job. If I were in school, I would not be avail- able. If I went to school, the government would sanction me and cut my welfare check from $408 to $258.... I began calculating how my kids and I could survive on $258 a month.... I was one of the lucky few who received help with housing costs. Only 14 percent of those who qualify for housing assistance receive it. Oth- ers are put on a wait list or turned away. (p. 29)

She continues, "The available assistance from government and social services barely helps people in poverty cope with their poverty conditions, let alone break loose from its grip" (p. 29).

Myth: People in poverty abuse drugs and alcohol more than people who are wealthy. Drug and alcohol abuse affects all socioeconomic classes. In fact, studies have demonstrated that drug abuse is a problem equally distributed among classes, and alcohol abuse is far more pervasive among wealthy people than among those who live in poverty (Gorski, 2008).

Myth: People in poverty do not work or have a poor work ethic. A pre- vailing belief in America is that if people work hard, they can pull themselves out of poverty. Socioeconomic mobility is thought to be possible for anyone with a strong work ethic, and people who live in poverty are often stereotyped as lazy. However, working adults who live in poverty spend more hours work- ing than do their wealthier counterparts (Economic Policy Institute, 2004, in Gorski, 2008). Two-thirds of people living in poverty work, on average, 1.7

full-time jobs (U.S. Census Bureau, 2004, in Beegle, 2006, p. 30). Although single mothers in the United States work more hours than do single mothers in any other wealthy nation, their rate of poverty is higher (Smedding, 2003, in Beegle, 2006, p. 30). It is not a matter of not working hard enough or enough hours, but rather the shortage of living-wage jobs available for people with little education or training.

Myth: Education, as a way out of poverty, is readily accessible to everyone. Despite the fact that children who attend Head Start are more likely to graduate from high school and go to college, the program's funding allows for service to only about 60 percent of eligible children. Problems related to accessibility to education compound when students who live in poverty attend K–12 schools, where they are often presented with substantial barriers to learning and achievement and school practices that perpetuate low achievement, such as tracking, retention, or low expectations (Barr & Parrett, 2007). Beegle (2006) suggests that "although some progress has been made in diminishing the educational barriers [to higher education] of race, gender, geography, and religion, poverty is the one barrier that has not been overcome" (p. 32). Drawing on Mortensen's (1993) research, she claims, "it is less likely today for a person born into poverty to go to college than it was in the 1940s" (p. 32).

Myth: Parents of students who live in poverty are uninvolved in their children's education because they do not value it. Rarely do low-income parents care little about education. Rather, it is more likely they do not know how to help, and the current system provides them with limited opportunities to be involved in ways that fit into the realities of their lives. Research has shown that people living in poverty have similar attitudes about their children's educations as do their more affluent counterparts. Conversely, they often have far less access to school involvement opportunities because they work multiple jobs, work evenings, do not have paid leave, are unable to afford child care, or do not have transportation (Gorski, 2008).

People living in poverty also may appear not to value education because of reasons related to its relevancy in their lives. In her study, Beegle (2006) suggests that education lacked meaning for many of the people she studied. They attended school for such reasons as "it was the law" (p. 69). For all of the participants, school was "a source of discomfort, unhappiness, and stress" and a place they felt they did not belong (p. 69). There is a strong link between parental education level and parental expectations related to education. Many in Beegle's study stated that during their formative years, they had limited communication with their parents about educational expectations, issues related to success in school, or higher education. This situation was

not attributed to devaluing education, but rather to their parents' limited frame of reference for discussing educational aspirations beyond their own experiences.

Why Confronting These Myths Matters

[In schools] there are other curricula besides the one being verbalized. There are the ones in the hallways with snide remarks from the peers, on the playground with put-downs learned from parents and in the celebration of holidays at school that can completely panic a happy family.... The third grade was a bad year. Third grade was the year I learned in school that I was poor.

—*Jeff Sapp,* Teaching Tolerance, *Spring 2009*

Mental maps underpin our professional practice as educators. What are mental maps? They are the images, assumptions, and personal perspectives that we hold about people, institutions, and the world in general (Argyris & Schön, 1974), and they are formed by our lived experiences. Often tacitly held, they may not be something we are aware of; consequently, they are often left unexamined. Although our mental maps (or mind-sets) may be invisible to us, they are important because they are the foundation for our behavior—how we plan, implement, and evaluate our actions. In other words, they influence the theories that guide our choice of action. These theories can be espoused (as, for example, in the rationale we give for our action) or they can be tacitly held (for example, the unspoken rationale for our action). These two kinds of theories are known as theories *of* action and theories *in* action. Effective leaders have only a small gap between the two (Argyris & Schön, 1974). In other words, effective leaders are reflective and introspective enough to have challenged their own mental maps, and most of the time the rationale they give for a chosen action is congruent with their mental maps.

The myths presented in this chapter represent commonly held biases and stereotypes about people who live in poverty. The biases and stereotypes we hold about people who live in poverty are part of our mental maps as educators, and to the degree they are unexamined, they can limit our effectiveness. The following story illustrates this point:

Harbor Middle School is located in a coastal community in the West. The economy of this community has suffered for decades, and teachers and administrators have seen their share of changes in the school. Eighty percent of the students are eligible for free and reduced-price meals. Eileen Showers, in her first

administrative position as the school's new assistant principal, made repeated attempts to address Sean's persistent tardiness, but failed. Over the course of the first two months of the new school year, she and the 7th grade teaching team had tried several things to ensure that Sean did not continue to miss 30 minutes of first period. Sean was relatively new to the school, enrolling in April of his 6th grade year. Sean was passing all courses except Pre-Algebra, which he took first period.

Principal Shores had reminded Sean several times that tardiness was unacceptable. "The school has the rule for a reason," she told him, "and you have to follow it like everyone else." She was most annoyed by Sean's reluctance to provide a reason for his frequent tardiness. "He won't explain why he can't manage to get himself to school on time," she explained.

She had attempted to call his parents, but the number was no longer in service. She had written a letter explaining the tardy policy (a student is suspended for one day after 5 violations and fails the course after 10). In the letter she had "made it clear" that the school required parents to "excuse" their child's tardiness by "signing them in." The letter was returned stamped as undeliverable. With the failure of these attempts to communicate with Sean's parents, Eileen sent another sealed letter with Sean, telling him he *must* give it to his parents. Eileen knew her success in this job was contingent on earning teachers' trust. She knew they wanted the administration to "crack down" on tardiness and truancy.

On the following day, Sean's parents walked into the school for the first time to "sign in." Sean was again 30 minutes late. Eileen, obviously frustrated, expressed her disappointment in Sean's parents' lack of responsiveness. Sean's mother began to cry, and his father explained that the family was living out of their car. Sean was late sometimes because they chose to wait until the shower facilities opened in a public campground. As Sean's father explained, "We just didn't want kids to make fun of him because he looked bad or wasn't clean." He was a smart boy. They thought he could make up whatever he was missing in class.

This story exemplifies how our mental maps can pose barriers to effective problem solving. Eileen and the 7th grade team's approach to Sean's tardiness was undoubtedly influenced by their mental maps. Some of the governing variables in their mental maps were explicitly stated and known; others were likely unspoken and tacitly held. Eileen and her colleagues believed school attendance was important, as was getting to school on time. This commonly held value was made explicit through policy. She and the faculty had also made explicit their belief that parents should take responsibility for their child's tardiness and established the "signing in" procedure. However, the educators' tacitly held assumptions about Sean and his parents (they didn't

care about education, were lazy, were absent, or were sleeping off a hangover) may have prevented them from rethinking the problem. Figure 3.2 illustrates how the theory of action and the theory in action played out in this case.

Although it can be difficult to surface our assumptions, a good place to begin is by asking the question "Are we sure we're solving the right problem?" If Eileen and the 7th grade team had brainstormed all the possible reasons Sean might be tardy, they may have surfaced some of their tacit assumptions, reframed the problem, and tried new strategies rather than continuing to solve the wrong problem. In fact, once Eileen and her team knew the problem was homelessness, they had an entirely new set of strategies at their disposal to help Sean succeed. For example, they connected Sean's family with community resources, allowed Sean to "make up" the seat time he missed in the mornings during lunch, and gave him access to a parent volunteer to help him with math.

FIGURE 3.2 Theory *of* Action—Theory *in* Action

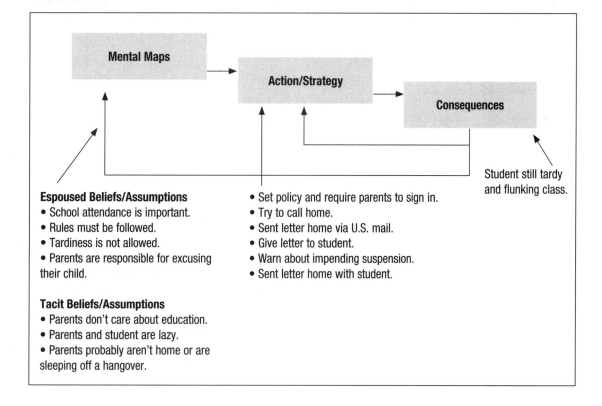

Espoused Beliefs/Assumptions
- School attendance is important.
- Rules must be followed.
- Tardiness is not allowed.
- Parents are responsible for excusing their child.

Tacit Beliefs/Assumptions
- Parents don't care about education.
- Parents and student are lazy.
- Parents probably aren't home or are sleeping off a hangover.

- Set policy and require parents to sign in.
- Try to call home.
- Sent letter home via U.S. mail.
- Give letter to student.
- Warn about impending suspension.
- Sent letter home with student.

Student still tardy and flunking class.

Mental Maps → Action/Strategy → Consequences

Whose Problem Is Poverty?

Some say we can't fix education until we fix poverty. It's exactly the opposite; we can't fix poverty until we fix education.

—*Kati Haycock, keynote address,*
2010 Education Trust Dispelling the Myth Conference

In the United States, intense public and policy debate related to poverty has occurred for decades. In the 1960s, the intent of welfare reform policy was to reduce poverty. But since the mid-1990s, policy has been focused not on reducing poverty but on reducing dependency on welfare and increasing work among the poor. In fact, changes in welfare policy accompanied by the economic boom of the late 1990s resulted in a decline of 70 percent in welfare recipients (Danziger & Danziger, 2008). However, a decline in the welfare rolls differs from a decline in poverty.

Antipoverty measures take many forms—some are intended to ease economic hardship by raising income (for example, cash welfare, food stamps), and others aim to ease the constraints that poverty poses (for example, subsidized housing and child care). Looking to successful policies in other industrialized countries, Danziger and Danziger (2008) point to the relatively modest increase in the level of income needed to turn the tide for families in poverty. They suggest that reasonable policy changes are possible and point to four specific strategies: (1) raising the minimum wage, (2) subsidizing health insurance, (3) reforming the unemployment insurance program, and (4) providing "transitional jobs of last resort" for those who are unable to find steady employment (p. 29). Working to change structures that perpetuate poverty is vital to its elimination; nonetheless, at the same time much can be done to improve the way in which institutions serve those living in poverty. Foremost among those institutions is public education.

James Coleman's (1966) conclusion that schools could have only a limited effect on students who live in poverty began a debate that has continued for decades. In an article published in *Educational Leadership* in April 2008, Richard Rothstein, research associate at the Economic Policy Institute, asked the question "Whose problem is poverty?" He suggests that schools can have only a limited influence on closing the achievement gap between students who live in poverty and their more affluent peers unless school improvement is combined with broader social and economic reforms. Without such a combined effort, he claims, the mandate for schools to "fully close achievement gaps not only will remain unfulfilled, but also will cause us to foolishly and unfairly condemn our schools and teachers" (p. 8). He is not alone in this logic. David Berliner (2007, as cited in Rodriguez & Fabionar, 2010) argues, "Without careful attention to the social conditions beyond schools, we will continue to encounter limitations in advancing educational equity and high achievement among diverse student populations within schools" (pp. 58–59). (See also Anyon, 2005.)

Others assert that schools can, and do, make a significant difference in the lives and the academic outcomes of students who live in poverty (Barr & Parrett, 2007; McGee, 2004). Kati Haycock contends, "It is very clear to me that even as we work to improve the conditions of families in this country, we can in fact get even the poorest children to high standards of achievement if we really focus in our schools on that goal" (in Holland, 2007, p. 56).

Eliminating poverty is a *both/and* proposition—reforms must occur in *both* the broader society and in schools—*and* schools do make a considerable difference. We encourage educators, and particularly educational leaders, to *both* become knowledgeable about issues related to eliminating poverty, joining forces with others who advocate for social and economic reforms, *and* summon the courage to do the much-needed work closer to home—in their own schools and communities. Successfully educating all students to high standards is critical to ultimately eliminating poverty. If, as educators, we feel powerless to address bigger issues such as living-wage jobs and health care reform, Gorski (2008) proposes that we ask ourselves, "Are we willing, at the very least, to tackle the classism in our own schools and classrooms?" Gorski (2007) provides the following 10 suggestions as a starting point:

- Assign work requiring a computer and Internet access or other costly resources only when we can provide in-school time and materials for such work to be completed.
- Work with our schools to make parent involvement affordable and convenient by providing transportation, on-site child care, and time flexibility.
- Give students from poverty access to the same high-level curricular and pedagogical opportunities and high expectations as their wealthy peers.
- Teach about classism, consumer culture, the dissolution of labor unions, environmental pollution, and other injustices disproportionately affecting the poor, preparing new generations of students to make a more equitable world.
- Keep stocks of school supplies, snacks, clothes, and other basic necessities handy for students who may need them, but find quiet ways to distribute these resources to avoid singling anyone out.
- Develop curricula that are relevant and meaningful to our students' lives and draw on their experiences and surroundings.

- Fight to get our students into gifted and talented programs and to give them other opportunities usually reserved for economically advantaged students and to keep them from being assigned unjustly to special education.
- Continue to reach out to parents even when we feel they are being unresponsive; this is one way to establish trust.
- Challenge our colleagues when they stigmatize poor students and their parents, reminding them of the inequitable conditions in our schools and classrooms.
- Challenge ourselves, our biases, and prejudices, by educating ourselves about the cycle of poverty and classism in and out of U.S. schools. (p. 35)

Reprinted with permission of *Teaching Tolerance* © 2007. All rights reserved. www.tolerance.org

The need for broader social and economic changes in our country does not provide an excuse for maintaining the status quo in schools. Three decades of research have demonstrated that schools can improve academic outcomes and other measures of success for children who live in poverty (Barr & Parrett, 2007; Education Trust, 2002; Teddlie & Stringfield, 1993). As Horace Mann asserted, public education is the most universal of institutions, and it can shape young minds and hearts. It is still our best hope. Although improvements in public education alone will not eliminate poverty, such improvements are an important part of the solution. The question is not whether too much is being asked of public schools, but rather, have we held up our end of the bargain?

Our Call to Action

We can reconfigure the world if we can reconfigure our way of thinking. This is where education, one that encourages us to challenge conventional wisdom, can try to play a significant role.

—*Muhammad Yunus, 2006 Recipient of the Nobel Peace Prize*

In the richest nation in the world, it is possible to eradicate poverty; and a vital step toward doing so is to provide a high-quality education for every child. We know there is a correlation between education and earning power. On average, a four-year college graduate earns two and a half times as much as someone without a high school diploma (San Antonio, 2008). As is true of more affluent children, those living in poverty attend schools of varying quality; however, for these students the quality of their school may be of greater consequence. In high-performing, high-poverty schools, excellence and equity are compatible goals, and the effects of poverty are not offered as an excuse to maintain the status quo; rather, such effects serve as "design parameters" for understanding how best to serve students (Calkins, Guenther, Belfiore, & Lash, 2007, p. 85). Too often schools have attempted to support students who live in poverty by attempting interventions that did not take into consideration their unique needs. By focusing on the constraints that poverty poses for students and their families, schools can more effectively develop multiple pathways for improving academic achievement and school success.

To understand these schools' commitment to excellence and equity, it is critical to understand not only what they do *but also what they no longer do*. Leaders in HP/HP schools are willing to examine data and ask questions in order to peel back the layers of the ways in which schools systemically perpetuate underachievement. Such critical inquiry provides the impetus for eliminating destructive policies and practices, such as inequitable funding, retaining and tracking students, and providing what Martin Haberman (1991) calls the "pedagogy of poverty."

This approach to working with students who live in poverty is different from other popular approaches. From leaders in HP/HP schools we have learned that the solution to the problem of poverty is not about fixing students and families so that they can "fit" into school; rather, it is fixing schools so that *all* students have a sense of belonging and the opportunity for success. A high-quality education has become increasingly important for all children. Without such an education, many are excluded from what is foundational to a democratic society—the opportunity to become responsible citizens, to contribute to one's economic well-being and to that of one's family and community, and to enjoy productive and satisfying lives. Indeed, a high-quality education has become so vital, it is viewed by many as the civil rights issue of our generation.

High-performing, high-poverty schools go beyond what is traditionally done in most schools to provide such an education to their students. How they do so is the focus of the remainder of this book. In the next chapter we describe our Framework for Action. This framework is our attempt to capture the tireless work of thousands of committed individuals who have collectively made a difference in schools across the United States and to provide guidance and support to the many dedicated educators embarking upon their own improvement journeys.

A Framework for Action:
Leading High-Poverty Schools
to High Performance

> We've put into place some of the research that Ron Edmonds did years ago. We have all the research we need. If you want to change a school, the research is there.... But as Ron Edmonds said, whether or not we do it depends upon how we feel about the fact that we haven't done it so far.
>
> *—Principal, HP/HP elementary school in the West*

> After eight years and a ton of work and reinventing wheels, we've really turned this school around.
>
> *—Principal, HP/HP high school in the West*

Which is it? As education leaders, do we have an extensive body of knowledge related to how low-performing, high-poverty schools become high performing, or are we primarily left to our own devices to figure it out?

To some extent the answer is both. Work from a wide-ranging group of scholars over the past three decades has clearly established that a low-performing, high-poverty school can improve. Much of this research has focused on elementary schools; there are far fewer high-performing, high-poverty high schools from which we can learn. Furthermore, there are no simple answers or fail-proof models for success. School improvement of this nature is comprehensive, complex, and somewhat subject to context-specific considerations.

The emergent body of knowledge related to how high-poverty schools can improve indeed may echo Almeida, Balfanz, and Steinberg's perspective that "we actually have more knowledge than we can apply" (2009, p. 22), or it may be that we have more knowledge than we have been *willing* to apply to this point. Again, based on what we know about high-performing, high-poverty schools, our intention in developing the Framework for Action is to provide understanding, guidance, and support to leaders from various vantage points, but particularly at the school level (principal and teacher-leaders).

Attempting to conceptualize the complex, nonlinear, messy nature of school improvement in high-poverty schools is fraught with problems. Over-simplifying the phenomenon can lead others to believe it can be reduced to a to-do list with a precisely sequenced set of activities or a cookbook filled with recipes guaranteed to succeed. The Framework for Action is neither a to-do list nor a cookbook. It is a source of research-based information about how improvement appears to happen in high-poverty schools; a collection of practical ideas offered by dedicated, hardworking educational leaders; and a set of tools that can be used to guide others' work. Our desire is to begin critical conversations, plant seeds of optimism and hope, as well as prompt action suited to a school's unique context. Using the information in this chapter, together with the rubrics in the action-oriented chapters that follow, leaders can access the existing knowledge base and learn from others' success while they consider the unique needs of their school and community.

Representing this complex work in the two-dimensional world of printed text presents another challenge. Thus, throughout this chapter, we have attempted to illustrate the dynamic nature of leadership in HP/HP schools and the interactions among the critical components of the framework. Refer to Figure 4.1 (p. 55), as we explain the relationship among the interactive components necessary to becoming a HP/HP school.

Leaders in HP/HP schools take action in three arenas: leadership capacity, the learning environment, and learning itself. It is complicated to explain precisely how actions in these arenas result in improvement; however, in most cases schools develop and build the *leadership capacity* needed to foster the creation of *healthy, safe, and supportive learning environments* and to support a relentless focus on *student, professional, and system learning*. These three arenas of action are represented in the Actions gear within Figure 4.1. The gear's circular shape represents the improvement process, which is fluid as all arenas work together without a true beginning or ending. Taking action is the necessary first step in making any kind of change; therefore, the Actions gear is the largest gear in the framework.

It is through strategic action in the three arenas of the Actions gear that the norms, values, and beliefs, which constitute school culture, begin to change. The School Culture gear provides a visual representation of the characteristics of culture in HP/HP schools. Interaction between changes in behavior and changes in beliefs is represented by the connection of the cogs between the Actions gear and the School Culture gear. In HP/HP schools, the school culture is characterized by caring relationships and advocacy for students; high expectations and support; professional accountability for learning; a commitment to equity; and courage and will to take action.

Finally, leaders' concerted efforts to take action and change the school's culture are targeted to affect the many Spheres of Influence (the final gear) on students' education, including their classroom, school, school district, family, and community. Leaders and the entire school community work in partnership and collaboration with stakeholders in any of these spheres to ensure that every student succeeds.

Collectively, the Framework for Action depicts a school's primary goal of all students learning to high standards. Figure 4.1 is an expression of the successful interaction of all components necessary to make every high-poverty school a high-performing school.

Taking Action: Building Leadership Capacity

As principal, I am a leader of leaders. At first, a lot of teachers did not want a leadership role. They didn't have the skills or the understanding of research.... I think one of the things that makes our success unusual is that we made it with a "bunch of old heads"—teachers who have been here 20 or 30 years. People say, "You've got to get rid of those people." No, my job is to grow those people. Were they hard to grow? Oh, you bet. Did they think I would leave before they did? Yes. I now have teachers who have a degree expertise in almost anything you can name.

—*Principal, HP/HP elementary school*

Throughout the research literature, the importance of leadership and leadership capacity is emphasized as being vital for organizational improvement. But what specifically does this leadership look like, and what does it mean to build leadership capacity? What is the relationship between leaders in a school? Can everyone be a leader? Might a school significantly improve without leadership capacity? How intense and pervasive must leadership be to prompt and sustain a significant degree of improvement?

In HP/HP schools, leadership capacity provides the necessary *infrastructure* to make and sustain improvements. Leadership capacity acts as the context for improvements in learning and the learning environment. Leadership capacity is both necessary infrastructure for high performance and the context for the other two domains in our Framework for Action (see Figure 4.1).

FIGURE 4.1 A Framework for Action: Leading High-Poverty Schools to High Performance

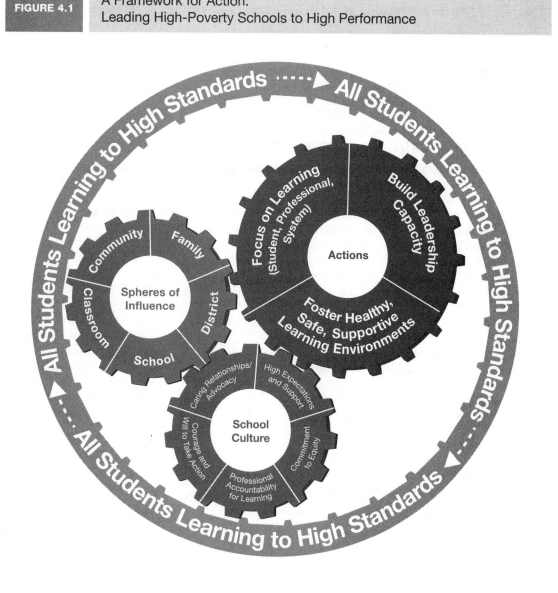

When such leadership infrastructure is present, HP/HP schools look much like what Linda Lambert (2005b) describes as "high leadership capacity" schools. She defines leadership capacity as "broad-based, skillful participation in the work of leadership" and further clarifies the term *work of leadership* as "reciprocal, purposeful learning together in community" (p. 38). According to Lambert (2005c), schools that develop high leadership capacity "take on a different character" than is true of schools with less leadership capacity (p. 65).

As was found in Lambert's (2005c) high leadership capacity schools, leadership in HP/HP schools is shared and distributed, a spirit of reciprocity flourishes, and principals embrace the role of lead learner. See Figure 4.2 for more information about characteristics of schools at three levels of leadership capacity.

FIGURE 4.2	Characteristics of Schools with High, Medium, and Low Levels of Leadership Capacity

High Leadership Capacity	Medium Leadership Capacity	Low Leadership Capacity
• Are learning communities that amplify leadership for all, learning for all, and success for all. • Develop a fabric of structures (e.g., teams, communities, study groups) and process (reflection, inquiry, dialogue) that form a more lasting and buoyant web of interrelated actions. • Principal is only one of the leaders in the school community and he/she models collaboration, listening, and engagement. • Features a shared vision for where the school is going and how it is getting there. • Individuals understand how they contribute to attaining the shared vision. • Quality of school is a function of the quality of conversations within the school. • Student success is revealed by multiple measures, including the presence of student voice in the direction of the school.	• Lack a compelling purpose and focus. • Are governed by norms of individualism. • Hold few conversations among the whole community. • Are fragmented and polarized. • Feature small groups of more skilled educators who are concerned that others are not "buying in" and may form an isolated inner core of decision makers. • Disaggregating student scores inevitably reveals a lack of success for the most vulnerable or challenged students.	• Are principal-dependent. • Have a lack of professional culture. • Are significantly unsuccessful with children. • Only principal as "top-down manager" is referred to as the leader. • Educators deflect responsibility while preferring blame. • Educators avoid focusing on teaching and learning while holding fast to archaic practices. • Professional relationships are congenial, but not collegial. • Test scores may be considered the only valid measure of success. • Void of internal accountability. • Subject to the whims, demands, and pressures of parents, districts, and states.

Shared and Distributed Leadership

A principal's position of formal authority affords that person a unique and vital role in the effort to turn around a low-performing school. In HP/HP schools, principals frequently acknowledge that they cannot go it alone, as leadership functions must be shared and distributed among many stakeholders. Recognizing the critically important opportunities others have to lead from various vantage points throughout the system (for example, other administrators, teachers, support personnel, school trustees, parents, families, and community members), HP/HP principals seek to share decision-making authority and governance of the school.

A Spirit of Reciprocity

Shared and distributed leadership depends upon a spirit of reciprocity. Autocratic leadership encourages a dependent relationship between leader and follower. Dependent relationships between principals and teachers can lead to blaming and abdicating responsibility for improvement (Lambert, 2005c). On the other hand, principals who embrace the approach of holding others accountable while holding themselves equally accountable present a dramatically different type of leadership. Harvard University professor Richard Elmore (2000) describes a relationship of reciprocal accountability between principal and teacher, saying, "If the formal authority of my role requires that I hold you accountable for some action or outcome, then I have an equal and complementary responsibility to ensure that you have the capacity to do what I am asking you to do" (p. 21).

Principal as Lead Learner

Interdependent relationships and reciprocal accountability characterize a new paradigm for the principal as lead learner among a community of learners. This was true of all of the principals we studied. As one principal in an HP/HP urban elementary school admitted:

> It's scary for me to think about everything I need to do and then to know that I am supposed to be an instructional leader too. Instead of being an instructional leader, I am a learning leader. I like that because it's about me bringing everything I can to the table and about empowering this community of learners to do the best job possible. It's about offering opportunities for collaboration and really honest, deep conversations about our practice.

Principals most often begin the conversation about what is truly possible in a high-poverty school. They facilitate the development of a common vision of high levels of learning for all—students and adults—and become the chief stewards in keeping it alive and in the forefront for the school staff, parents, and community. They act out of a commitment to equity, which often begins with an analysis of data. As a teacher in one of the schools we studied explained:

> We're a data-driven school. We use data a lot here, and we're lucky to have a principal who helps us target the students with the highest needs and helps us set goals for those students. We get a lot of training on how to use data. We use it to make curriculum decisions and to individualize instruction. Our principal can take credit for a lot of the success our school has had. She is an amazing leader and is learning with us. We haven't always had the best track record with our kids, but I like how things are done here now.

Sharing and distributing leadership functions, fostering a spirit of reciprocity, and viewing the principal as lead learner among a community of learners constitute the leadership capacity or "leadership infrastructure" necessary to maintain the constant focus on learning and the learning environment found in HP/HP schools. Chapters 5 and 6 provide detailed information about building leadership capacity, including advice about specific actions to take and practices to eliminate, as well as tools for assessing your school's current leadership capacity and planning your next steps.

Leadership capacity influences the level of collective efficacy with which the school is able to focus on improvements in the learning environment and learning itself. As improvements in these areas are made and sustained, the level of leadership capacity increases. Leadership capacity is a core component of the Actions gear (see Figure 4.1) and a central part of a process that intimately connects with the corresponding gears of focusing on learning and fostering healthy, safe, and supportive learning environments. As part of a gear, these three actions provide the impetus that makes all gears or domains of a student's life work together to improve his or her learning and outlook in life.

Taking Action: Fostering Healthy, Safe, and Supportive Learning Environments

> There was a sign in the cafeteria, "No Talking In Line." Not only were kids talking, but also pushing, shoving, and hitting. We had rules, but no expectations that they would be followed.... So I began gathering data and wrote down everything I saw. I met with every teacher, and we began to talk about the Correlates of Effective

Schools. The first correlate is safety and order. Creating a safe environment had to be addressed before we were going to be able to address anything else.

—Susan Williamson, principal, Taft Elementary School

More than three decades of research has demonstrated that schools can influence the outcomes for children who live in poverty and the concomitant situations that put them at risk behaviorally, emotionally, cognitively, and academically. High-performing, high-poverty schools provide *protective factors* that help build a bond between students and school. These factors include fostering caring relationships between adults and children, as well as among peers; setting high expectations and providing the support needed to meet those expectations; providing opportunity for meaningful involvement in school; providing a safe and orderly environment in which the rules are clear; and ensuring academic success (Benard, 1991). Chapters 7 and 8 present the many ways leaders foster a healthy, safe, and supportive learning environment and offer a way to assess your school's current learning environment, as well as plan for collective action.

Creating the kind of environment in which students living in poverty can flourish becomes possible when leaders, teachers, and other staff work collaboratively to meet each student's learning needs. But such collaboration is not always the norm; indeed, in many schools it is the antithesis of the way they do business. In far too many schools, teachers and other staff continue to work as independent contractors who share a building. This is not true of HP/HP schools. In these schools, learning is the focus and collaboration is the means.

Taking Action: Focusing on Student, Professional, and System Learning

We have a lot of kids who move in and out of the school, or they miss a lot of school. More of our kids are coming to school impacted by methamphetamines in the home. When we assessed our kindergartners at the end of last year, we had 20 kids start at the zero point. They didn't know even five sounds or letters. You might be wondering what's going to happen to those 20 kids this year. I'll tell you what's going to happen... they're going to learn to read.

—Teacher, rural HP/HP elementary school in the West

Leaders in HP/HP schools demonstrate a tenacious focus on learning. Despite the challenges that their students face and the odds against them, they maintain high expectations for their students, as well as for themselves.

Three Kinds of Learning

In high-performing schools, student learning is purposefully and intentionally linked to two other learning agendas—professional learning and system-level learning (Knapp et al., 2003). We are using the term *professional learning* to refer to the adult learning that occurs in schools. The term *system-level learning* provides a way to describe how the school as a whole "learns" to be more effective in accomplishing its mission and goals. In other words, as individuals learn, the school (or system) learns to do business differently and better.

The three types of learning—student, professional, and system—interact and influence one another (see Figure 4.1, p. 55). One of the greatest challenges that leaders face is to grasp the opportunity for learning that each agenda gives rise to—to see the connections among the various kinds of learning and the manner in which they mutually influence one another. Nonetheless, meeting this challenge is the "essential first step" for leaders to begin to improve learning (Knapp et al., 2003, p. 14). How does this look in practice? One of the schools we visited provides a good example.

Imagine a team of 4th grade teachers collaboratively examining the results of a classroom-based assessment that they recently administered (evidence of student learning) and discussing the classroom instruction that occurred before administering the assessment. The teachers conclude that they need to learn more about how to help students make inferences when reading fictional text. Now imagine that the school's literacy coach has been participating in this discussion and other previous discussions that have ended with similar conclusions. This information becomes "data" or "inputs," which in this case informed the system. In this school, leaders, teachers, and staff subsequently selected and engaged in professional development on the topic of making inferences from fictional text and received embedded coaching to reinforce what they had learned in a workshop format (evidence of system learning). Teaching improved (evidence of professional learning), as did student assessment results (evidence of student learning). Chapters 9 and 10 provide additional action-oriented information about how schools focus on the three kinds of learning, advice about actions to take, and tools for self-assessment and planning.

Learning—student, professional, and system—is influenced by attributes of the broader contexts in which it is nested, such as the size and location of the school and district, considerations related to the families and communities the school serves, as well as local, state, and federal policy (Knapp et al., 2003). Thus, schools that enroll a high percentage of students who live in poverty must understand how poverty influences student learning and how a concentration of students living in poverty can affect the learning conditions for teachers and staff, as well as the system's capacity to learn. A keen understanding of the link between learning and the influence of poverty is critical as leaders try to change the culture of the school. Leaders in HP/HP schools courageously engage their colleagues in collectively changing behaviors, which in turn prompts an examination of the existing norms, values, and beliefs.

Leading Change in School Culture

Let me tell you the one huge difference I see between this school and others I've worked in. Every single staff member cares about every single kid in this school, and the kids know it. The teachers care about each other too. I know they care about me; they care how I do. Parents know I care. Way back, when I first assembled an *F* list, I called each student in—all 93 of them—and also met with a parent of each student. I didn't care what time it was. Sometimes I stayed until 9 p.m. and I'd get here at 5 a.m., if that was when the parents could meet. We had to figure out why their child was failing. I'm not the only one who does that; it's the culture of this school. That's the difference.

—Assistant principal, HP/HP high school in the West

In high-poverty schools, changes in policies, practices, and structures are necessary but by themselves are insufficient to gain and sustain improvement in student achievement and other measures of student success. Leaders in high-performing, high-poverty schools take the next necessary step by sparking change in the fundamental ethos and culture of the school. A school's culture is defined by three elements: (1) norms, (2) values, and (3) beliefs or assumptions. These aspects of school culture exist on a hierarchy of abstraction. Norms are more easily observed and are more concrete than are values. In turn, values are less abstract than are beliefs and assumptions, which are often tacitly held (Hoy & Miskel, 2008).

Change of a Second Order

Changes in school culture represent deep systemic change for most schools. Such change is sometimes described as second-order change and is of a greater magnitude than first-order change (Marzano, Waters, & McNulty, 2005). First-order changes tend to be incremental and do not significantly depart from current conditions. Typically, processes used to make first-order changes, as well as their intended outcomes, are familiar to the individuals engaged in facilitating the change. Second-order change is change that results in conditions that are significantly different from the present reality. Individuals engaged in second-order change often use an "invent as you go" approach, and the outcome may be uncertain or unknown. Whether a change is of the first or second order (lesser or greater magnitude) varies from school to school; therefore, it is not possible to establish that certain kinds of changes will always be first-order changes and others will always be second-order changes.

Nonetheless, for example, in many if not most secondary schools, adopting the latest edition of a textbook would be a first-order change. Then again, in many if not most secondary schools, detracking math courses is likely to be a second-order change. Why might this be? In most schools, the process for adopting textbooks is familiar to teachers, and the use of a new edition is not likely to result in a fundamental change in pedagogy. Detracking all math courses, on the other hand, is apt not only to result in fundamental changes in school structure and pedagogy, but also to challenge long-held beliefs and assumptions (such as math is not for everyone; some students just can't learn math; most of our kids are poor, they aren't going to college, and they don't need much more than basic math).

The Mismatch of Leadership to Magnitude

All change can be difficult to facilitate, and second-order change is particularly challenging. There is no shortage of explanations about why this is true; volumes of information have been compiled on organizational change by scholars from a variety of fields. Drawing from this literature as well as our own study of HP/HP schools, we offer the following insight into the intractability of school culture: School leaders in high-poverty schools may fail to facilitate lasting and deep change in school culture because they do not recognize the magnitude of the needed change and, in doing so, underestimate the intensity of the leadership needed (Marzano, Waters, & McNulty, 2005). Differing dramatically from the culture of many schools, particularly perpetually low-performing schools, the culture of HP/HP schools suggests a confluence of five critical attributes: (1) caring relationships and advocacy, (2) high expectations and support, (3) an unwavering commitment to equity, (4) a sense of professional accountability for learning, and (5) the courage and will needed to take action. See Figure 4.1 (p. 55) for a graphic representation of the attributes that collectively drive dramatic improvements in school culture and student performance.

Low-performing, high-poverty schools are often distinguished by a toxic culture of low expectations, excuse making, blame, and resignation. In these schools, the degree of change needed to foster a culture conducive to high levels of learning for all—students, professionals, and the system—presents a formidable challenge. To improve these schools, leaders must match their leadership actions with the order of magnitude that the needed changes represent.

The Power of Mental Maps

Changing school culture is difficult, in part, because it requires people to challenge their mental maps or mind-sets—the images, assumptions, and personal perspectives we hold about people, institutions, and the world in general. These mental maps underpin both our theories *of* action and our theories *in* action (Argyris & Schön, 1974). Challenging and changing a mental map is difficult because we humans usually reject information that conflicts with or contradicts our mental maps. Leaders must understand the power of mental maps, particularly those who hope to lead cultural change in low-performing, high-poverty schools. As noted earlier, many educators cling to myths about people who live in poverty. These myths are shaped and perpetuated by mental maps. Separating myth from reality often entails challenging our mind-set. Leaders who are successful in courageously encouraging the examination of mental maps do not do so by challenging others' beliefs; rather, they encourage changes in behaviors and norms first. *Changes in behavior most often come before changes in beliefs.*

Leaders in the schools that we studied did not use the term *mental maps*, they use the term *mind-set*. No matter the word, leaders took action that prompted themselves and others to reflect upon their existing perspectives and assumptions about poverty. They used data and shared information to challenge long-held assumptions about students living in poverty, to build a shared vision of equity and excellence, and to create a sense of urgency. These leaders seemed to understand that their own values and beliefs could not be infused into others. Rather, these leaders engendered changes in beliefs and values by providing others with new experiences in a relatively nonthreatening environment.

Leaders in these schools allowed teachers and other staff to get on board by taking risks and trying new things. These changes in behaviors challenged the tacit assumptions underlying educators' mental maps and in turn seemed to prompt changes in beliefs and values. For instance, in some schools, leaders supported teachers and staff in conducting carefully planned home visits to promote a better understanding of low-income families and the challenges they face. Thoughtfully executed, these home visits became opportunities to explore stereotypes about students who live in poverty. They challenged the deficit perspective held by many and made teachers and staff more responsive to poverty's intervening factors that threaten students' well-being and readiness to learn.

As a result of better understanding the impact of poverty, another school provided supplies for every student and abandoned extracurricular pay-to-participate fees. Connecting with families helped to change expectations in another school, where the notion that all children can and will learn to high standards became the norm. In this school, when student achievement lagged, teachers took professional accountability rather than blaming children and families.

Working in Many Spheres of Influence

> It takes all of us—teachers, parents, community members. Leaders have to have a commitment to the community. We have to be stakeholders in the community. We can't just be a visitor or part-timer, or somebody passing through. You have to have that combination of things, some experience in and knowledge of the community, caring about kids, and then the money. We can't just throw money at the problem if we don't have the commitment and the caring, but when we do, the money sure helps!
>
> —*Rural school board member*

Leaders in HP/HP schools do not work in isolation. In addition to taking action that influences the classroom and the school at large, these schools often develop positive and productive relationships with district office leaders, students' families, and the broader neighborhood and community. See the Spheres of Influence gear in Figure 4.1 (p. 55). For instance, in many schools, leaders use the school as a community center, which affords them greater opportunity to build relationships with families and other members of the community while providing needed resources. Many high-performing, high-poverty schools also establish community-based learning programs, which have demonstrated particular effectiveness for students living in low-income homes and for those with other risk factors (Barr & Parrett, 2007).

In practice, leaders develop effective partnerships, in part, to garner resources from sources external to the school. One of the most important partnerships that school leaders can establish is with district office personnel to leverage support for the unique needs of their school.

The sustained success of an HP/HP school depends on a multitude of factors related to the core components reflected in the Framework for Action. Part II, Leading Together: Taking Action to Lead Underachieving Students in Poverty to Success, presents a contrast of what to *eliminate* and what to *initiate or improve* related to the three focal points of leading HP/HP schools: building leadership capacity; fostering a healthy, safe, and supportive learning environment; and focusing on student, professional, and system learning.

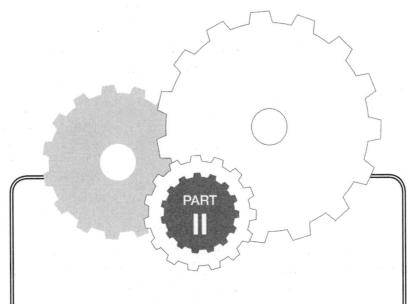

Leading Together:

Taking Action to Lead
Underachieving Students in Poverty
to Success

PART
II

Building Leadership Capacity: HP/HP Schools *Eliminate* What Doesn't Work

We thought we were doing what was best for Devon. He didn't have the reading skills to move on to 7th grade. Another year in 6th should help him catch up. We had no idea that he would stop coming. Now he's gone.

—*Middle school principal in the Southwest*

Devon dropped out of school at age 13. No one knows where he is today. Most likely, he's not in school. Devon was going to be retained to spend another year in the 6th grade as a 13-year-old. He was embarrassed and felt alone. He didn't want to be with a new group of kids who were younger. Truth was, Devon had been passed along with low reading skills for years. Now, in the beginning of his adolescent years, he was told he was going back. He gave the class a try... for three weeks... and then disappeared. With good intentions, Devon's teachers had recommended an intervention—retention—that resulted in the opposite effect of what they had hoped.

Retention as an intervention for underachievement does not work. Sixty years of research bear out this conclusion; thus we view it as the "poster child" for the many mind-sets, policies, structures, and practices entrenched in schools that are commonly employed to "allow a student to catch up" and, at times, as a punishment for not keeping up.

High-poverty schools become high performing in part by *abandoning* what does not work and replacing those approaches with those that *do work*. A number of counterproductive strategies and beliefs about educating students, particularly those who live in poverty, actually perpetuate underachievement by working against the development of leadership capacity.

Our Framework for Action builds on Lambert's (2005c) definition of leadership capacity as the ability of a broad base of stakeholders to engage in "the work of leadership," which she defines as "learning together in community" (p. 38). Further, leadership capacity is described as shared decision making and a spirit of reciprocity, together with the principal's assuming the role of lead learner. In this chapter and Chapter 6, we extend this conceptualization to include the mind-sets, policies, structures, and practices that serve either to *impede* the development of leadership capacity in high-poverty schools or to *support* it.

High-performing, high-poverty schools endeavor to build leadership capacity to better meet the needs of students like Devon. As part of committing to that work, leaders aggressively confront entrenched, counterproductive strategies and beliefs. They are relentless in this effort. They know that inaction perpetuates low achievement and undermines other effective practices. But where do they begin? Because there is no one right answer to that question, we have designed the tools in this book to help you and your fellow leaders tailor the information and ideas to your unique context. To guide learning and to help in reflecting on the current situation in your school, use the rubric in Figure 5.1, which isolates seven specific mind-sets, policies, structures, and practices that HP/HP schools have helped to identify as barriers to building leadership capacity and improving achievement.

Perpetuating Underachievement

We had to get to a point where we were all on board with the belief that every kid was going to learn, that every family mattered, and that regardless of the condition of the home, this child would learn and reach proficiency. We would do whatever it took... all of us. Did it mean several teachers chose to transfer or leave? Did it mean it took a couple of years to get there? Yes, but now everyone's on the same page, and that makes all the difference.

—*Principal, HP/HP high school in the West*

FIGURE 5.1 Barriers to Building Leadership Capacity

Are We Perpetuating Underachievement? What Have We Eliminated?				
Progress Indicators/Evidence →	**No Action Yet**	**Getting Started**	**Gaining Momentum**	**Sustaining Gains, Refining**
		• People are aware of counterproductive mind-sets, policies, structures, or practices. • Urgency is apparent. • People acknowledge the need for change.	• People are empowered. • Barriers are being removed. • Commitment to elimination is increasing. • Pressure and support for change continues.	• Counterproductive mind-sets, policies, structures, or practices have been eliminated. • New mind-sets, policies, structures, and practices are in place.
Counterproductive Mind-Sets and Practices ↓	**0**	**1**	**2**	**3**
Inequitable distribution of resources.				
Low expectations for students.				
Low expectations for professionals and staff.				
Lack of courage or will to confront inequities and improper practices.				
Lack of support for effective leaders and teachers.				
Failure to retain effective leaders and teachers.				
Ineffective data systems.				

A common characteristic of public education in the United States is the tendency to rarely, if ever, abandon policies, structures, and practices that have become mainstream. If adopted and kept in place for a nominal amount of time, it is likely that the policy, structure, or practice will be around for a long time, even if it yields only marginal positive results. In many respects, this reluctance to change has served our systems well by supporting what works. Yet when something does not work, even when refuted by overwhelming research, we often have a difficult time changing a course of action or abandoning something we are used to doing.

Retention, tracking, misassignment to special education, out-of-school suspensions, ineffective teaching, placing inexperienced or improperly credentialed teachers with underachieving students, ignoring ELL needs, and failing to counter cultures of low expectation represent only a few of the policies, structures, and practices that continue to exist in many schools. These approaches yield predictable negative results for underachieving students, particularly those who live in poverty.

Several reasons seem likely for the perpetuation of these approaches, not least the inertia found in bureaucratic systems. Still, organizations are composed of people, and people have to change before "systems" change. Underlying the perpetuation of these counterproductive approaches are the mental maps discussed in Chapters 3 and 4. These mind-sets often result in the underserving of students who live in poverty and can be seen in schools in the form of indifference, ignorance, classism, racism, and at times simply anger or annoyance. They impede progress toward improving the learning conditions and achievement of underperforming students.

Such mind-sets are manifest foremost in low expectations for students living in poverty. In a culture of low expectations, three other practices that perpetuate underachievement and work against building leadership capacity are often present in low-performing schools: inequitable funding, lack of support for or the failure to retain effective educators, and data systems that are nonexistent or ineffective. A lack of willingness and courage to tackle these issues is what fundamentally differentiates low-performing, high-poverty schools from high-performing, high-poverty schools.

Tolerating Low Expectations

When we hire new teachers, we check out their expectations of kids. The kids help us with the interviews and are the first to spot anything less than high expectations in an applicant. We will not employ or tolerate any staff member who demonstrates otherwise.

—*Principal, HP/HP middle school in the Southeast*

A toxic atmosphere of low expectations permeates everything in a low-performing school. Low expectations are well intended at best and prejudiced, biased, classist, or racist at worst. No underperforming school that enrolls students who live in poverty will ever reverse trends of underachievement without explicitly addressing the expectations held by all staff. High expectations are simply paramount to success.

Leaders in HP/HP schools, particularly the principal, model high expectations for themselves. To counter the existence of any mind-set that reflects less than the very best for every student, they tackle the insidiousness of low expectations head-on. They do not tolerate excuses for underachievement, including those made by the students themselves. They are relentless in their efforts to help all students feel safe and develop a sense of belonging at school, they honor the effort required of students, and they celebrate the students' accomplishments. This mind-set of high expectations and resulting action often begins with the development of a common vision of what powerful learning looks like for all students and a verbalized belief that every student can and will achieve at high levels and experience other types of success in school. A culture of high expectations appears to be accomplished, in part, by building relationships with students and their families; seeking to understand their needs, strengths, interests, and assets; and in turn accessing whatever support is needed to succeed.

The importance of high expectations, as noted author Rhonda Weinstein (2002) has stated, is critical to our children's future:

> When we respond to the individual differences among students by lowering our expectations and providing inferior educational opportunities, we underestimate the capacity for all of our children to grow intellectually, and we fail to provide adequate tools for learning. In these ways, we confirm our own predictions. To prevent such educational tragedies—a particularly urgent goal given the growing diversity of our children attending our schools—we need to both embrace and support pedagogically a vision of possibility regarding the educational achievement of all our children. (p. 2)

High expectations hold incredible power, often single-handedly determining the fine line or enormous chasm between success and failure. Schools routinely serve as a broker to parcel out both types of expectations, high and low, and student success follows accordingly. High-performing, high-poverty schools are places of high expectations. Creating and sustaining this element of the school's culture requires educators to eliminate blaming, excuse making, and a host of other counterproductive practices that not only perpetuate low achievement but also serve as barriers to building leadership capacity within the school. Such barriers include inequitable funding, lack of support for and failure to retain effective educators, and ineffective data systems.

Lacking a Commitment to Equity— Inequitable Funding

> Far too many of our kids arrive at school with less... vocabulary, preschooling, educational learning experiences, books in the home, parents in the home, supplies and materials associated with learning and school, safe environments, and more. And what do we give them? They come with less and, in return, we give them less.
>
> —*Kati Haycock, President, the Education Trust*

At the top of the list of the villains that rob students of the opportunity to catch up with their more advantaged peers is inequitable funding. While acknowledging that the formulas used by states and districts to finance schools are complex, leveling the playing field for students in poverty comes down, in part, to this simple question: Do we provide equitable funding to our students who live in poverty?

The answer is more complex than merely calculating per-pupil or per-teacher expenditures; yet such figures are indeed revealing. Through a decade of research, Ed Trust has continued to document the fact that high-poverty schools in the United States on average receive substantially less (around $900) in per-pupil funding than do low-poverty districts. Ed Trust's recent analysis of teacher salary discrepancies in the 50 largest districts in Texas found the gap between high- and low-poverty districts ranged from $975 for elementary schools to $1,089 for high schools. In some cases, the gap was as great as $3,834 per teacher. Such funding gaps have proven persistent and appear to some degree in all states (Education Trust, 2006).

Countless decisions related to the use of resources influence whether underachieving students in poverty will catch up and whether students from low-income homes (underachieving or not) will have the opportunity to fully participate in school. Instead of arriving at schools that provide opportunities to accelerate their learning and catch up, too often these students are greeted by inexperienced teachers (often teaching out of their area of expertise), in schools that are substandard and sometimes unhealthy, unsafe, and full of chaos and disorganization. The students who need more resources often come to schools that receive less.

In addition, students living in poverty are confronted with a barrage of hidden costs that serve as reminders that they simply "don't belong" and diminish the necessary bond between school and student. For example, in one particular middle school, the background colors on students' ID cards (which students were required to wear on lanyards around their necks) were chosen by the photography company and depended on whether the student had purchased a photo package. Staff did not notice the difference in IDs until a student told one of his teachers, "You know who bought pictures and who didn't by the color of the background."

The hidden cost of attending school often includes fees for participation in athletics, band, choir, and various clubs, as well as materials and supplies related to homework assignments, athletic uniforms, yearbooks, school pictures, social activities, and school supplies. Student who are poor usually do without these aspects of school, which most students consider standard. High-performing, high-poverty schools commit to the equitable use of resources. They create and maintain budgets that become moral documents intended to target support where it's needed most. The schools' priorities drive the budgeting process and are aimed at leveling the playing field for students from low-income families.

Lack of Support for and Failure to Retain Effective Educators

> Our school was a revolving door for principals—in the past two years we've had three. How are we supposed to get better with that going on?
>
> *—High school teacher in the Midwest*

Stability of leadership is a hallmark of effective schools. When transitions do come, these schools usually have a unique ability to rely on the leadership capacity throughout the school and their sustained accomplishments to successfully adjust. When a leader leaves a successful school of any type, it is not unusual for a period of instability to follow as the incoming leader establishes relationships with the staff and often creates new routines for the school.

But frequent changes in leadership are disruptive to the trust building and sustained focus is needed to improve low-performing schools. District leaders' failure to support and retain the most effective leaders in low-performing schools can precipitate a recipe for maintaining the status quo, or worse.

Stable leadership characterizes HP/HP schools. It is not unusual for principals to remain for multiple years. Of the seven schools we studied, the average principal tenure was more than eight years. Although some of these effective principals would suggest that they stayed because of district support, most would acknowledge that the trust and collaboration established among the staff and with families was a key factor in their returning to the school year after year.

Similarly, if a school consistently loses effective teachers each year and must continuously engage in the search and selection of personnel, the trajectory of student achievement usually will remain flat at best. The revolving door, often found in low-performing, high-poverty schools, clearly perpetuates low student achievement. There may be pockets of excellence among remaining faculty; still, research demonstrates that the drastic changes needed to gain and sustain improvement in teaching and learning require trust—and trust building requires time and continuity in staffing (Bryk & Schneider, 2002).

High-performing, high-poverty schools recruit and retain excellent and effective educators. Why? In part, such educators seek positions in these schools and stay for years despite the challenges they face because excellent and effective teachers prefer to work with other excellent and effective teachers, and the leadership infrastructure (capacity) is present to support collaborative relationships. The following observation from a superintendent provides a specific example of how stable and supportive leadership can make a difference in retaining excellent teachers:

> We used to lose a lot of teachers every year to the surrounding districts because, in part, they paid more but also because our schools were not well led. Now, three years later, we have effective, stable leadership in every building, and our teacher attrition rates have dropped substantially.

Ineffective Data Systems

There was a time in the not so distant past when the only data teachers had to deal with related to their classroom grades. Teachers rarely used or understood yearly norm-referenced national tests (which were usually administered in select grade levels), largely because such tests had little connection to the classroom curriculum. Teachers were not expected to be data literate. Much has changed in this area.

Today, teachers must be proficient in the use of data. In low-performing, high-poverty schools, this skill is especially critical for establishing targeted, needs-based interventions that require accurate data analysis and diagnosis. Additionally, effective interventions must be carefully monitored to sustain achievement gains.

An effective data system is user-friendly, designed appropriately for its intended purpose, and easily deployed in the classroom and school. Systems that are too complex or not readily accessible simply do not get used. Under these circumstances, it is much more likely for students to slip through the cracks and school improvement efforts to, at best, become random acts of good deeds. An effective data system supports the development of data and assessment literacy that is fundamental for informed short-cycle and long-term improvement planning, instructional decisions, and the guidance of students' understanding of their learning.

Lacking the Courage and Will to Act

Leaders in HP/HP schools confront the brutal facts that result from the perpetuation of practices that yield unsatisfactory results for their underachieving students. They tirelessly endeavor to eliminate such counterproductive practices. This effort requires that they have the will and courage to challenge some of the most entrenched mind-sets, policies, structures, and practices that are often found in schools. But their work does not end there. In Chapter 6 we discuss the actions school leaders need to take to build the leadership capacity necessary to focus on the improvement of learning and the learning environment.

Action Planning/Next Steps

Use the action planning template in Figure 5.2 (p. 78) to help you and your colleagues reflect on the content and ideas from Chapter 5. What commitments do you need to make, and what actions do you need to take, to build leadership capacity?

FIGURE 5.2	Action Planning Template for Building Leadership Capacity

1. What new information, insights, and ideas did we gain from this chapter?

2. Based on our assessment of the school or district, what change needs to occur and what might be our next steps?

3. Are the changes needed in our school or district structural (time, resources), cultural (norms, beliefs, values), or both? What is the evidence?

4. What is the magnitude of change this represents for our school—first order or second order? What is the evidence?

Action Plan		
Next Steps	**Lead Person Responsible**	**Timeline**

Building Leadership Capacity: How HP/HP Schools Do It

[Our school has] a culture of learning, a culture of dialogue, a culture of reflection.... I need to grow the teachers to be leaders of leaders, and I do that by listening to them. We do that by listening to each other.

—*Susan Williamson, principal, Taft Elementary School*

At William Howard Taft Elementary School in Boise, Idaho, a 3rd grade teacher marveled, "Within five minutes of the bell ringing, classrooms were running smoothly. The kids knew exactly what the expectations were. They came into the classrooms ready to learn." She was referring to how well 58 students who had recently emigrated from 16 different countries and spoke 14 different languages had successfully transitioned into the "Taft family" in fall 2008. Taft made the transition possible through initiatives tailored to address the challenges refugee students and their families faced as they entered an unfamiliar school.

Principal Susan Williamson learned in April 2008 that the school district had designated Taft as an ELL site. Forty refugee students were slated to be transferred to Taft from other schools in the district (and an additional 18 enrolled in September). The school, which serves 360 students, went from serving only 1 English language learner to serving nearly 60.

The teachers, staff, and neighborhood community of Taft are no strangers to challenges. Taft's student body is 73 percent low income, and when

Williamson arrived at the school, test scores were low, morale was dismal, and student behavior was out of control. Ten years later, student achievement had increased significantly and Taft had been recognized as a National Blue Ribbon School.

Nonetheless, ensuring that a group of newcomers—half of whom had minimal English language proficiency—would achieve at high levels posed a formidable expectation. The district assigned Taft a certified ELL teacher and a paraprofessional, and it provided the services of an ELL consultant and the director of the district's ELL program. These services were vital, but the school knew it would have to put forth effort to forge trusting relationships with students and their families.

With fewer than 45 days remaining in the 2007–08 school year, a small team began to welcome the refugee students. They learned as much as possible about the youths and their families, set aside time at the faculty meetings to devote to this welcome effort, and used two half-day professional development opportunities to devour information about the needs of English language learners—refugees in particular. They also launched Tiger Pride Summer Camp, a two-week nonacademic team-building experience designed to develop a sense of belonging and introduce students to the traditions of their new school.

Taft's "whatever it takes" attitude turned what could have been a difficult transition for its new students into a smooth success, and the school year began better than anyone could have anticipated. The camp made a tremendous difference in easing the students into their new environment. But its success depended on the relationships of mutual trust that Principal Williamson and Taft's teachers had built through summer home visits with families. The Taft faculty continues outreach to the school's newest families through ongoing home visits. With the input of a parent—once one of the most resistant to the transfer of her child to Taft—the school team recently launched the Tiger Pride Family Saturday Learning Academy for the newcomer parents and their children.

In another high-poverty school, this same scenario might have been disastrous for students and teachers. How was it possible at Taft? The quick answer might give all the credit to Principal Williamson. But one heroic leader's effort was not the key to Taft's success. This is not to say that Principal Williamson's leadership wasn't critical—it was. From the beginning of her tenure at Taft, she created conditions that built leadership capacity in herself and others, as well as in the school itself. In essence, Taft's story is one of building leadership capacity. When confronted with the challenge of transitioning nearly 60 refugee students into the school, they had the leadership capacity (or infrastructure) to do so successfully.

In Chapter 4 we conceptualized what it means to build leadership capacity by expanding upon Lambert's (2005b) definition, which posits that when a school has a high degree of leadership capacity, leadership functions and tasks are shared and broadly distributed, reciprocal accountability is the norm, and the principal assumes the role of lead learner. The notion of the principal as lead learner is critical to understanding that in HP/HP schools the work of leadership *is* learning—learning as individuals, as a community, and as a system.

By building leadership capacity throughout the school, leaders construct the infrastructure needed to focus intensely on the work of improving learning and the learning environment. Use the rubric in Figure 6.1 to focus your learning and to reflect on your school's current situation.

Asking the Right Questions and Finding the Leverage Points

Because HP/HP schools are places of reflection and inquiry, leaders' work in these schools is better characterized in the form of questions than formulaic lists of strategies. These questions span the three interrelated core elements in the Framework for Action discussed in Chapter 4: (1) building the necessary leadership capacity; (2) fostering a healthy, safe, and supportive learning environment for all; and (3) focusing the staff's everyday core work on student, professional, and system learning. If a school's primary goal is to significantly improve achievement, particularly of low-income children, the questions discussed in this chapter, as well as those in Chapters 8 and 10, should provide valuable, insightful direction.

Three guiding questions can serve as leverage points for building leadership capacity: (1) Are we deploying financial, material, and human resources effectively? (2) Are we optimizing time—extending it for underachieving students and reorganizing it to better support professional learning? (3) Do we have a data system that works for classroom and school leaders?

Are We Deploying Resources Effectively?

Principals in high-performing, high-poverty schools ensure that the necessary financial, material, and human resources are available for students and adults to succeed (Ball, 2001; Leader, 2010). Leaders in the schools we studied began their remarkable turnarounds by making tough calls—and many of

FIGURE 6.1	Building Leadership Capacity

Do We Have Structures and Processes for Building Leadership Capacity?				
Progress Indicators/Evidence →	**No Action Yet**	**Getting Started**	**Gaining Momentum**	**Sustaining Gains, Refining**
		• Urgency is apparent. • School status is understood. • A vision for improvement is shared. • Implementation strategies are selected. • Staff is prepared to begin.	• People are empowered. • Barriers are being removed. • Implementation is becoming routine. • Commitment is increasing. • Progress is monitored. • Initial gains are being made and celebrated. • Support for improvement continues.	• Improvements are embedded in daily practice. • Collaboration continues. • Refinements are made. • Gains continue to be made and sustained.
What is my school's progress? ↓	**0**	**1**	**2**	**3**
Does our budgeting process reflect our priorities?				
Does our interviewing and selection process result in high-quality personnel who match the needs of the school?				
Does our workplace encourage high-quality personnel to stay?				
Do we optimize time by extending it for our underachieving students?				
Do we optimize time by using it for job-embedded professional learning?				

FIGURE 6.1	Building Leadership Capacity (*continued*)

What is my school's progress? ↓	0	1	2	3
Do we have a learning-centered schedule and do we protect learning time during the school day?				
Do we use multiple forms of data to make instructional decisions at the class and school levels?				
Have we conducted an equity audit?				
What is my district's progress in supporting schools in these areas?				

those decisions were about how to use resources. They not only used the school's existing resources innovatively, but also often secured additional funding from the district office and capitalized on relationships with external stakeholders to garner support for the school.

SCHOOL CULTURE ALERT

As a matter of practice, leaders in HP/HP schools guide the use of resources by holding fast to the school's vision and goals. The budget in an HP/HP school becomes a moral document, reflective of the school's commitment to equity, as well as its values and beliefs about the conditions necessary to sustain success for all students and the adults who serve them.

Approximately 70 to 80 percent of a typical school's budget is dedicated to personnel, so it stands to reason that recruitment and retention of talented staff is a top resource-management priority. Too often principals have limited influence over personnel decisions. Teacher assignments are often made by district personnel offices and guided by factors that are not necessarily related to the needs of a particular school. These factors can include school closings and openings, boundary changes that influence school size and consequently staff size, collective bargaining agreements that favor seniority over teacher and staff qualifications, and "the dance of the lemons" (transferring ineffective teachers from school to school).

When decision making about resources, chiefly personnel, is decentralized to the school level, the principal and other site-based leaders can further their improvement efforts by hiring teachers and staff with qualifications that match the school's needs. Three phases of the personnel process are critical to consider: (1) recruitment, (2) selection, and (3) retention.

In the recruitment phase, principals should consider factors that attract excellent teachers to high-needs schools. Using strategies such as hiring bonuses and housing supplements may be beyond the purview of most principals; however, principals often do have some degree of control over other factors that may lure excellent faculty and staff to their schools. According to a study of 1,700 National Board-certified teachers, ensuring that teachers have updated technology, lower class sizes, and opportunities to work with colleagues as a regular part of the school day may entice highly qualified teachers to schools with greater challenges (Berry, 2008). Teachers who participated in this study maintained, "Supportive principals, freedom to use professional judgment, and a guarantee to work with like-minded and similarly skilled colleagues mean more to good teachers than extra pay" (p. 769).

When hiring teachers to work with students living in poverty, Tish Howard, Sandy Dresser, and Dennis Dunklee (2009), authors of *Poverty Is Not a Learning Disability*, suggest school leaders (1) begin by identifying the characteristics they are seeking in a candidate, (2) conduct an analysis of their current faculty and staff strengths and weaknesses to clarify what the school needs, (3) seek support from district-level human resource personnel by clearly communicating the school's needs and interests, (4) structure the interview questions to elicit responses that will reveal the candidate's attitudes and values, and (5) take candidates on a short tour of the school to observe how they interact with others and relate to the environment.

Using behavior-based interviewing (BBI) may also be helpful. Mary Clement (2009) claims that BBI provides a "clearer sense of the candidate's suitability for the position, based on the premise that past behavior is the best

THE DISTRICT'S "AD-VANTAGE POINT"

Supporting Schools in Resource Management

District office personnel often have the opportunity to support a high-poverty school's efforts to improve through the effective use of resources. Resource management is an area in which district leadership can be particularly helpful. W. Norton Grubb (2009) suggests four strategies district leaders can use to support better resource management at the school level:

• Decentralize decision making about resources to the school level and adopt school-based budgeting.

• Carry out routine "waste audits," especially at the school and district level, to see where funds are being misspent.

• Use professional development to make school leaders and teachers more sophisticated about effective resources.

• Create a What Works Institute that provides user-friendly information about effective and ineffective resources.

Source: Strategies from "Correcting the Money Myth: Re-thinking School Resources" by W. Norton Grubb, 2009, *Phi Delta Kappan, 91*(4), p. 51–55. © 2009 Phi Delta Kappa International.

predictor of future performance. BBI questions begin with the phrases 'tell me about a time when,' 'how have you,' or 'describe your experience with'" (p. 23). Ascertaining candidates' attitudes and values, as well as understanding how their past experiences might shape their future performance, could be especially valuable in determining who would likely be most successful working with students who live in poverty.

Once excellent teachers and staff are hired, the challenge then becomes retaining them. Again, principals may have greater control over this dynamic than they believe. Schools with a high percentage of students who live in poverty can be tough places to work. Retaining faculty and staff begins with providing a healthy, safe, and supportive environment in which to work and learn. The challenges are greater than in more affluent schools, but the rewards also can be greater. The work becomes deeply personal for those who stay in such schools—both an asset and a liability for educators.

UNCOMMON SENSE

Osmond A. Church K–8 School in Queens, New York, has set a priority for decision making regarding all school resources: "We simply always target the lowest-performing kids," stated Principal Valarie Lewis. "For example, we know maintaining a low student-teacher ratio is key to our caring relationships that are essential for these kids. So that drives personnel decisions and budgeting. We also know that if we don't first address their needs, we well may lose them." Subsequently, Osmond A. Church considers this priority in every decision regarding the precious resources of the school. By basing all resource decisions on priority needs, schools stand a far greater chance of meeting the learning needs of all of their students.

Nathan Eklund (2009) studies teachers' job satisfaction and maintains that teachers' sense of calling to the profession both compels them to persist under stressful conditions and places them at risk for burnout. For this reason, leaders in high-poverty schools must make a positive staff climate a high priority if they hope to retain the high-quality personnel necessary to ensure that leadership capacity can be developed and sustained. Eklund stresses the need for leaders to create an environment in which teachers can regularly tap into the reason they became a teacher in the first place. He argues that for most educators, teaching is a calling. He states, "Teachers come to this work laden with strong beliefs about the work and deeply held convictions about their own self-image" (p. 26). He maintains, "Dedication is admirable, but martyrdom is unsustainable" (p. 27). To avoid burnout and maintain a balance between home and work, educators who teach in high-poverty schools must attend to their own health and well-being.

Eklund (2009) provides specific suggestions for how schools can improve the climate of the workplace for teachers and staff, as well as how individuals can better maintain a balance between their work and their life outside of school. He encourages teachers and school staff to work together to set norms of behavior, learn how to resolve conflict, celebrate their work, and use collegial hiring processes.

 ## SCHOOL CULTURE ALERT

Leaders in HP/HP schools manage to retain high-quality faculty and staff using multiple and varied approaches, but they make all relationships a priority and establish norms of personal regard and mutual respect.

Effective leaders celebrate individual and schoolwide accomplishments on a regular basis. They create spaces for learning not only for students but also for teachers. For instance, although space was tight at Taft Elementary, Principal Williamson insisted that teachers have a pleasant space in which to learn together, as well as a place to rest and rejuvenate during the day. Several staff members pitched in to repaint, decorate, and furnish a teachers room as part of a large-scale cleanup of the school.

Another way leaders attend to teachers' emotional well-being is to make certain everyone has the knowledge and skills to be successful. Teachers do not want to teach in a school where they cannot be successful. In a high-poverty school, this means everyone is given an opportunity to develop an accurate understanding of poverty so that they are prepared for the complex challenges that poverty poses. It also means opportunities for learning are job-embedded, focused on student work, and conducted in collaboration with peers. Developing an accurate understanding of poverty is discussed at greater length in Chapter 8, and research-based models for professional learning are further elaborated in Chapter 10.

Rarely does a principal take the helm of a high-poverty school with the opportunity to wipe the slate clean and hire an entirely new faculty and staff of like-minded individuals. In *Good to Great*, a study of leadership in successful private and public organizations, author Jim Collins (2001) says "getting the right people on the bus" is vital to an organization's success. This goal can require leaders to move some of the current occupants off the bus.

Principals in HP/HP schools model reciprocal accountability. "I think he's probably the first principal I've worked with who actually cared about the kids," explained one of the teachers in an HP/HP school in the Northwest when asked about her principal. She continued:

> He will go around at lunchtime and ask kids, "Do you know what your reading level is?" And then he would tell them, "Well, your English teacher does, so you better find out. You need to know that." Sometimes he will have a list of kids who aren't doing well in a class, and he finds them at lunchtime and asks what they need.

This principal held teachers to the same standard he held himself. He modeled his expectation that everyone is accountable for ensuring that kids don't fall through the cracks. He explained, "I told the teachers, 'Yes, we have a counselor, but you're all going to be quasi-counselors. If we're treating students like they are our own kids, we want them to graduate, right?'" He described times when faculty challenged him:

> One teacher told me, "I didn't go to school to be a counselor, and I'm not doing home visits. I'm not a social worker." I told him, "You're a good teacher; you just

happen to have a different philosophy. I do not have any problem writing you a letter of recommendation so you can find a school that's a better match for you."

He continued:

There was another time when I said to the faculty, "You know how long it would take me to evaluate you out of the job you hold? It would take me a good three years; but it says right here in the contract that you can be fired for insubordination. If I ask you to do something because it's good for kids, you will do it, or you will be fired."

 SCHOOL CULTURE ALERT

Although they use different approaches, principals in HP/HP schools challenge teachers who do not hold high expectations for their students or themselves and suggest that they need to get on board, find another school, or pursue another line of work if they can't change.

In tough economic times, effective resource management becomes increasingly important. Principals sustain the school's success by working collaboratively with staff to stay focused on the priorities that guide their work. They know that cuts in critical resources can jeopardize their hard-won gains. Countering these challenges becomes their top leadership priority—particularly as they work to recruit and retain talented staff.

Are We Optimizing Time?

The manner in which time is used is closely linked to retention of high-quality staff. In *The Principal as Curriculum Leader*, Allan Glatthorn and Jerry Jailall (2010) assert, "[T]hey who control the schedule control the school's resources" (p. 87). All students are likely to benefit from improving the quality of academic learning time, and those who live in poverty may require additional high-quality time. Teachers also need time to learn, especially time to learn collaboratively with others. The manner in which time is used can influence teachers' working conditions and their sense of efficacy. Teacher learning and student learning are two sides of the same coin. When teachers are afforded time to learn collaboratively, they can in turn optimize academic learning time within the school day and best plan for student learning outside the school day.

Extending academic learning time can occur in at least two ways—literally extending the available time for students to learn or better using the time within the traditional school day. High-performing, high-poverty schools do both. Underachieving students living in poverty often require more instructional time to catch up to their higher-achieving peers.

High-performing, high-poverty schools find a way to extend learning time for students who need it. The schools offer a blend of before- and after-school tutoring, weekend and vacation catch-up sessions, summer school, full-day kindergarten, and sheltered classroom support. At Osmond Church P.S./M.S. 124, for example, school is in session "pretty much five and a half days per week," according to Principal Valarie Lewis. On Saturday mornings, middle school students who need to catch up attend small learning academies.

Summer instruction in particular may be as important as any extended-time intervention, as it serves to maintain continuous learning, counters the loss of achievement gains caused by long gaps in school, and provides needed nutrition and other auxiliary supports (Borman & Dowling, 2006). Extending learning time for underachieving students is discussed in greater depth in Chapter 10.

THE DISTRICT'S "AD-VANTAGE POINT"

Transformational Strategies for High-Performing Schools

For more than a decade Education Resource Strategies Inc. (ERS), a nonprofit organization, has worked with large urban school districts to transform the manner in which those school systems organize and manage resources (people, time, money) to ensure equity. The organization's mission is "to be a catalyst for positive change by helping educational leaders rethink how they use system- and school-level resources—people, time, and money—to support strategies for improved instruction and performance."

They have identified the following Core Transformational Strategies that support the development of high-performing schools: (1) ensure equitable, transparent, and flexible funding across schools adjusted for student need; (2) restructure teaching to foster individual and team effectiveness and professional growth; (3) support schools in organizing talent, time, and money to maximize learning; (4) ensure access to aligned curriculum, instruction, assessment, and professional development; (5) build school and district leadership capacity; (6) redesign central roles for empowerment, accountability, and efficiency; and (7) partner with families and communities.

ERS has developed a variety of tools and other resources to support district-level leaders in aligning resources with the transformational strategies. One such tool is the "ResourceCheck" questionnaire designed to assist district leaders in analyzing current practices and identify areas in which the district could provide greater support to schools through better use of resources. More information is available at http://erstrategies.org.

UNCOMMON SENSE

The Caldwell School District in Idaho provides the 25 lowest-performing students in each of its elementary schools with 12 weeks of supplemental after-school tutoring with funds provided through federal and district sources. Each student is pre-tested, and the results are used to determine the appropriate needs-based curricular materials and teaching approach; students then meet twice a week with their classroom teachers, who serve as their tutors. Tutors receive just-in-time professional development to help with planning and delivery of tutoring. Communication with parents occurs weekly, and the students are post-tested at the conclusion of the 12-week program to determine growth and additional needs. "To date, the results have been remarkable for these kids," explained the superintendent. "The kids would never have caught up without this intervention, and our teachers continuously benefit from the PD and parent contact."

In addition to extending learning time, leaders in HP/HP schools are vigilant about protecting time for learning during the school day. In schools in general, time for academic learning is lost to holiday celebrations, assemblies, announcements, testing, and too much review of old information. In a study of teachers' classroom practices conducted by Richard Elmore (2006) and his colleagues from Harvard, teaching new content occupied between 0 and 40 percent of the scheduled instructional time. Elmore claims that teachers spend a great deal of time on tasks other than instruction of new material, such as overseeing student seatwork, administrative tasks, and listening to announcements on the intercom. He argues:

> [T]he use of time in classrooms is a measure of the respect adults have for the role of learning in the lives of students. It would be an enormous step forward if adults in the schools treated the time that children and their families give to schools as a precious gift rather than an entitlement. (p.7)

Academic learning time also is lost to the "end-of-year letdown" common in many schools when instruction of new content ceases two to four weeks before the end of the school year (Elmore, 2006). When considering these classroom and school practices, together with the instructional time lost to state- and district-mandated testing, Elmore and his colleagues estimated that during a school year, between 245 and 450 hours (50 to 90 days) of academic learning time are lost.

As is true of a school's budget, the schedule is a reflection of what the school values and how it prioritizes competing objectives. Leaders attempting to create the conditions necessary to raise the achievement of all students—particularly those living in poverty—might begin by developing a learning-centered schedule that encompasses a commitment to protect academic learning time.

Some schools and districts raise their consciousness about how time is used by taking a blank calendar and blacking out all the days that have traditionally been used for activities other than academic learning, such as weekends, holidays, summer vacations, parent-teacher conferences, holiday celebrations, school assemblies, testing, and other events. Schools may also want to conduct their own study of the use of classroom time by observing classrooms bell-to-bell on a sampling of days throughout the school year. Gathering such data might develop the sense of urgency needed to stimulate action.

Developing a learning-centered schedule is important not only to support higher-quality academic learning time for students, but also to provide time for professional learning. Time for collaborative professional learning, while important in any school, is especially important in HP/HP schools, because the traditional culture of isolation may actually put students who live in poverty at greater risk than would be true in schools where students come from more affluent families (Chenoweth, 2009b). Karin Chenoweth, Ed Trust, explains:

> The traditional organization of schools, which relies on isolated teachers doing their jobs with little interference and less support, means individual students are totally reliant on the knowledge and skills of their individual teachers.... Because middle-class students bring more social capital than students of poverty, this tradition of isolation, on average, hurts them less.... For the most part, parents living in poverty leave education to the schools—not because they don't care about their children's education but because they often don't feel competent to challenge the knowledge of teachers and because they're more likely to be overwhelmed with the daily logistics of life. This means low-income children are often completely reliant on their schools for their education. When schools understand that and step up to the challenge... and set up the structures and systems that allow teachers to work together, even students burdened by poverty and discrimination can achieve remarkable success. (pp. 42–43)

Schools must find ways to reorganize time to support the development of communities of practice (Wenger, 1998) that are consistent with the unique circumstances found in their context. They can repurpose time that is traditionally set aside for faculty meetings, reorganize the schedule to accommodate common planning time, bank time for professional development, or locate funds for ongoing released time. Principal leadership in this area is critical. Improving student learning requires more than competent individuals. To build leadership capacity throughout the school, principals need to focus their energy on creating the conditions necessary for teachers to work collaboratively.

Andrew Collins, principal of Dayton's Bluff Elementary, provides substitute teachers as needed for each grade-level team to engage in collaborative professional learning. Every six weeks, teacher teams spend a full day reviewing classroom-based assessment data, discussing instructional strategies, and planning for the next six-week period. As teachers discuss students' performance and specific teaching strategies, the school's literacy coach and a district-level instructional coach look on and take part. By participating in collaborative planning sessions, coaches are better able to provide just-in-time support. (A variety of research-based models for professional learning are discussed in Chapter 10.)

District-level leaders can support site-based leaders' better use of time by collaborating with them in the development of a learning-centered schedule. Scenario planning is a strategy that district personnel might find useful. Scenario planning is a process by which policy-level leaders work with those who will implement the policy to lay out multiple possibilities—in this case, multiple master schedules with their accompanying policy options and budget implications. Scenario planning provides practitioners a voice in the process and policymakers with an opportunity to better understand the implications of various policies.

THE DISTRICT'S "AD-VANTAGE POINT"

Supporting Learning-Centered Schedules

District leaders play an important role in creating coherence in improvement efforts by aligning the district's learning goals with the realities of the day-to-day operations of each school. Some districts support the development of school schedules by providing consultation and technical assistance to school leaders. This process usually begins with district leaders identifying a desired outcome, such as "Each school will provide 60 minutes for collaboration weekly." District leaders then work with school-based teams to develop a variety of scenarios that address the unique needs of each school. In her article "Think Inside the Clock" Crawford (2008) provides a step-by-step process for supporting such learning-centered scheduling.

Do We Have a Data System That Works for Classroom and School Leaders?

Effectively managing resources—money, people, time—requires accurate information. All schools in our study implemented data systems to guide their decision making. In fact, using data-based decision making was one of the two most common explanations offered for the schools' success (the other was fostering caring relationships).

Constructing and implementing a data system is an essential function that moves a school toward addressing the underachievement of students living in poverty. In HP/HP schools, leaders facilitate an ongoing, courageous look in the mirror. These schools have access to accurate, timely data that allow school and classroom leaders to set goals and benchmarks, monitor progress, make midcourse corrections, and perhaps most important, design and successfully implement needs-driven instruction and interventions.

Victoria Bernhardt (2005), a nationally respected authority on data use in schools, suggests four different types of data should be accessible: (1) data related to student learning (for example, classroom-based assessments, standardized test data, teacher observations); (2) data related to perceptions held by stakeholders about the learning environment, as well as values, beliefs, and attitudes; (3) data related to school and student demographics (for example, attendance, graduation rate, race/ethnicity, class, gender, level of teaching experience, level of education of teachers); and (4) data related to structures, processes, programs, and policies (for example, after-school tutoring programs, RTI Tier 2 intervention programs, summer schools).

 UNCOMMON SENSE

Building on a decade of hard work to develop an effective and usable data system, Lapwai Elementary staff turned to the system for help with improving parent-teacher communications. The staff implemented a schoolwide goal to have weekly contacts with every family and agreed to keep themselves accountable by working with the principal to log all contacts and report them at school board meetings. "The number and quality of contacts significantly increased," reported the principal, "and as you could imagine, we were able to show that student performance increased for most of the kids as well. Maintaining an effective data system was critical to all aspects of this effort, and being able to explain how we accurately kept track of our work and compared it to individual student performance really helped all of us have confidence in what we were doing."

A comprehensive data system uses three types of data tools: student information systems, data warehouses, and instructional management systems. For more information, see Figure 6.2. Bernhardt (2005) says, "[T]he hard part in selecting data tools is figuring out what you want the tools to do, which tools do what you want, and which tools you need first" (p. 66).

FIGURE 6.2	Data Tools Defined

What Is It?	What Does It Do?	What Is the Purpose?
Student Information System	Collects and organizes data concerning characteristics of the student population and processes/programs used by the school.	Provides information about many factors, such as student attendance, discipline referrals, student demographics, student course assignments, and specialized school programs.
Data Warehouse	Connects multiple databases, usually through individual student and teacher identification numbers.	Allows for longitudinal and comprehensive data analysis with multiple variables from multiple sources.
Instructional Management System	Provides resources to support standards-based instruction and assessment. Collects data related to ongoing assessments of students in relationship to standards.	Supports alignment of curriculum with content and assessment standards in individual classrooms, as well as among and between grade levels.

Gaining access to high-quality data tools can be expensive, requiring significant district support. Bernhardt (2005, pp. 68–69) provides six suggestions that can guide the selection of effective data tools:

• Be clear about what type of tool you are looking for. Are you hoping to find one company that can provide all three types of tools? Do you want to buy them all at once or one at a time?

• Be sure the tools can talk with one another.

• Involve a team with broad membership in the [decision-making] process.

• Research the history and financial stability of possible vendors and invite them to show the data tools in your environment.

- Stay aware of what you need a data tool to do, and don't automatically go to the lowest bidder.
- Talk with current users.

We know that high-performing, high-poverty schools are concerned with both excellence and equity. To ensure excellence in teaching and learning, schools need to assess how equitably they serve their students. Conducting an equity audit might result in useful data for high-poverty schools aiming to improve. An equity audit provides a "systematic way for school leaders—principals, superintendents, curriculum directors, and teacher leaders—to assess the degree of equity or inequity present in three key areas of their schools or districts: programs, teacher quality, and achievement" (Skrla, McKenzie, & Scheurich, 2009, p. 3). Equity audits can provide useful data for confronting and eliminating policies, practices, and programs that are likely to perpetuate underachievement for students living in poverty. Confronting and eliminating such inequitable policies, practices, and programs (as described in Chapters 5, 7, and 9) often provides clear focus and a starting point for any school concerned with addressing barriers to improvement.

The Principal's Role

Although the development of leadership capacity requires that leaders from various vantage points within the school work together (such distributed and shared leadership is inherent to leadership capacity), the principal's role is vital. Principals, by virtue of the authority typically granted them, are in a unique position to be the catalyst for improvement through the creation of conditions that make it possible to create further capacity in leadership. Figure 6.3 (p. 96) describes the actions that principals in HP/HP schools take to ensure that resources are effectively managed, time is well used, and data-based decision making becomes the norm.

 ACTION ADVICE

- Consider your school's budget. Do you consider your budget a moral document? Does it reflect your values, goals, and priorities as a school?
- Evaluate your current hiring practices. Do they result in hiring personnel who match the needs of the school?
- Take action to retain talented personnel. Have you taken stock of the ways your school encourages talented people to stay?

- Hold high expectations. Have you evaluated current practices that ensure all teachers hold high expectations for their students and themselves?

- Provide extended learning time. Have you explored ways to extend learning time for underachieving students?

- Analyze your school calendar. Is it learning centered and focused on the needs of underachieving students?

- Provide time for professional learning. Have you reorganized the schedule and calendar to provide job-embedded professional learning opportunities?

- Analyze the way decisions are made. Are multiple forms of data used to make instructional decisions in the classroom and systemic decisions schoolwide?

- Conduct an equity audit. Have you assessed how equitably your school is meeting all students' needs?

FIGURE 6.3	The Principal's Role in Building Leadership Capacity in HP/HP Schools

The principal—

- Begins the conversation about what is possible.
- Guides the development of a shared vision of high levels of learning for all.
- Is the chief steward of the vision, keeping it alive and in the forefront.
- Acknowledges that he/she cannot "go it alone," recognizing the important opportunity others have to influence (lead) from various vantage points throughout the system.
- Shares decision-making authority and governance of the school.
- Acts out of a commitment to equity.
- Fosters interdependent relationships of reciprocal accountability with other stakeholders.
- Uses his or her formal authority to ensure school structures and processes are in place to build capacity in individuals and in the system, including the following:

  o Management of the school's budget in a manner that reflects collectively identified priorities, values, beliefs, and goals;

  o Personnel practices that recruit and retain high-quality teachers, not the least of which is an emphasis on trust building through relationships of mutual respect;

  o Construction of school schedules and calendars that are learning focused—for students and adults;

  o Use of data that allows for informed, shared decision making in the classroom and schoolwide; and

  o Use of data that encourages critical conversations about equity and the elimination of counterproductive practices.

Action Planning/Next Steps

Use the action planning template in Figure 6.4 (p. 98) to help you and your colleagues reflect on the information and ideas from this chapter. What commitments do you need to make and what actions do you need to take to build leadership capacity?

| FIGURE 6.4 | Action Planning Template for Building Leadership Capacity |

1. What new information, insights, and ideas did we gain from this chapter?

2. Based on our assessment of the school or district, what change needs to occur and what might be our next steps?

3. Are the changes needed in our school or district structural (time, resources), cultural (norms, beliefs, values), or both? What is the evidence?

4. What is the magnitude of change this represents for our school—first order or second order? What is the evidence?

Action Plan		
Next Steps	**Lead Person Responsible**	**Timeline**

Fostering a Healthy, Safe, and Supportive Learning Environment: HP/HP Schools *Eliminate* What Doesn't Work

Six years ago, we were really a different place, and a lot of kids were not doing well. School attendance and tardiness were problems, student cliques were strongly influencing behavior, and many of our lowest-performing kids were not catching up enough to meet state proficiency standards. We really didn't have a clear focus on the needs of individual kids, and our results showed that.

—*Randy Dalton, principal; David Luce, assistant principal; and Therese Gerlits, dean of students, Molalla High School*

Creating a healthy, safe, and supportive learning environment entails identifying and countering the mind-sets, policies, structures, and practices that directly work in opposition to this effort and ultimately perpetuate underachievement. These include lack of safety; low levels of trust and collaboration; lack of understanding of the effects of poverty; lack of positive school, family, home, and community relationships; failure to establish a needs-based approach for all students; ineffective transitions; inattention to student attendance and mobility; and inappropriate behavioral interventions, such as suspensions and expulsions.

Figure 7.1 is a self-assessment rubric that isolates specific mind-sets, policies, structures, and practices that HP/HP schools have helped to identify as barriers to improvement. Use the figure to guide your learning and to help in reflecting upon the current situation in your school.

Lack of Safety

A number of the 3rd graders were afraid to be on the playground with the older kids. We put another staff [member] out, but it hasn't fixed the problem. We still haven't got it figured out; maybe we need even more staff out there.

—*Elementary school counselor in the Southwest*

In a school that cannot ensure safety, parents do not engage, communities members will be reluctant to become partners, teachers will not stay, and most important, students will not focus on learning and achieve. Many HP/HP schools trace the origins of their journey to high performance to times when safety was the immediate concern. In many of the schools we studied, leaders related stories of abusive students, hallway violence, bullying, rampant graffiti, frequent property damage to the school and its vehicles, fights, verbal abuse, the dangers posed by aging facilities, unhealthy conditions in restrooms... the list went on. Carmen Macchia, former principal at Port Chester Middle School, described the situation at his school:

> When we arrived, it was like the Wild West around here. Intimidation was everywhere, classroom instruction was regularly interrupted, and there was a revolving door of staff every year. No one wanted to be here. We thought we were going to focus on math and reading those first months. What we had to do instead was first establish law and order.

The school did just that, with the entire staff working cooperatively to target key areas for behavioral improvement such as bathrooms, hallways, and entryways into the school. They also focused on creating positive behavior in classrooms. Several years later, Port Chester Middle School transitioned from one of the lowest-performing and most unsafe schools in its state to an award-winning school. Is your school safe?

Becoming a safe school requires not only structures and processes that immediately and decisively address physical, emotional, and psychological well-being, but also those that create a bond between school and students,

FIGURE 7.1	Barriers to a Healthy, Safe, and Supportive Learning Environment: What Have We Eliminated?

Are We Perpetuating Underachievement? What Have We Eliminated?				
Progress Indicators/Evidence ⟶	**No Action Yet**	**Getting Started**	**Gaining Momentum**	**Sustaining Gains, Refining**
		• People are aware of counterproductive mind-sets, policies, structures, or practices. • Urgency is apparent. • Staff acknowledges need for change.	• People are empowered. • Barriers are being removed. • Commitment to the elimination is increasing. • Support for change continues.	• Counterproductive mind-sets, policies, structures, or practices have been eliminated. • New mind-sets, policies, structures, and practices are evident.
Counterproductive Mind-Sets and Practices ↓	**0**	**1**	**2**	**3**
Our school is unsafe.				
Misunderstanding the effects of poverty on learning and achievement.				
Distrust between staff and students.				
Distrust among staff, parents, and families.				
Avoiding opportunities to foster positive relationships among school, home, and community.				
Failure to establish a needs-based approach for all students.				
Ineffective transitions.				
Inattention to student mobility.				
Inappropriate use of suspension and expulsion.				

such as a caring relationship with teachers or other adults in the school and interventions that ensure that individual learning needs are met.

Low Levels of Trust and Collaboration

No one but the principal talks at faculty meetings... it's toxic.

—*Middle school teacher in California*

Trust building is a necessary component of school improvement. Through a longitudinal study of schools in Chicago, Anthony Bryk and Barbara Schneider (2002) found that when high levels of trust (defined as mutual respect, personal regard, competence to do one's job, and integrity) existed among teachers, teachers and administrators, teachers and students, and teachers/administrators and families, then a school had a 50-50 chance of improving student achievement. If that sounds like the bad news, it's not. When trust levels were low, a school had a 1-in-7 chance of improving student achievement.

Trust cannot be developed when teachers work in isolation. Trust will also be difficult to achieve when relationships between the staff and leadership are strained. Yet in some schools a positive community among the staff, caring relationships with students, and mutual respect between educators and families have become the norm. Without a trusting environment, most schools and educators simply go through the motions of school, rarely extending beyond what is required.

Do the stakeholders in your school (students, parents, families, teachers, administrators) trust one another? Are relationships characterized by mutual respect, personal regard, integrity, and an assurance that everyone has the competence to fulfill their role in educating the students? If not, do teachers in your school have an opportunity to collaborate with each other? Do educators have an accurate understanding of poverty from which they can successfully reach out to parents and families?

Collaboration and trust are hallmarks of HP/HP schools. Leaders in these schools model trusting behaviors and establish structures that guarantee that teachers have an opportunity to work together and provide protocols to ensure collaborative efforts are successful. They also nurture trust among teachers, students, and families by providing opportunities for teachers to develop an accurate understanding of poverty's influence on the lives of their students and families.

A Lack of Understanding of the Effects of Poverty on Learning and Achievement

> I watched the kids line up to get their yearbooks yesterday. Everyone was excited. The school had planned an early release signing party for the students on their last day of the year. Then I noticed a number of others who silently were leaving the building without a yearbook. Didn't anyone notice them? I felt horrible. The yearbook cost $60. I wonder how many kids just couldn't afford to buy one.
>
> —*High school parent in Idaho*

Students from low-income homes have typically had fewer experiences that develop school readiness than their middle-class counterparts. Life for families in poverty is often about day-to-day survival. Living in poverty affects students' health and well-being, language and literacy development, access to material resources, and stability of housing. Unfortunately (as discussed in Chapter 3), stereotypes of people who live in poverty are commonplace. Educators who have not challenged their own bias and who do not understand how poverty affects lives and learning are less likely to develop authentic relationships with students and their families who live in poverty. They are also more likely to make harmful assumptions about students' capabilities that lead to low expectations and unrealistic or counterproductive demands on families. Do the adults in your school have an accurate understanding of poverty and its influence on learning?

Leaders in HP/HP schools find ways to help teachers learn about the constraints placed on people in poverty, and they provide opportunities for teachers to develop the skills and knowledge necessary to meet students' needs, which in turn leads to changes in beliefs about students' capabilities and improved relationships between educators and families.

Lack of Positive School, Family, Home, and Community Relationships

> The kids get zero help at home. I really don't think their parents could give a rip about how hard we try to help them. They really don't value education.
>
> —*Elementary teacher in the Midwest*

Many believe the "secret" to helping an underperforming student lies in developing a positive relationship with the student's family. This belief emanates from numerous successful experiences by educators who have participated with families and seen dramatic positive results in students' lives. Yet in far too many schools, establishing these positive connections remains at best an afterthought, or at worst a waste of time because of the ill-founded perception that families who live in poverty do not care about education.

But people who live in poverty *do* care about both their children and education. Lived realities, such as the number of hours spent at work, limitations on leave time, and limited access to transportation and child care all result in parents who live in poverty having far fewer opportunities to be involved in school in ways characteristic of middle-class families. What is the nature of the relationship between educators in your school and the families it serves? In HP/HP schools, educators understand the challenges that poverty presents. One principal says it best:

> We knew we had to get to the families... it was our best chance... so I started going door to door and inviting them to come to their kid's school conference. That led to other staff joining me, and soon we all were canvassing the community, talking to the parents and families—and they came to the conferences. That started everything for us. That's what got us going.

Like other HP/HP schools, this school found a way to connect with families, which the staff credits for years of academic achievement gains and other measures of student success. A willingness to authentically engage families living in poverty is part of an HP/HP school's needs-based approach to providing an excellent education for every student. At the heart of this mission is a "whatever it takes" attitude.

Failure to Establish a Needs-Based Approach for All Students

> The little kid sat in the back of my class. He never talked, wouldn't volunteer any answers, and just wasn't engaged. I was so busy with the rest of the kids, and he never caused any problems, so I guess I just left him alone. When it came out later in the year after he left school that he had been regularly intimidated by other boys, I felt sick that I hadn't gotten to know him earlier.
>
> —*Middle school teacher in the South*

For too many students who live in poverty, achievement gaps grow as their school experience unfolds. This experience often reflects a journey of unmet needs. First, the core instruction they receive is not powerful. Often characterized by teacher-dominated choices and decontextualized learning, such teaching has been characterized as "the pedagogy of poverty" (Haberman, 1991). Second, these students likely had teachers who were not literate in data and assessment. Failure to collect the meaningful data necessary to analyze individual student proficiency and diagnose deficiencies prohibits educators from prescribing and providing effective interventions.

Educators who fail to establish a needs-based approach also fail to take professional accountability for learning. In such schools, the mind-set is "I taught it" rather than "Did students learn it? If not, what am I (the teacher) going to do about it?" In many low-performing schools, teachers feel accountable for teaching, but not necessarily for learning. This mind-set can be underpinned by a conviction that there is insufficient time and unavailable resources to do everything they would like to do for kids.

Therein lies a key difference between high-performing, high-poverty schools and low-performing, high-poverty schools. A needs-based approach is not viewed as one of the "things" they do; it is viewed as *the thing* they do. The equation that follows is logical. If they want every child to succeed, they have to address each child's individual learning needs and situation. If students need help with a place to do homework, they provide it. If students are hungry, they feed them. If students' decoding skills are weak, they provide focused, skill-building intervention. If students need to talk, they take the time to listen. And when students succeed, they recognize and celebrate their efforts.

What is the mind-set in your school related to meeting the needs of every student? When students fail to learn, who do teachers in your school believe is responsible, and what do they do about it? High-performing, high-poverty schools are all about their kids' needs, and a "whatever it takes" mind-set is bedrock. This disposition is foundational not only to what occurs in their school, but also to ensuring that students successfully transition into or out of their school.

Ineffective Transitions

We know the students who are getting mostly *D*s and *F*s in the 8th grade. Yet we make them go to the high school for 9th grade instead of allowing them access to our Academy that does a great job with the kids who don't fit the traditional schools. We require them to fail an entire year at the high school before we intervene. What's up with that?

—*Alternative high school teacher in the West*

What happens when kids leave their elementary school and head to the larger, more impersonal middle school? What about the students who move from that school to what can be a larger, even more impersonal high school? Is the accumulated knowledge about students' learning needs shared with receiving teachers and staff? Do we have safety nets and interventions in place for those students entering far behind? Do we welcome them with a culture of inclusion, high expectations, and support? Do we get to know them? How would you answer these questions for your school or school district?

For students who live in poverty and are underachieving, successful transitions are often key to keeping them in school. High-performing, high-poverty schools intentionally plan for transitions. Leaders develop processes for providing pertinent information and opportunities to connect with staff in the school or schools that will next be serving their students. Additionally, they often provide structured experiences that immerse incoming students into the supportive culture of their school and afford time for teachers to get to know students as individuals. Effective transitions from school to school are important for all students, but particularly for underachieving students who live in poverty. High-performing, high-poverty schools also plan for another type of transition for students in poverty. Knowing mobility is concomitant with poverty, HP/HP schools address the needs of students whose education is disrupted by numerous changes in the schools they attend.

Inattention to Student Attendance and Mobility

How can we teach these kids if they aren't here?

—*Middle school teacher in the Midwest*

Last year 60 percent of my class turned over. How am I supposed to keep the kids who stay with me doing well when I'm getting a new student every couple of weeks? At times I feel like I teach in a bus station.

—*Elementary teacher on the West Coast*

Poor attendance and mobility often are ways of life in high-poverty schools. Teachers in these schools are acutely aware of the challenges posed by absenteeism and mobility to their students and themselves. Every few weeks they usher in a new student or witness a departure. Their record-keeping systems require constant revision. Their prep periods turn into catch-up meetings, orientation sessions, or times to interact with new or sometimes departing parents. Lesson planning, instruction, and assessment are more complex, and classroom management is an ongoing challenge as new students join the classroom community and those familiar with routines leave. Poor attendance and mobility are tough not only on teachers but also on a school's administrative staff, who must deal with intake issues and frequently build time into their schedules to welcome and familiarize new families with the school. Does your school or school district have systems in place to improve attendance and to ensure that your mobile students succeed?

High-performing, high-poverty schools brace themselves for challenges related to attendance and mobility. Leaders budget time and resources for addressing these issues, including ensuring that staff are both knowledgeable and prepared for the continual influx of new students. These schools develop routines to aid students in feeling welcome; commit to meeting parents and families on arrival; and in the first weeks after a child enrolls, carefully monitor the student's progress. High-performing, high-poverty schools consider mobility to be part of the landscape; and by addressing the challenges it presents, they increase the odds of success for their mobile students.

Inappropriate Behavioral Interventions— Suspensions and Expulsions

> She screwed up and got suspended for a week. I saw her at noon the other day at the hangout for lunch. She didn't seem even to mind being kicked out.
>
> *—High school teacher in the Southeast*

One of the most entrenched contradictions in our current system of schooling relates to the importance we place on attendance and our disciplinary decisions. Attendance is compulsory in most states until the ages of 15 to 17. Why is this so? Why make attendance compulsory? As a nation, is it not a statement about the value of schooling and the learning we believe occurs particularly in schools?

Yet when a student misbehaves, a decades-old strategy has been to remove that student from the learning environment. Many schools also routinely suspend students for the benign offense of too many absences. Suspensions in particular serve as short-term responses to disciplinary problems with little known benefit other than relieving the school of the challenge of dealing with behavior issues. The student's separation from the culture of the school, from friends, and most important, from the place of learning results in a benefit for the adults, but not for the student.

Suspension removes "the problem" from the teacher's classroom and school campus and is used to set a public example from which other students are meant to learn. For lesser offenses, some schools use in-school suspensions, in which students are encouraged to study on their own or sit quietly. For the most serious offenses, a district will exclude or expel a misbehaving student for a longer term or permanently. Do these practices work to change students' behavior, or do they primarily exist for the classroom teacher, school, or system? What is the ultimate purpose of discipline in schools? Is it to teach or to punish? What is the purpose of discipline in your school?

Although a common characteristic of HP/HP schools is a dramatic decline in behavioral problems, sometimes kids do act out. When they do so in HP/HP schools, a collective effort on the part of the adults and often the students has resulted in the establishment of a healthy, safe, and supportive environment in which the vast majority of individual disciplinary issues are proactively and productively resolved. Relationships of mutual respect between students and educators go a long way toward eliminating disruptive behavior, as does the development in all students of a sense of belonging to the school. In such a school culture, when behavioral problems arise, the students themselves often intervene. When adults take disciplinary action, it is focused on teaching new behaviors and does not deprive students of the opportunity to continue academic learning. As a teacher in an HP/HP school explained, "Ornery kids can do both—they can learn from their mistakes *and* stay in class and learn from us!"

Action Planning/Next Steps

Use the action planning template in Figure 7.2 to reflect on the information and ideas in this chapter. What commitments do you need to make and what action do you need to take to foster a healthy, safe, and supportive learning environment?

FIGURE 7.2	Action Planning Template for Fostering a Healthy, Safe, and Supportive Learning Environment

1. What new information, insights, and ideas did we gain from this chapter?

2. Based on our assessment of the school or district, what change needs to occur and what might be our next steps?

3. Are the changes needed in our school or district structural (time, resources), cultural (norms, beliefs, values), or both? What is the evidence?

4. What is the magnitude of change this represents for our school—first order or second order? What is the evidence?

Action Plan		
Next Steps	**Lead Person Responsible**	**Timeline**

Fostering a Healthy, Safe, and Supportive Learning Environment: How HP/HP Schools Do It

I don't care about all the things that went wrong in your other school. They're history. Now you're here. You go to work, you show us what you've got, and believe me, we'll get you there... you'll catch up and walk across that stage.

—*Pat Swift, assistant principal, Port Chester Middle School*

To learn, children and adolescents need to feel safe and supported. Without these conditions, the mind reverts to a focus on survival. Educators in high-performing, high-poverty schools have long recognized the critical importance of providing a healthy, safe, and supportive classroom and school environment. At Port Chester Middle School and other HP/HP schools, this means all forms of safety and security while at school—food if hungry, clean clothes if needed, medical attention when necessary, counseling and other family services as required, and most of all caring adults who create an atmosphere of sincere support for the students' well-being *and* academic success. When students who live in poverty experience comprehensive support that works to mitigate the limiting, sometimes destructive poverty-related forces in their lives, the likelihood for success is greatly enhanced.

Comprehensive support uses the needs-based approach and "whatever it takes" mind-set discussed in Chapter 7. Striving to create and maintain a healthy, safe, and supportive learning environment for every child, leaders in HP/HP schools adhere to the key principle of continuous improvement—acknowledging that the work is never completely done—and ask questions such as these to guide their actions: Is our school safe? Do we understand the influence of poverty on student learning? Have we fostered a bond between students and schools? Do we engage parents, families, and the community in authentic ways?

In this chapter, we provide background helpful in answering these questions. These same questions serve as leverage points for improving the learning environment in any high-poverty school.

A healthy, safe, and supportive learning environment enables students, adults, and even the school as a system to learn in powerful ways. Such an environment promotes innovation, inquiry, and risk taking. Moreover, such an environment reinforces and enhances the leadership capacity in the school because competent, excellent, and dedicated educators want to work under such conditions. Is your school fostering a healthy, safe, and supportive learning environment? Use the self-assessment rubric in Figure 8.1 to focus your reading and reflect on your school's current situation.

Is Our School Safe?

> I was scared at times when I first arrived here. The gangs seemingly had control of the place. Teachers were afraid to discipline kids because their cars would get keyed. Neighboring schools had to hire security folks to escort their teams here for athletic events, and the worst was that a lot of our kids did not have a safe place to learn.
>
> —*Principal, HP/HP high school on the West Coast*

A school must be safe. Creating this condition requires thoughtful and constant attention to the security and safety of the facilities; creation of clear policies and procedures for student and staff conduct; frequent and effective communication with parents, families, and the school community; and attention to classroom management as well as the requisite professional development. Without these conditions in place, learning cannot become a school's focus.

The knowledge base on HP/HP schools is consistent with the practices of the schools we studied, particularly the secondary schools, in which leaders emphasized safety for students and staff as a prerequisite for learning.

FIGURE 8.1	Fostering a Healthy, Safe, and Supportive Learning Environment

Do We Have Structures and Processes for Fostering a Healthy, Safe, and Supportive Learning Environment?

Progress Indicators or Evidence ⟶	No Action Yet	Getting Started	Gaining Momentum	Sustaining Gains, Refining
		• Urgency is apparent. • School status is understood. • A vision for improvement is shared. • Implementation strategies are selected. • Staff is prepared to begin.	• People are empowered. • Barriers are being removed. • Implementation is becoming routine. • Commitment is increasing. • Progress is monitored. • Initial gains are being made and celebrated. • Support for improvement continues.	• Improvements are embedded in daily practice. • Collaboration continues. • Refinements are made. • Gains continue to be made and sustained.
What is my school's progress? ↓	0	1	2	3
Is our school safe?				
Do we understand the influence of poverty on student learning?				
Are we addressing student mobility?				
Are we fostering a bond between students and school?				
Do we foster trusting relationships with all students?				
Do we offer student advisories?				

| FIGURE 8.1 | Fostering a Safe, Healthy, and Supportive Learning Environment (*continued*) | | |

What is my school's progress?	0	1	2	3
Have we created small learning environments?				
Have we removed economic barriers to school participation?				
Do we provide service learning opportunities?				
Do we engage parents, families, and the community in our school?				
Do we foster trust among parents, families, and school?				
Do we ensure effective communication between the school and families?				
Do we conduct home visits for all students?				
Do we assist our students and families in accessing needed social services?				
Do we make our school available as a community center?				
Do we foster trust among parents, families, and school?				
What is our district's progress in supporting schools in these areas?				

At Port Chester Middle School, the previous principal, Carmen Macchia, explained, "In the beginning, kids would hold their bladders all day out of fear of what might happen to them in the bathrooms." To help students become accountable for their actions, the school established structures, such as the frequent presence of school staff in bathrooms and hallways. By clearly setting expectations and modeling appropriate behavior and good citizenship, staff encouraged students to help promote school safety, which authentically contributed to changing students' perspectives from one of "ratting out" their friends to one of civic responsibility to their school.

Every student needs and deserves to feel respected and free from physical harm, intimidation, harassment, and bullying. To ensure a safe learning environment, leaders attend to all aspects of daily life in schools. They ensure safety at bus stops and on playgrounds, as well as in lunchrooms, bathrooms, hallways, and classrooms. Matthew Mayer and Dewey Cornell (2010) refer to teasing, hateful language, and social exclusion as factors of "low-level incivility that impact a student's adjustment and psychological well being" (p. 8). Through daily vigilance, consistent consequences, and continual monitoring of progress with frequent midcourse corrections by the adults, HP/HP schools wage war on such low-level incivility. Still, leaders of these schools report that the school did not become truly safe until the students came to believe that destructive behaviors would not be tolerated. Only then did they feel comfortable enough to trust each other and to join the adults in collectively working against inappropriate behavior. As a principal of an HP/HP school on the West Coast explained, "Once the kids let the other kids (particularly new kids) know that we don't do that stuff in our school, it all began to change. They were taking responsibility for their school and liked the way that felt."

SCHOOL CULTURE ALERT

While staff must be aware of early warning signs of harassment and bullying and act swiftly to intervene if warranted, this awareness, action, and timely intervention will only happen when trust has developed and relationships of mutual respect have been formed between students and adults. Establishing daily contact and demonstrating concern for each child provides a comfort zone for communication between teacher and student.

Leaders in the HP/HP schools we visited and those in other studies report that their concerted mission to eliminate aberrant behavior required daily attention in the early weeks and months. Their tenacity in successfully addressing students' negative behaviors paid off. Discipline referrals dropped, overall behavior improved, and relationships of mutual respect became the norm in the school culture.

They also explain that as instruction became more focused and relevant, student engagement in learning improved, which in turn had a positive effect on behavior. When children and adolescents willingly engage in productive learning experiences in their classrooms, such as solving a challenging math problem or writing a compelling introduction to an essay or grasping how a consonant blend works, they begin to see value in learning and experience success, and their need to act out or disengage diminishes. The negative behavior is replaced by a newfound confidence that success in a classroom or course is something they can attain. This phenomenon accounts for why, even in a highly dysfunctional school characterized by rampant misbehavior, some teachers are still able to maintain respectful, productive classrooms. These environments become islands of safety for the kids fortunate enough to be in them. High-performing, high-poverty schools strive to create a similar atmosphere of safety and security schoolwide.

Ensuring school safety goes hand in hand with the development of optimal working conditions for teachers and staff. In 2006, Eric Hirsch and Scott Emerick examined working conditions for teachers in North Carolina and produced a report entitled *Teacher Working Conditions Are Student Learning Conditions.* Not surprisingly, they found that student learning increases when schools create safe, supportive, and trusting school climates. They also found that teachers and staff viewed such a climate as directly related to their working conditions; when safe and trusting, they felt compelled to do all they could to enhance student learning. Leaders in HP/HP schools optimize the link between professional learning and student learning. They understand that teachers' working conditions *are* students' learning conditions, and as such, ensuring safety for all learners (students and adults) becomes a priority.

Once the establishment of a safe learning environment is under way, the challenging work of improving instruction can happen. As an HP/HP high school principal in the West explained: "Once we reestablished law and order, we were poised to take off. It's our foundation… we had to get it fixed, and we did."

THE DISTRICT'S "AD-VANTAGE POINT"

Expect Safety—Support Schools

Establishing policies and procedures does not, in itself, ensure that every school in the district will be safe. District leaders not only hold a valuable advantage in this arena but also have an obligation to actively support a school's efforts to ensure safety.

Specifically, district leaders can assist with assessing a school's safety needs, support training and acquisition of materials and equipment, facilitate the development of community partnerships, and aid in the selection and evaluation of particular programs.

Do We Understand the Influence of Poverty on Student Learning?

> This morning I was asked to join two officers from our county health and welfare department on a visit to the home of three of our kids. What we found was a small trailer house where our three students, their baby sister, two of their adolescent siblings, and five adults were living—11 people in a two-bedroom trailer. There was very little food, a blaring TV, a blue haze of cigarette smoke, and a very unhappy baby. I wanted to cry. How in the world can we expect these three kids to come to school every day ready to learn? Yet they do... and we will teach them!
>
> —*Principal, rural HP/HP school*

A second question that drives the establishment of a safe, healthy, and supportive learning environment relates to understanding the effects of poverty on student learning. Although the concept of a culture of poverty has been refuted (Gorski, 2008), too many educators continue to believe that people who live in poverty share a common set of beliefs, values, attitudes, and behaviors (such as a poor work ethic, alcohol or drug abuse, or apathy toward school). To counter these myths, leaders in the schools we studied and in other HP/HP schools use data and research to support high expectations of students.

SCHOOL CULTURE ALERT

An ethos of professional accountability for learning is tangible in all of these schools, standing in stark contrast to the many educators in public schools who continue to blame students and families for poor achievement.

How Does Poverty Influence Lives?

Although some scholars and practitioners contend that educators can better understand the daily realities of poverty by focusing on "patterns or traits" ascribed to people who live in poverty, this stance can be a slippery slope that perpetuates damaging stereotypes. No one theoretical framework can completely describe the life experiences of those living in poverty. People in poverty are as diverse as people in any other socioeconomic class (Bane & Ellwood, 1994). They present, like other groups, a wide array of values, beliefs, dispositions, experiences, backgrounds, and life chances. This diversity makes ascribing specific characteristics to people who live in poverty at best challenging and at worst harmful.

A better approach considers the constraints that poverty often places on people's lives, particularly children's, and how such conditions influence learning and academic achievement. As witnessed in HP/HP schools, this approach is not about "fixing" students; rather, it is about transforming schools so that they better serve students who live in poverty—students who are as worthy of excellent schools as are their middle-class peers.

As we've already noted, living in poverty does not inherently result in a shared culture. Rather, poverty affects *intervening factors* that, in turn, affect outcomes for people (Duncan & Brooks-Gunn, 1997). These intervening factors or constraints are wide ranging and complex, and they can compound one another. They can be experienced directly or indirectly as an individual, a family, a neighborhood, or a community (Calkins, Guenther, Belfiore, & Lash, 2007). What do we mean by intervening factors? They can include students' health and well-being; literacy and language development; access to physical and material resources; level of mobility; and degree of continuity between home and school in terms of expectations, values, and beliefs.

On a fundamental level, for instance, with an income at or below the federal poverty level, it is very difficult to provide for one's basic needs. Under such circumstances, choices in housing and the quality and quantity of food available as well as access to health care are all severely circumscribed.

Uninhabitable living conditions, perpetual hunger, and sporadic access to health care can result in poor physical and emotional health, which in turn can inhibit cognitive development and one's readiness to learn. As also noted in Chapter 3, one in five children comes to school living in such circumstances.

Having money provides a sense of power and control over one's life and the means to make choices for one's self and family. This situation contributes to the development of personal agency, which is a belief in one's capacity to effect change or action and in one's ability to act on behalf of one's self, family, or community. By definition, people who live in poverty have limited economic capital (money). Nonetheless, it is not only lack of money that can compromise the ability to develop personal agency. Three other types of capital often affect personal agency: human, social, and cultural. Limitations in each of these forms of capital can also adversely influence students' success in school.

Limited Opportunity to Develop Human Capital. Human capital refers to the skills, abilities, and knowledge that an individual brings to the table, including the "capacity to deal with abstractions, to recognize and adhere to rules, and to use language for reasoning" (Putnam & Feldstein, 2003). Poor communities offer fewer opportunities to develop human capital than do wealthy communities because, for example, they often have inadequate schools, libraries, and medical facilities to promote healthy development.

Limited Opportunity to Develop Social Capital. Social capital can be a valuable resource to parents. It is gained by forming relationships in formal and informal social networks, although participation in such networks necessitates understanding the group's norms and gaining members' trust (Coleman, 1987). These networks often benefit parents with middle and upper incomes as they negotiate the bureaucracy of schools and advocate for their children. People who live in poverty, for a variety of reasons, are often isolated from such networking.

Limited Opportunity to Develop Cultural Capital. Students living in poverty often do not begin school with the same kind of cultural capital as their more affluent peers. Upper-middle- and upper-class students have a cultural advantage because they have often been socialized to the cultural benefits of exposure to libraries, museums, books on Western civilization, theater, or travel. Such knowledge is rewarded in schools (Parker & Shapiro, 1993). Studies have shown that parents, regardless of income level, often share similar aspirations for their children in terms of cultural capital. Some families simply have more means (money), leisure time, and resources (such as transportation) to achieve their goals (Lareau, 1987).

How Does Poverty Influence Learning?

In general, children and adolescents living in poverty are not nearly as prepared to benefit from school as their more affluent counterparts. Poverty-related factors that intervene in students' ability to learn include health and well-being, limited literacy and language development, access to material resources, and level of mobility.

Health and Well-Being. As previously mentioned, these factors are inter-related, and one factor can compound another. For instance, substandard housing, inadequate medical care, and poor nutrition can affect the rate of childhood disease, premature births, and low birth weights, all of which affect a child's physical and cognitive development. Such factors influence students' ability to benefit from schooling. Living in daily economic hardship can also adversely affect students' mental health (Winters & Cowie, 2009), self-efficacy (Conrath, 1988, 2001), self-image (Ciaccio, 2000a, 2000b), and motivation to do well in school (Beegle, 2006).

Language and Literacy Development. Children who live in poverty often come to school behind their more affluent peers in terms of literacy and language development. In *Educating the Other America*, Susan Neuman, (2008) states that more than 50 years of research "indicates that children who are poor hear a smaller number of words with more limited syntactic complexity and fewer conversation-eliciting questions, making it difficult for them to quickly acquire new words and to discriminate among words" (p. 5). A significant body of literature also points to differences in access to reading materials by students from low-income families in comparison to their more affluent peers (Allington & McGill-Franzen, 2008).

Material Resources. Poverty often places constraints on the family's ability to provide other material resources for their children as well. For example, they may have limited access to high-quality day care, limited access to before- or after-school care, and limited physical space in their homes to create private or quiet environments conducive to study. They may not own a computer or have the fiscal resources necessary to complete out-of-class projects.

Mobility. Poverty often places another kind of constraint on families—the ability to provide stable housing. Students often move from one location to another because their parents are in search of work or are dealing with other issues that require them to move. Frequent moves almost always have a negative academic and social impact on students.

UNCOMMON SENSE

Dayton's Bluff Elementary School, where 40 percent of the student body is mobile, takes an aggressive approach to counter the ill effects. The school plans for mobility as opposed to reacting to it when it occurs, lessening the adverse effect that moving in and out of school creates for so many under-achieving kids who live in poverty. Staff consider student mobility as a daily, expected occurrence, and intervene as they do with any other immediate student need. A staff member stands ready with intake materials, and the principal reserves daily time for meeting every new student and family the day they appear to provide tours, explain available resources, and introduce new teachers. Skill and placement diagnostics begin on arrival, but most important, the new student and family are met in a friendly, welcoming manner. The goal is for everyone to positively embrace the move and position the student for success.

Much is known about the far-reaching influences of poverty on a student's learning. An understanding of these factors provides invaluable knowledge to educators in their efforts to support and teach students who live in poverty. Like HP/HP schools, every school that enrolls such children must seek to acquire as much understanding as possible about the life circumstances of their students.

SCHOOL CULTURE ALERT

When children and adolescents know that their teachers care about them and are trying their best to relate to the realities of their lives, they become far more inclined to trust and actively engage in learning.

Have We Fostered a Bond Between Students and School?

If my kids don't get through this class, they won't graduate, and that means losing their dreams. We have to help them keep those dreams... we have to. It's the most important work we do.

—*Principal in a rural HP/HP high school*

It's 6 a.m. and three kids are waiting at the door for their math teacher to arrive. They had each received a call on their cell phones the night before reminding them that their work was late and they needed to get in early to finish it before zero hour. Reminders like these are not unusual from their math teacher. The kids know he keeps close track of their progress, and while not always appearing appreciative of those reminders, they show up.

SCHOOL CULTURE ALERT

High-performing, high-poverty schools provide "protective factors" that help build a bond between students and school. These factors include fostering caring relationships between adults and children as well as between peers, and setting high expectations and providing the support needed to meet those expectations.

Furthermore, these schools provide opportunities for meaningful involvement in school. To do this they use specific strategies such as advisory periods, small learning environments, and student clubs and other extracurricular opportunities.

UNCOMMON SENSE

Students at Molalla High School, concerned with the growth of school cliques and their negative influence on students, approached school leaders for support. Their plan was to launch several student clubs that would foster a more inclusive environment and develop a sense of belonging for students, particularly those who were feeling excluded. They created four clubs: a leadership club, a sports club, a club led by Latino students called UNITO, and a Gay/ Straight Alliance. These clubs provide opportunities for students to become more engaged in their school. The success of these clubs at Molalla High School is a reflection of the school's celebration of diversity and unity.

Foster Caring Relationships

"They didn't know my name; they didn't care if I slept in class or even if I came" is a statement that reflects a common refrain voiced by students in large comprehensive high schools of the United States. Yet this refrain is not heard in HP/HP schools, where a premium is placed on relationships.

SCHOOL CULTURE ALERT

The HP/HP schools that we studied considered "protective factors" as paramount to their successes. Central among these factors is the promotion of caring relationships between adults and students as well as among peers. Far too many of our children, particularly at the secondary level, attend school in large impersonal settings where students can too easily become lost.

Start Student Advisories

> I love my advisory—it gives me a chance to keep track of where I am and know what is important for me to be doing. [My advisor is] also great to talk to… she cares about me.
>
> —*11th grade student in the Northwest*

Positive, productive, and caring relationships are indeed possible in secondary schools; but they don't just happen, as illustrated by the case of one small school in the rural western United States. Although the school served fewer than 400 students, many of the kids felt disconnected from school. A principal's commitment to making the school more personal for kids led the staff to reorganize the school day to include a well-designed advisory program. All professional staff members, including the principal, advise a small group of 18 to 20 students four days each week and stay with those students for four years, navigating their path toward graduation and beyond.

UNCOMMON SENSE

At Tekoa Secondary School (grades 7–12) a peer mentoring program supports entering 7th graders as they acclimate to the "secondary" experience by connecting the "sprouts" with older students as guides, mentors, and friends. "Sprouts" is an apt name in this largely agricultural, rural community, where phone calls before the first day of school from their "mentors" both welcome new students and assure them that another student will be looking out for them when they arrive. Older students assist younger students with the myriad of details required upon entry to the new school and continue to meet with their "sprouts" throughout the year.

The school refined its data system to allow each teacher to receive biweekly progress reports for each of his or her advisees for the express purpose of staying on top of every student's achievement, which is critical to the advisors' credibility and success. The school's faculty agreed to enter daily grades into their school's data system, allowing advisors to work on immediate needs with each student.

Advisory teachers regularly review each student's progress through school-generated biweekly reports, holding students accountable for staying on track. Advisors identify any student who falls behind and work with the student's teachers to intervene. The most effective advisories meet daily for at least 30 minutes a day, providing support in content subjects, homework, career guidance, and individual needs.

 UNCOMMON SENSE

Begin by providing each advisor with a biweekly progress report for each advisee for the express purpose of staying on top of every student's achievement. Agree as a faculty to the timely entry of grades into the school's database, which in turn processes and provides the accurate biweekly reports for each advisor.

Create Smaller Learning Environments

> We are saving 90 of our kids that we used to lose every year when they moved from our middle schools to our large 1,700-student high school. Starting our new 9th grade Academy is all we had to do!
>
> —*Superintendent in the West*

Many HP/HP schools provide additional protective factors, such as restructuring into small learning communities. These schools create focused learning environments that help keep smaller groups of students connected with each other as well as to a smaller group of core teachers throughout the day. In large or moderately sized high schools, this approach may be in the form of 9th grade academies. In effect, these academies "protect" 9th graders from the impersonal nature of the large, comprehensive high school experience in which it is too easy to get lost. Academies are a strategy for easing the transitions from middle school to high school. Creating smaller learning environments and communities of practice has the potential to authentically connect students with adults every hour of every day.

Increase the Likelihood of Participation in Extracurricular Activities

> When we removed the fees to participate and supplied the outfits, the number of girls who came out to join our cheer squad quadrupled!
>
> —*Principal in the Southwest*

High-performing, high-poverty schools provide a protective factor when they find ways to ensure that their students living in poverty will be able to participate in extracurricular activities. The importance of such participation to the creation of a bond between students and school has long been known. Whereas middle-class children have opportunities to develop their skills and talents through private lessons and participation in community-based activities in their elementary years, kids who live in poverty generally do not. Poverty poses a variety of barriers to participation for many students, such as the cost of fees, equipment or instruments, uniforms, and transportation home after participation.

In addition, kids who live in poverty often face responsibilities that prevent participation, such as holding down a job and caring for younger siblings. Highly competitive "cut policies," which dramatically reduces the number of kids allowed to make the team, pose another barrier to participation. Waiving fees, supplying equipment or instruments, covering the cost of uniforms, providing transportation, partnering with community-based entities to offer scholarships for specialized skill and talent development, and eliminating "cut policies" are a few of the ways in which HP/HP schools work diligently to ensure that all kids have access to the benefits of extracurricular participation.

Do We Engage Parents, Families, and the Community?

> I was headed to the home of one of my 2nd graders to let the parents know that Luis was coming to after-school tutoring on time and doing well. When I knocked on the door, Grandma and Dad greeted

me warmly in Spanish, inviting me in. Luis's mom was preparing dinner. Dad asked me to come directly to the kitchen to show me what Luis had begun doing at home since he started the tutoring program. On the cupboards were taped a mishmash of cereal boxes, pasta containers, dairy product holders, and simple drawings. All were in English. Dad smiled and explained, "He's teaching all of us to read English! We learn 5, maybe 10 words every day!

—*Elementary teacher, HP/HP school in the Northwest*

The story of Luis is a good example of the benefits of engaging parents and families. A simple home visit by the teacher revealed how, previously unbeknownst to the school, a young ESL student was connecting his tutoring and schoolwork with his family. In turn, Luis's family was most appreciative of their son's progress in school and welcomed his newly gained English skills that were helping them learn. His family was also both surprised and pleased that the teacher had come to their home.

 SCHOOL CULTURE ALERT

High-performing, high-poverty schools do not go it alone. Instead, they build positive and trusting relationships with students, their families, and the broader neighborhood and community. They know the success of their efforts often hinges on the relationships they can foster with and among these groups.

The success of HP/HP schools in addressing the learning needs of their underachieving students who live in poverty does not always solely focus on academics. Instead, helping students' families meet their basic needs, which include housing, food, medical attention, and in some cases safety, can be part of teachers' or administrators' jobs. Leaders in HP/HP schools are not naïve about their inability to solve the myriad of problems their kids face, but they often can help families connect with the community resources available. They do not concern themselves with whether or not such a task is in their "job description." If it helps kids learn, they do it.

In HP/HP schools, educators commit to engaging other stakeholders—parents, families, community members, patrons, and anyone else who holds an interest in the student or the school who may be a potential source of support if engaged in a positive manner. Families living in poverty often work multiple jobs, may have limited English language skills, and in some cases may have had few positive experiences with their children's teachers or schools. These factors frequently work against a school's attempts to form relationships with families who live in poverty and authentically engage them in their children's education. Even in high-performing schools, this problem is an ongoing concern. Leaders in HP/HP schools continually look for ways to provide opportunities for involvement and to gain back their trust.

The Critical Importance of Trust

In a recent study of the Chicago public schools, Anthony Bryk, president of the Carnegie Foundation for the Advancement of Teaching, and his colleagues concluded, "Relationships are the lifeblood of activity in a school community" (Bryk, Bender Sebring, Allensworth, Luppescu, & Easton, 2010, p. 137). Their previous work targeted trust as the essential building block in the positive relationships that foster authentic school improvement. He concludes, "In short, relational trust is forged in day-to-day social exchanges. Through their actions, school participants articulate their sense of obligation towards others, and others in turn begin to reciprocate. Trust grows over time through exchanges in which the expectations held by others are validated by actions" (p. 139). This pervasive sense of trust characterizes the relationships found in HP/HP schools among educators, students, families, and other stakeholders.

 SCHOOL CULTURE ALERT

Educators in HP/HP schools endeavor to establish, and at times rebuild, trust between the school and the families it serves. Trust develops and the learning environment of the school improves as parents, families, and community members are welcomed, begin to feel "listened to," and connect in meaningful ways with the learning and success of their children and those of others.

In one HP/HP elementary school, a teacher remarked, "Without a trusting environment in our classroom and with the families of my kids, it's all uphill. We never make the progress we could... we never can 'click.' Trust is what makes it all happen for us."

The development of trusting relationships lies at the heart of successfully engaging parents, families, and the community. To do this, HP/HP schools employ a variety of strategies and practices. They operate full-service schools, hire school/family/community liaisons, offer adult mentoring, connect the school and community through service learning, conduct home visits, ensure effective two-way communication between the school and the family, and use the school as a community center.

Create Full-Service Schools and Safety Nets

Many HP/HP schools connect needed social and medical services with their students. These "full-service schools" typically provide services such as social workers, physicians, dentists, vision and hearing specialists, and mental health and family counselors on site. Some schools provide a child care center and a family resource center to assist families in meeting their basic needs. Joy Dryfoos, noted scholar and longtime advocate of full-service schools, has studied these models for decades and concludes that when a full-service school works well, student achievement increases, attendance rates go up, suspensions drop, and special education placements decrease (Dryfoos, 1994; Dryfoos & Maguire, 2002).

Another critical purpose of a full-service school is to provide needed safety nets to catch kids in crisis and keep them from falling through the proverbial cracks of life. Leaders in HP/HP schools develop processes through which needs can be identified in a timely manner. Homelessness, hunger, medical issues, social and emotional distress, imminent physical danger, and coping with illness and death can interfere with learning. High-performing, high-poverty schools often establish networks within their school community to stay on top of these issues on behalf of their students. Once challenges are identified, teachers and staff move quickly into intervention mode, using all of the resources available to them.

Create Links Between School and Home

Strengthening the family's ability to support their children's academic achievement and other forms of success in school is a priority in HP/HP schools. One school organizes a learning academy on Saturday mornings to assist families of refugee students. Other schools employ school-family liaisons who connect families with schools in a variety of ways. Sadowski (2004) identifies six activities a school might consider to establish linkages between students' homes and school: (1) dual-language classes for students; (2) English as a second language, GED, and parenting classes; (3) home-school liaisons (with fluency in the home language); (4) preschool and early literacy programs; (5) early assessment; and (6) community and school activities and events.

UNCOMMON SENSE

Taft Elementary in Boise offers a voluntary (and very well-attended) Saturday morning learning academy for all families of refugee students. Building on the success of their summer Tiger Pride Orientation Camp for new refugee students (see Chapter 6), the staff wanted to continue connecting with the families throughout the school year. Various topics fill the Saturday morning agenda, such as English language classes, skill-building and catch-up sessions, continued orientation and support, and opportunities for refugee students to spend time with their camp buddies, all of which inevitably enhance the connection between these families and their children's school.

THE DISTRICT'S "AD-VANTAGE POINT"

Leading from the Broader Picture: The Importance of Knowing the Students

District leaders are positioned to maximize schools' efforts to mitigate the ill effects of poverty. In the same manner that educators in high-poverty schools seek to know and understand the circumstances of their students' lives, district-level leaders must genuinely know the schools they serve to make informed decisions and take action. In addition to thoughtfully deploying resources—particularly federal funds appropriated for the purpose of creating equity in schools—district leaders who genuinely know the strengths and challenges that characterize each school can provide support by coordinating efforts among schools, such as leveraging community partnerships, providing matching or seed funding for special projects, and helping with grant writing.

Offer Adult Mentoring

Mentoring works. Most educators have long known that a meaningful relationship with an adult is what kids want and need most. Mentors provide such a relationship. The National Dropout Prevention Center identifies mentoring as one of the most effective strategies to keep kids engaged and in school. The Western Regional Center for Drug-Free Schools and Communities identifies five positive outcomes of mentoring programs: (1) personalized attention and care, (2) access to resources, (3) positive/high expectations for staff and students, (4) reciprocity and active youth participation, and (5) commitment (Jackson, 2002). Many HP/HP schools draw from this knowledge to create and operate their own programs with local staff and volunteers; others access the help of Big Brother/Big Sister programs, local YMCA/YWCA services, and a host of other community-affiliated programs that offer adult mentoring.

Provide Opportunity for Community-Based and Service Learning

> Our kids actively work to support their community. Through clubs and classes, they raise money for families in need, work on a "coats for kids" project, plant trees, build park benches, help with efforts of the Northwest Blood Center, Children's Miracle Network, American Cancer Society, March of Dimes, Red Cross, and many others. They rake leaves in our parks and do yard work for our elderly folks in need. Our students feel better because of these efforts, and our community values the extra help that the school gives back to them. When everyone is supporting one another, it makes Tekoa a great place to live and raise children.
>
> —*Wayne Roellich, principal, Tekoa High School*

At Tekoa High School, all kids are expected to participate in community service. Noted for connecting academic learning to real-world problems beyond school, community-based learning, particularly service learning, has become common in HP/HP schools. Many benefits accrue from service learning, including the following: enhanced academic achievement, increased school attendance, improved student motivation to learn, decreased risky behaviors, increased interpersonal development and student ability to relate to culturally diverse groups, and improved school image and public perception (Billig, 2000a, 2000b).

Community-based learning also provides an excellent means to initiate career exploration, internships, shadowing, and in some cases jobs.

 UNCOMMON SENSE

Twenty-five thousand dollars—that is how much money Molalla High School students raised in four weeks in their 2010 Share the Love fundraiser. Each year the funds raised by students are dedicated to a pressing school or community need as identified by the students. The 2010 recipient was a fellow student with overwhelming medical costs for cancer treatment. Their enthusiasm is contagious as they take on leadership roles and organize multiple projects to raise money and request donations. This annual tradition is a month-long effort by students to give back to their community. Working together, diverse groups of students not only become better connected with their community, but also become more unified as a student body.

Conduct Home Visits

I was worried and very nervous about visiting my students' homes. But I've learned that making that connection with the family has made all the difference in how well my kids are doing at school. I now view them as part of my work... my job.

—*Elementary school teacher, HP/HP school in the Northwest*

Many HP/HP schools encourage and conduct some form of home visits. Ten years ago, test scores in the Mason County School District in Kentucky ranked in the lowest quartile of all districts in the state. Inspired by a theory of action that held that to improve achievement, educators had to build closer connections to students' home lives. Therefore, the district, with a cadre of volunteer teachers, embarked on a goal of visiting every home of the 2,800 kids enrolled. Maintaining this commitment over the years, together with positive administrative and collegial support and the requisite professional development, has resulted in every family's receiving at least one home visit from their child's teacher annually.

Since the home visits began, the district has experienced consecutive years of student achievement growth and a 50 percent drop in discipline referrals, as well as reduced achievement gaps and increased attendance. Mason County leaders consider "getting to know the individual talents and interests of the students" to be the "true benefit" of the home visits. "These visits go a long way toward bridging the barrier created when predominately middle-class teachers find themselves teaching in a system where 57 percent of the students qualify for free or reduced-priced lunch and an even greater percentage are from single-parent households," explained the assistant superintendent. "By taking the time to actually go to the homes to meet the students and their families, we begin to build the relationships that research suggests are a foundation of student success" (Middleton, 2008, p. 58).

Sometimes these visits have a truly transformational effect on teachers. Here's a descriptive account from an elementary school teacher:

I stood at the front door of the small clapboard house. Black garbage bags were stacked beside me. A barking dog was chained to a post in the bare yard behind me. The weathered door didn't seem to completely latch. I had sent a note home indicating that I could come by after school since she had missed our conference at school. As my student's mom opened the door and smiled, I wondered what kind of life this family had. I was invited into a front room—more garbage bags in the corner along with a mattress on the floor next to a TV, which sat on an empty shipping box. We sat at a bare table with three rickety chairs and had our conference. Three younger kids ran through the house as we talked about Michael. Mom said she didn't like coming to the school. But she appeared pleased that I had come to her home and truly cared about her son, and was happy to hear he was improving. We had a good talk. I learned that Michael had no father at home, that his mom had never finished elementary school, that his older brother was in jail, that his family—mom and three other siblings—lived on state assistance, and that he had no positive relationship with another adult male in his life. As I walked down from the front stoop to my car, I realized that I had been teaching a kid whom I didn't know really anything about. I left in a strange state of unrest, but also one of hope. I knew that when I looked at Michael tomorrow I would see him differently, and that alone would help us develop a better relationship to guide his learning. I was glad I went.

Ensure Effective Two-Way Communication

We had to figure out how to make sure that the family understood what we were trying to do. The telephone was disconnected, translated letters mailed home yielded no response, and notes sent through the student didn't work either. Two attempts to drive by the apartment and knock on the door found no one home. Finally, we reached them through a neighborhood connection one of our paraprofessionals had with the family. We had our conference in the community building at their apartment complex. It went great!

—*Middle school teacher, HP/HP school in the South*

We know that a "whatever it takes" attitude prevails in HP/HP schools. This is especially true in their efforts to communicate with the parents and families. Despite often limited resources, educators in these schools do not make excuses or settle for less than authentic connections with students' parents and families. The goal of fostering two-way communication between school and home requires leaders in HP/HP schools to be relentless in their insistence that communications be respectful, honest, and timely.

Use the School as a Community Center

Many HP/HP schools engage parents, families, and other community members by opening their doors and expanding their schedules to offer clubs, parent support and education, early childhood activities, GED programs, advisory groups, community education classes, and a host of other events and activities of interest to the community. These HP/HP schools partner with community or city organizations, local foundations, state and municipal agencies, service clubs, universities, and businesses to host these valued endeavors in their buildings, as well as offer services at times that better fit families' work schedules.

As an example, in partnership with the City of Saint Paul and the Amherst H. Wilder Foundation, Dayton's Bluff Elementary provides students and families with a recreational facility and the services of a nurse practitioner, dentist, and social worker at the school. According to the principal, "The payoff has been huge... our parents and kids see us as way more than a school. It helps in so many ways that all connect to learning."

The Principal's Role

Principals, working with teacher-leaders and staff leaders from various vantage points within the school, are positioned to address the wide spectrum of environmental needs that confront high-poverty schools. Figure 8.2 (p. 133) describes the actions that principals in HP/HP schools take to ensure that every student is surrounded by the positive supports and scaffolds necessary to ensure his or her individual success.

High-performing, high-poverty schools don't go it alone—and they don't reinvent the wheel. They access support, resources, and guidance whenever and wherever they can to foster a healthy, safe, and supportive learning environment. The resources and organizations listed in Figure 8.3 (p. 134) can guide a school's efforts to build strong relationships with parents and families.

Perhaps the most widely respected and accessed of these organizations is the National Network of Partnership Schools at Johns Hopkins University. This network of more than 1,500 schools originated from the work of the Center on School, Family, and Community Partnerships and its founder and senior scholar, Joyce Epstein. Guided by more than two decades of research and practice, the network offers what Epstein calls "a new way" to authentically incorporate parent and community involvement into a school's improvement process. The network helps member schools organize and implement action teams within their school communities, with the goal of increasing quality partnerships. In addition to creating new partnerships and supporting

| FIGURE 8.2 | The Principal's Role in Fostering a Healthy, Safe, and Supportive Learning Environment in HP/HP Schools |

The principal—

- Relentlessly ensures the school is safe.
- Initiates conversation and supports professional learning about the influence of poverty.
- Organizes collaborative efforts to address student mobility and other poverty-related factors that negatively influence learning.
- Initiates and promotes policies, structures, and practices that link students and families with medical, dental, and mental health services, as well as other sources of support in the community.
- Promotes the development of positive relationships and a bond between students and school by doing the following:

  - Modeling caring;
  - Facilitating strategies that strengthen the student-adult connections, such as advisories and small learning groups; and
  - Examining data related to barriers to student participation in extracurricular activities and leading collaborative efforts to address them.

- Initiates and promotes policies, structures, and practices that develop trust between school and family, such as hiring a school-home liaison and visiting homes.
- Initiates and promotes policies, structures, and practices that connect schools to families and the community, such as service learning and using the school as a community center.
- Ensures effective, frequent communications between school staff, students, families, and the community.

existing ones, the teams—composed of 6 to 12 volunteers, including the principal, teachers, staff, and parents—review school data to determine and prioritize needs.

Many HP/HP schools belong to the Johns Hopkins Network or other similar organizations to support their work. Any school concerned with furthering efforts to engage parents and families and associate activities at home that support a child's learning might consider Epstein's conclusion regarding the value of these partnerships and endeavor to create something similar in their school. According to Epstein, "The greatest impact on student achievement comes from family participation in well-designed at-home activities—and this is true regardless of the family, racial, or cultural background or the parents' formal education" (Jones, 2001, pp. 18–22).

Fostering a healthy, safe, and supportive learning environment is an essential function of leadership in HP/HP schools. Creating such an environment is inherently connected to its paramount mission—the improvement of learning.

FIGURE 8.3	Resources for Connecting with Parents, Families, and Schools

Boys and Girls Clubs of America—www.bgca.org
Coalition for Community Schools—www.communityschools.org
Communities in Schools—www.communitiesinschools.org
National Network of Partnership Schools—www.csos.jhu.edu/p2000/
YMCA/YWCA Programs—www.ymca.net, www.ywca.org

 ACTION ADVICE

• Relentlessly monitor data related to ensuring a safe learning environment. Are we making sure every student is always safe?

• Build a commonly held understanding of the influences of poverty on learning among the adults in the school. Do we all understand how living in poverty may negatively influence the ability of our underachieving students to catch up?

• Plan for mobility. Are we ready for mobile students' arrival—providing welcome packets, diagnostic testing, and appropriate placements? Do we develop "catch-up" plans if needed? Do we provide built-in opportunities for new friendships with peers? Do we make it a practice to communicate with parents during the first six weeks after enrollment? Do we address transportation issues if a student is mobile within our district? Have we marshaled schoolwide support from staff?

• Make sure all students are connected to a caring adult. Do we know which students come to school without the support of a caring adult?

• Start student advisories. Is every secondary school student connected to an adult at school who regularly monitors his or her progress?

• Personalize relationships through creating small learning environments and communities of practice. Is the size of our school presenting problems for some students and preventing us from forming caring relationships?

• Provide opportunities for all students to participate in extracurricular activities. Do our students have an equitable opportunity to participate?

• Work to engage every family with school. Do we have a plan in place to guide our efforts to build trust and connect with our families?

• Personalize the connection between school and the student's home. Who among our staff visits the homes of our kids?

THE DISTRICT'S "AD-VANTAGE POINT"

Creating Full-Service Schools

High-poverty schools are typically located in high-poverty neighborhoods where a full-service model can be particularly effective. But garnering the resources necessary to implement such a model is often beyond the purview or capacity of school-level leaders. District leaders are better positioned to establish partnerships with community-based agencies and organizations for the provision of services on the school site.

District-level leaders in a midwestern school district garnered resources to establish a family resource counselor (FRC) program and staffed each school with a counselor assigned to specifically work with the families in highest need. "Never did I imagine the level of support needed, and when we started working with families, in almost every case the student began doing better in school," explained the district coordinator. Family resource counselors assisted families in accessing services for which they were eligible. As liaisons between home and school, they helped with everything from required immunizations to homework. One FRC actually helped trap a marauding rat that had been terrorizing one of his student's families.

Each of the district's FRCs provided multiple and varied supports to families. Perhaps equally important was the deepened understanding they brought to educators back at their school regarding the unique and considerable challenges their students faced.

- Initiate an effective adult mentoring program. How are we connecting students with caring adults and positive role models?
- Offer community-based learning and service-learning opportunities to all students. Are we connecting students with the community? Are we teaching students about the value of giving back? Are we providing opportunities for students to explore career options in the local community?
- Visit every student's home. Do we have a plan in place to guide us in conducting productive home visits?
- Ensure two-way communication between homes and school characterized by the following:

  o Language-appropriate written and verbal contacts
  o Translation assistance when needed
  o Respectful and clear communications
  o Frequent contact through the most effective mode
  o Authentic requests for feedback/response
  o Willingness to help with requests and family needs
  o Personal invitations to participate in school conferences
  o Timely invitations to activities and events

- Open the school to the community. Have we created a plan to provide welcome and needed services to our community?

- Join a network to enhance school, family, and community relationships. Can we improve our connections with our families and communities?

Action Planning/Next Steps

Use the action planning template in Figure 8.4 to help you and your colleagues reflect on the information and ideas in this chapter. What commitments do you need to make and what actions do you need to take to foster a healthy, safe, and supportive learning environment?

| FIGURE 8.4 | Action Planning Template for Fostering a Healthy, Safe, and Supportive Learning Environment |

1. What new information, insights, and ideas did we gain from this chapter?

2. Based on our assessment of the school or district, what change needs to occur and what might be our next steps?

3. Are the changes needed in our school or district structural (time, resources), cultural (norms, beliefs, values), or both? What is the evidence?

4. What is the magnitude of change this represents for our school—first order or second order? What is the evidence?

Action Plan		
Next Steps	**Lead Person Responsible**	**Timeline**

Focusing on Student, Professional, and System Learning: HP/HP Schools *Eliminate* What Doesn't Work

When we looked at our performance data several years back, we realized that only 35 percent of our students were meeting the state standard for high school math. While we know our elementary and secondary teachers are really working hard to better teach math... 65 percent of our kids not getting there just wasn't acceptable. Our math curriculum and instructional approach was really all over the board... not connected... and the kids' performance clearly demonstrated that.

—*High school math teacher, Tekoa High School*

Graduation at Tekoa High School is more than a culminating ceremony for graduating seniors and their families; it is a community event. "We have a progressive party for graduation, moving from home to home to celebrate each student's accomplishments as a community." Although the concept has become a cliché, Tekoa is a place where the village has raised the children. As one of the district's elementary teachers explained, the students who graduated were "my sons and daughters." As is tradition, each senior's future plans are shared with the family and community members who attend the graduation ceremony. Many students will go to college—80 to 85 percent; others will join the military, and some will stay in the community on family-owned farms. If possible, many who go away will find a way to come back, because Tekoa is a good place to live.

Graduates of Tekoa High School are well prepared for their future, in part because teachers, administrators, staff, and other stakeholders are tenaciously focused on learning, not only of academic subjects, but also on helping each student learn to be a better person. As one teacher explained: "The first thing you need to do is make a connection with the students. Build rapport with them and let them know you're rooting for them. I tell them failure is not an option, and I'm on their side. I've had kids move in that were far behind the students who'd been here and we had PGT—personal growth time—because it's not just about getting better academically; it's about becoming a better person. One kid I'm thinking about is at the top of the class now."

Tekoa High School is a place where the structures and practices that work against a focus on learning are simply not present. Instead of a fragmented curriculum, the curriculum at Tekoa is aligned to state standards. Rather than working in isolation, teachers work together regularly to improve what they do in their classrooms. Rather than segregating students into various tracks, special education students are educated, for the most part, in the general education classroom, and all students have access to college-prep curriculum. Instead of professional development that seems to have little relevance to what goes on in the classroom, professional learning is linked to student learning. And instead of seeing the school and the community as separate entities, Tekoa removes the barriers. As one teacher explained: "We are aiming high, and for kids who struggle we talk to each other and to their parents. We get the parents on board and we let them know that we are willing to stay after school or come to school early. At our Friday meetings we'll ask each other, 'Does anyone know what's going on with Joey?' and most of the time someone knows." Another teacher remarked, "I guess we're kind of a positive Peyton Place, because we usually know what's happening in students' lives. We can offer support and get them help."

Ten specific policies, structures, and practices directly undermine a school's efforts to focus on student, professional, and system learning—and ultimately perpetuate underachievement. These include the lack of an instructional framework; misalignment of curriculum, instruction, and assessments; ineffective instruction; teacher isolation; inability to approach student and professional learning as two sides of the same coin; misassignment of teachers; retention, tracking, and misuse of pullouts; lack of a powerful curriculum for all; lack of extended learning time for underachieving students; and misassignment of students to special education.

The self-assessment rubric in Figure 9.1 isolates these mind-sets, policies, structures, and practices that HP/HP schools have helped to identify as barriers to improvement. Use the rubric to guide your reading and to help you reflect upon the current situation in your school.

Lack of Instructional Framework

> Our state helps us with selecting the right textbook. We try to get new ones every five to seven years. They're all our teachers need to teach the subject to the students—curriculum, teaching content, study guides, and tests.
>
> —*Principal, rural high school in the Southwest*

When a ship loses its compass, getting to port becomes a game of chance. It's no different for a school. When a school, particularly one characterized by high poverty and low performance, lacks an instructional plan or framework, progress will be anything but systematic, and more than likely patterns of low performance will continue. Too many of these schools continue to rely on textbooks to guide curriculum and assessment. Too often, isolated teachers provide instruction, purportedly aligned to district and state standards. In reality, they're driving without a map on an uncertain course to a misunderstood location.

Through the collaborative efforts of the leaders and staff, HP/HP schools design or adopt an instructional framework. These frameworks reflect the development of a common vision of powerful teaching and learning, support curriculum alignment and the adoption of research-based materials, guide the use of classroom-based assessments, and inform and support the learning environment of the classroom. In HP/HP schools, these frameworks are not static. Teachers and administrators continually analyze data and adjust practice to address student needs.

Misalignment of Curriculum, Instruction, and Assessments

> We've just been told that the spring tests were not aligned to the state standards and they are under revision. What are we supposed to do in the meantime?
>
> —*Elementary teacher in Idaho*

FIGURE 9.1	Barriers to Focusing on Student, Professional, and System Learning

Are We Perpetuating Underachievement? What Have We Eliminated?				
Progress Indicators or Evidence →	**No Action Yet**	**Getting Started**	**Gaining Momentum**	**Sustaining Gains, Refining**
Counterproductive Mind-Sets and Practices ↓	**0**	• People are aware of counterproductive mind-sets, policies, structures, or practices. • Urgency is apparent. • Staff acknowledges need for change. **1**	• People are empowered. • Barriers are being removed. • Commitment to the elimination is increasing. • Support for change continues. **2**	• Counterproductive mind-sets, policies, structures, or practices have been eliminated. • New mind-sets, policies, structures, and practices are evident. **3**
Lack of instructional framework.				
Misalignment of curriculum, instruction, and assessments.				
Ineffective instruction.				
Teacher isolation.				
Inability to approach student and professional learning as two sides of the same coin.				
Misassignment of teachers.				
Retention, tracking, and misuse of pullouts.				
Lack of a powerful curriculum for all.				
Lack of extended learning time for underachieving students.				
Misassignment of students to special education.				

When learning targets are unclear to students, it is likely they will be unable to meet them. This may seem like a blinding flash of the obvious, but when content and instruction are not aligned to state and district standards (both content and performance standards), we should not be surprised when students are not able to demonstrate what we have asked them to learn. Lack of alignment between curriculum (standards), instruction, and assessment has historically resulted in lower student achievement and performance—and will continue to do so.

High-performing, high-poverty schools work diligently to connect the learning expectations of the state and district to the curriculum and instructional delivery. They seek to create assessment-literate classrooms in which all teachers and students understand learning goals and expectations. Educators in these schools relentlessly pursue good instruction.

Ineffective Instruction

> Dee Dee has taught 9th grade technical reading and writing forever. Few students like the class. Many decide to pay a $120 fee to take the required course online from a statewide digital learning academy. Long tenured, Dee Dee does the minimum. She never volunteers for activities and doesn't seem to have much passion, if any, for her teaching, the kids, her colleagues, or the school. She says she has six more years to retirement. Her kids earn *A*s, *B*s, and *C*s as long as they go to class and turn in assignments. When they take the 10th grade state reading and writing test, 30 percent don't make proficiency.
>
> —*Middle school teacher in the Northwest*

No student should be subjected to an ineffective teacher. Unfortunately, many will experience poor instruction during their school years. For students who are low performing and live in poverty, ineffective teachers can have a particularly harmful effect, because in many cases these students are more dependent upon the quality of their educational experience than are their more affluent peers. Numerous studies indicate that when students are assigned an ineffective teacher for two consecutive years, dramatic gaps will develop and grow between these students and students assigned to competent teachers.

Leaders in HP/HP schools do not tolerate poor teaching—at least not for long. Collaborative efforts, positive relationships, coaching, and other forms of assistance are used to support underperforming teachers who appear to have the potential to improve. Nevertheless, if improvement does not occur in the context of the high expectations found in HP/HP schools, as one principal put it, "Ineffective teachers need to do one of the three *R*s—rethink, relocate, or retire." If necessary, principals in HP/HP schools initiate appropriate legal processes to dismiss a teacher, regardless of tenure status.

Teacher Isolation

> We used to close our doors and rarely did we collaborate. We really didn't know what the other teachers were doing. Like somebody once said, we were independent operators united only by a common parking lot.
>
> *—Teacher, HP/HP high school on the East Coast*

A core body of knowledge (or way of thinking) represents a hallmark of any profession. Professionalism requires that we continually, and collaboratively, inquire into the core body of knowledge; therefore, even if all teachers were competent, experienced, and caring, the historic isolation of the teaching profession would be problematic. This concern is especially the case in schools with high enrollments of students who live in poverty. Far too many teachers in high-poverty schools spend the majority of their day in overcrowded classrooms behind a closed door in which the quality of learning and the level of achievement run the gamut. Karin Chenoweth (2009a) perhaps summarizes it best, saying, "The fact that teacher isolation is the core of a school's organization structure means that the kids have always been incredibly reliant on which teacher they get every year. A good teacher means a good year of learning, and a bad teacher means the opposite" (p. 10).

A high level of professionalism defines HP/HP schools, in part. Leaders facilitate shared expectations of high performance from everyone—staff and students—and work diligently to provide structures and processes that ensure productive conversations about teaching and learning, as well as collaboration. In HP/HP schools, cooperation and working together become the norm.

Inability to Approach Student and Professional Learning as Two Sides of the Same Coin

> Our budget cuts forced us to eliminate most of our teacher work days. We'll just have to do without most of our staff development this year.
>
> *—Superintendent in the Northwest*

Another hallmark of any profession is the need for continuous professional development, although most educators will attest that the quality and range of opportunity vary greatly. Educators' access to effective professional development may well be the difference between success and failure with their students, and success and failure as a school. This development assumes even greater importance when the challenges increase, as is often the case in low-performing, high-poverty schools.

Leaders in HP/HP schools consider professional learning and student learning as two sides of the same coin. Driven by the needs of their students, these schools constantly seek the most effective approaches and interventions to serve their students. They link what students need to know and be able to do with what the adults in the school need to know and be able to do. This linkage requires an understanding of the importance of teacher-directed collaboration, shared problem solving, and inquiry. Leaders structure schedules to provide time for educators to collaboratively analyze student work and identify their own learning needs. When budgets are reduced in an HP/HP school, the essential components of success, including professional learning, remain a priority as reductions are considered.

Misassignment of Teachers

> We do our best. We have to balance academic hiring with our other needs in athletics, extracurricular activities, clubs, etc. We provide so much for kids and have to have teachers who can both teach their areas and take on these other jobs. The new ones really bear the brunt of this, but that's part of getting your foot in the door here.
>
> —*High school principal in the Midwest*

When teachers instruct out of their area of expertise, students are often shortchanged. Unfortunately, higher proportions of low-income students are taught by teachers who are not certificated in the subject to which they are assigned than are their more advantaged peers (Haycock, 2010). The same is true for years of teaching experience.

This egregious injustice, seemingly entrenched in our system, perpetuates underachievement. In contrast, in HP/HP schools, the most effective teachers are routinely placed with the highest-need students. In these schools, a commitment to equity means the kids who need the most get the most. But this assignment strategy does not happen at the expense of ensuring excellence for all students. The result of this practice is that HP/HP schools succeed in closing achievement gaps and raising overall achievement, central tenets of the mission of public schooling in the United States.

Retention, Tracking, and Misuse of Pullouts

We've had to open up more sections of pre-algebra. There seem to be more and more of our students who just can't learn algebra. I don't know what we're going to do to get them through our 10th grade state test.

—High school assistant principal in the Midwest

Retaining students who are low performing and live in high-poverty situations does not work. Decades of research on the topic have failed to produce support for this long-standing practice. In fact, retention of low-performing students who reside in low-income families seriously compromises the students' chances of ever catching up and graduating. Likewise, tracking students by ability also significantly works against low-performing students, particularly those who live in poverty.

Pullout instruction, a form of tracking as traditionally deployed, is also not in the best interests of low-performing students who live in poverty. The exception is carefully designed approaches that use pullouts for targeted "skill shots" of instruction with the goal of frequent assessment and reassignment to appropriate groupings, together with minimal time away from classroom instruction and the student's higher-performing peers.

High-performing, high-poverty schools do not employ traditional forms of retention or ability-based tracking and pullouts. Their instructional design focuses on providing excellent core instruction for all students and on high-quality classroom assessment to make instructional decisions. When students fail to learn, these schools focus on the individual needs of their students with a goal of catching them up. As students begin to make progress, interventions are modified or eliminated as appropriate.

Lack of a Powerful Curriculum for All

Approximately 28 percent of students in high-poverty schools attend four-year colleges, compared with 52 percent from low-poverty schools (Haycock, 2010). One factor contributing to this difference is the curricular offerings provided to students. Students cannot learn content that they are not taught! High-performing, high-poverty secondary schools eliminate courses that are, in essence, a repetition of curricula provided in lower grades. These courses, with titles such as Consumer Math, Opportunity Math, or Workplace English, often do not offer the curriculum and instruction students need to meet standards or be ready to continue their education after high school should they choose to do so. In secondary schools, offerings such as honors, advanced placement (AP), and International Baccalaureate (IB) courses are usually only available to high-achieving students, not for any student who wishes to enroll. Students who live in poverty are also underrepresented in gifted and talented programs. Ensuring a powerful curriculum for all students can involve removing traditional barriers to participation in such programs.

Lack of Extended Learning Time for Underachieving Students

> The kids come to us with little vocabulary, and many don't even know their *ABCs*. It's sad, but many of them start behind and never catch up.
>
> —*Kindergarten teacher in the South*

Underperforming students who live in poverty will not catch up with their higher-performing peers without additional, targeted instructional time. For the most part, our public schools focus instruction on the larger group of students who achieve proficiency and keep moving through the curriculum. For those who are behind, catching up means largely being left to their own devices. This approach results in underachievement that compounds with each passing week, month, and year. Many educators earnestly attempt to provide support to students who are behind; however, the system as a whole is not structured to effectively address this problem.

Educators in HP/HP schools consider the need to extend learning time as the utmost priority. They focus their individual, collaborative, and school-wide resources first and foremost on helping students who need additional time. As a teacher-leader in an HP/HP school in New England put it, "We only have so much time and energy to get these kids where they need to be... we can't afford to spend any of it on things that don't directly help them."

School schedules are designed with multiple interventions in mind; an extension of the school day, week, and year to provide additional learning time and a continual focus on the learning needs of their underachieving students define these schools. In HP/HP schools, extended time for learning represents the norm.

Misassignment of Students to Special Education

I was diagnosed with a learning disability in the 6th grade and was sent to the resource room every day for two hours… same for junior high and an hour a day through high school. I never got out of special ed, and now I've learned that I really don't have any disability… and never did. I just never was taught to read.

—*College student in a midwestern university*

How often are students from low-income homes referred for testing and assessment by teachers who believe some type of learning disability exists? Once diagnosed with a disability, how often are they removed from general education classrooms for their core instruction? How often do they leave special education programs and succeed in general education? The answers to these questions paint a bleak portrait of the school experience for far too many low-income children. If a student's family is poor, the chance of that student being referred to and placed in special education programs increases significantly. Having been placed in special education, these students rarely transition back into general education (Howard, Dresser, & Dunklee, 2009).

Leaders in HP/HP schools recognize that far too many students living in poverty are misidentified as "disabled" and placed in special education programs. Educators in HP/HP schools prevent disproportionate placement in special education by (1) providing excellent core instruction and follow-up interventions as needed; (2) fostering healthy, safe, and supportive learning environments in the classroom and schoolwide; and (3) developing a culture of high expectations and support for every student.

Action Planning/Next Steps

Use the action planning template in Figure 9.2 (p. 148) to reflect on the information and ideas in this chapter. What commitments do you need to make and what actions do you need to take to focus on student, professional, and system learning?

| FIGURE 9.2 | Action Planning Template for Developing a Focus on Learning |

1. What new information, insights, and ideas did we gain from this chapter?

2. Based on our assessment of the school or district, what change needs to occur and what might be our next steps?

3. Are the changes needed in our school or district structural (time, resources), cultural (norms, beliefs, values), or both? What is the evidence?

4. What is the magnitude of change this represents for our school—first order or second order? What is the evidence?

Action Plan		
Next Steps	**Lead Person Responsible**	**Timeline**

Focusing on Student, Professional, and System Learning: How HP/HP Schools Do It

---

If you don't know what an education should be, only what it is, you'll never get there.

—*Valarie Lewis, principal, Osmond A. Church P.S./M.S. 124*

In 1999, Osmond A. Church P.S./M.S. 124, a K–8 school in Queens, New York, received a $784,000 Comprehensive School Reform grant from the state department of education, and teachers agreed to adopt Core Knowledge. According to Principal Valarie Lewis, "Core Knowledge provided a framework for teaching much more content than we'd ever taught before. We have had to ensure that basic skills are taught, and they are, but in context. Teachers have learned to think like scientists and historians."

Osmond A. Church is a Core Knowledge Demonstration School—and so much more. "We're open six days a week because we run a Saturday Academy for students and parents," says Lewis. "We have after-school programs until 5:30 Monday through Friday. We can do all this because teachers believe in what they are doing. People don't leave here. And we're running a tight ship in terms of the budget. We have two assistant principals, and we qualify for four. Instead of more administrators, we use that funding for programs that extend learning for our students who need it."

During their improvement journey, Lewis has learned to buffer teachers from initiatives that might have had the potential to distract from their vision. She relentlessly keeps the focus on learning. "I have learned to protect my teachers from distractions. I know what might stay around long enough to make it worth sharing. The assistant principals and I spend four days per week in classrooms; the paperwork will wait. We stay true to the vision."

As noted earlier, leaders in HP/HP schools focus on three kinds of learning—student, professional, and system. These learning agendas influence each other, and leaders in HP/HP schools make the most of this connection to facilitate sustainable improvements in teaching and learning. Again, the term *professional learning* denotes the adult learning that takes place within a school, whereas *system learning* conveys how the school as a whole learns to be more effective. In other words, as people within the school learn, the system learns.

At Osmond A. Church, leaders are focused on each of the three learning agendas. Teachers and principals in this school are continuously engaged in inquiry related to what is working for students and what is not. This, in turn, informs what needs to be learned by the adults in the building and how the school, as a system, can get better at what it does. At times, opportunity for professional learning occurs outside the classroom through the assistance of external experts; however, most professional learning is embedded in the daily practice of teachers and principals.

Is your school focusing on all three kinds of learning? Are you making the most of the links between the three? Use the rubric in Figure 10.1 (pp. 152–153) to guide your reading and to help you reflect on the current situation in your school.

Asking the Right Questions, Finding the Leverage Points

Throughout this chapter, we explore five questions that can support leaders as they make the three learning agendas the focus of their actions: (1) Does our instructional framework guide curricula, teaching, assessment, and the learning environment? (2) Do we provide targeted interventions for students who need them? (3) Are all students proficient in reading? (4) Are we using research-based models for professional learning and encouraging reflective practice? (5) Are we engaging in continuous data-based inquiry as a school? In the following sections we examine each of these questions in turn.

Instructional Framework

Question 1: Does our instructional framework guide curricula, teaching, assessment, and the learning environment? What is an instructional framework? In the broadest sense, an instructional framework consists of the theories, policies, structures, processes, and practices used in a school to guide what happens in the classroom—the dynamic interaction between content, student, and teacher referred to as the *instructional core*. Creating a common vision of what excellent (or powerful) teaching looks like, aligning curriculum with state and district standards, selecting materials, selecting and using research-based instructional practices, and developing and using common assessments are all part of creating an instructional framework that brings coherence to teachers' professional practice and positively influences the instructional core.

Comprehensive School Reform Models as a Jump Start to a Framework

Leaders in HP/HP schools credit much of their success to a high level of coherence in the instructional program. Several of the schools we studied began their improvement efforts by adopting a Comprehensive School Reform (CSR) model but later customized the reform model to better fit their needs. For example, Osmond A. Church selected Core Knowledge, whose framework emphasizes building students' knowledge base in world history, geography, civics, literature, science, art, and music. Finding the content to be "too Eurocentric," teachers at Osmond A. Church have added content relating to Africa, Latin America, and Asia. They also incorporated knowledge about the specific ethnicities and cultures represented by their student body.

The CSR models are developed using a research-based rationale for the suggested instructional practices. Some models include curricular materials and formative and summative assessments. Most require specific professional development. This level of structure can be advantageous in jump-starting improvement. Over time, based on data, leaders and teachers often tweak these models to better meet the needs of their students or specific groups of students. At Lapwai Elementary, a highly prescriptive CSR model was customized to incorporate teaching students to use new technology to write a school newspaper and ensuring that the Nez Perce language and culture continued to be taught.

FIGURE 10.1 Focusing on Student, Professional, and System-Level Learning

Assess Current Status				
Progress Indicators or Evidence $\longrightarrow$	**No Action Yet**	**Getting Started**	**Gaining Momentum**	**Sustaining Gains, Refining**
		• Urgency is apparent. • School status is understood. • A vision for improvement is shared. • Implementation strategies are selected. • Staff is prepared to begin.	• People are empowered. • Barriers are being removed. • Implementation is becoming routine. • Commitment is increasing. • Progress is monitored. • Initial gains are being made and celebrated. • Support for improvement continues.	• The improvements are embedded in daily practice. • Collaboration continues. • Refinements are made. • Gains continue to be made and sustained.
What is my school's progress? $\downarrow$	0	1	2	3
Does our instructional framework guide curriculum, teaching, assessment, and the learning climate?				
Do teachers understand the attributes and functions necessary to succeed with students living in poverty?				
Does our instructional framework include research-based strategies for students who live in poverty?				

FIGURE 10.1	Focusing on Student, Professional, and System-Level Learning (*continued*)

What is my school's progress? ↓	0	1	2	3
Do we use common formative and summative assessments to measure student learning?				
Have we ensured that teachers are assessment literate and can use assessments to guide instruction?				
Have we developed assessment literacy in students?				
Are we collaboratively analyzing student work and collectively improving teaching?				
Do teachers have a common vision of good teaching?				
Are we using research-based models for professional learning?				
Have we ensured all students are proficient in reading?				
Do we provide targeted interventions?				
Are we engaging in continuous data-based inquiry as a school?				

UNCOMMON SENSE

Learning about and understanding the Nez Perce culture reflects an important goal of the Lapwai community for its children and adolescents. The early grades incorporate elders as teachers of their native heritage and traditions. As the students progress through secondary school, they have opportunities to learn the Nez Perce language and participate in local and regional annual traditions, such as salmon fishing, sweat lodges, and the gathering of camas roots. High school students travel the trail of Chief Joseph, retracing the migration of their ancestors during the fateful war with the U.S. Army. The school, the Nez Perce tribe, and the Lapwai community work together to support these learning priorities for the students, believing the acquired knowledge leads to the development of a sense of place, which helps students come to better know and understand themselves.

When we visited Dayton's Bluff, Principal Collins explained, "We recently took the sign down that identified Dayton's Bluff as a demonstration school for America's Promise," which was the CSR model they had chosen in the early years of their improvement effort. He explained:

> We had the luxury of having an implementation rubric [based on the CSR model] that provided a strong structure for transitioning into the work our district is doing now. It helped us begin the conversation about leveled libraries and how a book room is set up. We've transitioned into the use of tables rather than desks, and we now better understand the idea of what reading, writing, and math workshop are all about. [The CSR model] was the organizing structure for this school to really gather some momentum and achieve initial success.

An HP/HP school's ability to "innovate on the innovation" and to sustain high levels of achievement points to the leadership capacity it has built and the healthy, safe, and supportive learning environment it has created for students and adults. These schools develop a sense of efficacy that appears to stem from collectively knowing their content, their students, and themselves as teachers. It is likely that these achievement gains would not have been possible had the principal of each of these schools required strict fidelity to a model. Valarie Lewis of Osmond A. Church perhaps said it best: "Our success depended upon building trust and allowing flexibility. We had fidelity with flexibility."

Once again, the news is not new. No one-size-fits-all, silver-bullet approach to the improvement of teaching and learning exists. Yet a body of research from which instructional frameworks might be developed at the local level is available. Figure 10.2 lists websites for school leaders seeking more information about CSR models.

FIGURE 10.2	Comprehensive School Reform

Excellent and pertinent information about comprehensive school reform can be found on the following websites and in the following reports.

Alliance for Excellent Education
www.all4ed.org/files/PolicyBriefWholeSchoolReform.pdf

American Institutes for Research
www.air.org/expertise/index/?fa=viewAllReports&tid=143

Center for Comprehensive School Reform and Improvement
www.centerforcsri.org/

Center on Innovation and Improvement
www.centerii.org

Comprehensive School Reform Models (part of the National Forum to Accelerate Middle-Grades Reform)
www.mgforum.org/ImprovingSchools/ComprehensiveSchoolReformModels/tabid/102/Default.aspx

Evaluating Comprehensive School Reform Models at Scale (a report of the RAND Corporation)
www.rand.org/pubs/monographs/2006/RAND_MG546.pdf

Schools Moving Up
www.schoolsmovingup.net/cs/smu/view/rs/24079

SEDL (formerly the Southwest Educational Development Laboratory)
www.sedl.org/re/experience-improvingschoolperformance.html

Other Paths to an Instructional Framework

More than half of the HP/HP schools that we studied did not select a comprehensive reform model as their framework. Instead, these schools used a homegrown approach. They constructed instructional frameworks based upon students' needs, local data, community assets, and an examination of research. In the early years, these frameworks began to emerge as schools aligned curriculum to state and district standards and implemented specific research-based instructional strategies schoolwide, such as higher-order questioning, explicit academic vocabulary-development strategies, teaching reading across the curriculum, and explicitly teaching thinking skills. In addition, assessment and data literacy for adults and students became the focus in most HP/HP schools. In the later years, use of common, classroom-based assessments greatly enhanced instructional coherence, as teachers collaboratively analyzed student work and discussed teaching practices.

To varying degrees, all HP/HP schools developed structures and processes that supported the development of communities of practice (Wenger, 1998). This collaborative structure enabled schools to create, implement, continuously improve, and sustain a coherent instructional framework. Communities of practice are groups of people who work together over a period of time. They are neither a team nor a task force. They are people who perform the same job and are therefore peers in the execution of that job. What holds them together is a common sense of purpose and a real need to know what one another knows.

In schools, communities of practice are groups of people who work together to hone their professional practice. Although similar to professional learning communities (PLCs), we use the term *communities of practice* to describe the structures and processes observed in the HP/HP schools we studied for two reasons. First, most of the schools we visited did not use the term *PLC*. Second, the term *communities of practice* emphasizes *practice*, which is a term used to describe the work of professionals. Physicians *practice* medicine. Attorneys have a legal *practice*. Education is a profession, and those who work in HP/HP schools are consummate professionals. They draw on, and contribute to, a core body of knowledge, hone their skills in collaboration with each other, hold themselves accountable for student learning, and view their work as much more than a job. As one teacher told us: "I could work in another school, a more affluent school. Most of us could. But we work here. Why? Because every day when I go to work, I know I make a difference. A lot of people don't feel that way about what they do every day."

The Importance of Curriculum Alignment

Findings from almost every study of HP/HP schools indicate that school leaders intensively focus on the curriculum as part of creating coherence in the instructional program. This work includes aligning the written curriculum with state and district standards; vertical and horizontal planning to articulate the curriculum across subjects and grade levels; identification of benchmarks and development of common assessments; collaborative unit and lesson planning; and differentiation of curriculum and instruction, as well as monitoring the taught and tested curriculum through some form of instructional walk-throughs.

From a Pedagogy of Poverty to Powerful Teaching and Learning

Too often, schools continue to use ineffective curricular approaches and instructional practices with students who live in poverty. Such practices have been described as "a pedagogy of poverty" (Haberman, 1991; Padrón, Waxman, & Rivera, 2002). This pedagogy is characterized as an overuse of teacher-controlled discussions and decision making, lecture, drill and decontextualized practice, and worksheets. Other researchers have documented differences in the intellectual quality of tasks required of students in high-poverty schools in contrast to schools where most of the students are middle- or upper-middle-class (Anyon, 1981; Finn, 1999). This contrast can be seen within a single school when students are tracked into courses such as Consumer Math or Opportunity Math, usually provided for students who are thought to be "unable" to learn algebra. Rather than a pedagogy of poverty, what students who live in poverty need is "powerful pedagogy"—powerful instruction resulting in powerful (or deep) learning. Such pedagogy is consistent with a large body of research related to how people learn (Bransford, Brown, & Cocking, 2002).

 UNCOMMON SENSE

All students at Tekoa High School take Algebra I in 8th grade. To prepare them to be successful, the high school math teacher, who teaches all secondary math courses in this rural district, met with the elementary teachers to ask for their help. His goal was to have every 8th grader successfully complete algebra and be positioned to take the advanced mathematics courses needed to pursue higher education should they choose to do so when they graduate. Elementary teachers agreed to teach math for a 90-minute period each day, which has greatly enhanced students' readiness for algebra and other advanced math courses. With the goal of all students successfully completing Algebra I in 8th grade, this school, enrolling fewer than 100 students, is able to offer a full continuum of advanced math courses.

Powerful pedagogy has been conceptualized in various ways—as relevant to the learner (Brandt, 1998); meaning centered (Knapp & Adelman, 1995); supporting the development of various kinds of understanding (Wiggins & McTighe, 2005); accelerated, strength based, and empowering (Levin, 1989); as well as encompassing higher-order thinking, deep knowledge, and connections beyond classrooms (Newman et al., 1996). When a powerful pedagogy is employed, students are actively engaged in meaning making and developing understanding not only of content but also of one's self as a learner. Problem solving, reasoning, critical and creative thinking, and inquiry are integral. Lessons and units access and build upon students' prior knowledge and focus on understanding. Students are empowered through choice and given a voice in decision making.

The staff of the Center for Educational Leadership at the University of Washington in Seattle has developed a 5D Framework focused on five dimensions of powerful teaching and learning: (1) purpose, (2) student engagement, (3) curriculum and pedagogy, (4) assessment for student learning, and (5) classroom environment and culture. This framework, supported by a comprehensive research base, includes the key instructional elements from which coherence in practice can be developed. Additional information regarding this instructional framework, as well as other resources linking powerful teaching and learning with leadership, can be accessed at www.k-12leadership.org.

Begin with a Common Understanding of Good Teaching

As a profession, education lacks a clear definition and a common language for describing good teaching. According to Robert Pianta (Wiltz, 2008), who has conducted studies of thousands of classrooms in hundreds of schools across the United States, our definition of good teaching "is all over the map" (p. 1). Charlotte Danielson (1996), author of *Enhancing Professional Practice: A Framework for Teaching,* highlights this important problem of practice, saying, "Indeed, other professions—medicine, accounting, and architecture among many others—have well-established definitions of expertise and procedures... such procedures are the public's guarantee that the members of a profession hold themselves and their colleagues to the highest standards" (p. 2). Although progress has been made, as witnessed through the work of Pianta, Danielson, and others, the field of education continues to be plagued by the lack of an "established definition of expertise." Having spent decades studying teachers in high-poverty, diverse urban schools, Martin Haberman (1991) who, as noted earlier, coined the term "pedagogy of poverty," describes "good teaching" as a "core set of teacher acts" (p. 293) that tend to be more evident in what students are doing than in what the teacher is doing. He suggests good teaching is going on when students are

- Working on problems and issues they care about and in experiences that help them make sense of their world and their place in it;
- Focusing on big ideas rather than the pursuit of isolated facts;

- Planning what they will learn;
- Wrestling with ideals such as fairness, equity, and justice;
- Learning from real-life experiences;
- Thinking creatively, questioning common notions, and connecting ideas to prior learning or new problems;
- Revising, polishing, or perfecting their work;
- Using technology to solve problems; and
- Reflecting on themselves, their beliefs, and their feelings. (Adapted from Haberman, 1991, pp. 293–294)

Even in schools employing a CSR model, where the notion of what constitutes good teaching is, at least partially, conscribed by the model itself, the time spent on topics, the focus of skill development, and the use of instructional practices vary greatly from classroom to classroom. Furthermore, such variation in instructional practice is often not linked to students' needs, such as socioeconomic background or prior achievement (Correnti & Rowan, 2007).

This is an area in which HP/HP schools appear to stand in stark contrast to the norm. Teachers and administrators in HP/HP schools collectively make modifications to meet the needs of their students. Believing the work is never done, these schools endeavor as a community of practice to develop a common understanding of what good teaching looks like; establish clear expectations for students and teachers; use research-based instructional strategies; and monitor what happens in the instructional core through coaching, classroom walk-throughs, and a variety of other informal means.

Knowing and Using Practices That Address Underachievement and Poverty

High-performing, high-poverty schools include strategies, curricular approaches, or instructional processes in their instructional framework to specifically address the learning needs of students who are underachieving and in poverty. Such strategies, approaches, and procedures not only focus on improving students' academic achievement but also speak to the needs of the "whole" child. Figure 10.3 provides a synthesis of practices, supported by empirical evidence, that appear to work because they mitigate the poverty-related factors that adversely affect learning (discussed in Chapter 9). Many of the studies included in this synthesis examine the effectiveness of the practice not only with students living in poverty but also with culturally and linguistically diverse populations of students.

FIGURE 10.3	Practices That Address the Needs of Underachieving Students Living in Poverty

Effective Practice	Examples Used in Classrooms and Schools	30 Years of Research
• Create a bond between students and school. • Foster a sense of belonging.	• Class meetings • Home rooms • Advisories • Placement in higher-level courses • Athletics/clubs	• Smerdon (2002) • Lareau (1987) • Murray & Malmgren (2005) • Kovalik & Olsen (1998)
• Teach, model, and provide experiences that develop creative and critical thinking skills.	• Higher-order questioning • Problem-based learning • Socratic seminars • Multidisciplinary units	• Langer (2001) • Johannessen (2004) • Ornelles (2007) • Lalas (2007) • Eisenman & Payne (1997) • Pogrow (2005) • Schlichter, Hobbs, & Crump (1988)
• Provide opportunities to build short-term working memory.	• Multisensory instruction • Memory aids (e.g., mnemonic devices)	• Jensen (1998) • Jensen (2009) • Fogarty (2009)
• Provide specific opportunities for the development of social skills.	• Cooperative learning • Peer tutoring • Mentoring	• Langer (2001) • Lalas (2007)
• Access and build on prior knowledge to expand knowledge.	• Brainstorming • Semantic mapping • Advance organizers • Tuning and reconstruction • Autobiographical activities	• Lareau (1987) • Johannessen (2004) • Rockwell (2007) • Kovalik & Olsen (1998)
• Mediate and scaffold learning experiences.	• Reciprocal teaching • "Think-alouds" • Visual organizers/models • Guided practice • Shelter instruction	• Johannessen (2004) • Palinscar & Brown (1985) • Echevarria, Vogt, & Short (2004)
• Personalize based upon diverse learning needs.	• Learning styles • Multiple intelligences • Differentiated instruction • Tiered structures for learning (Response to Intervention)	• Honigsfeld & Dunn (2009) • Tomlinson and others (2003) • Campbell & Campbell (1999)
• Accelerate and enrich rather than remediate learning.	• Talent development • College-prep courses for all • Advanced placement/honors for all • Arts education	• McCormick & Williams (1974) • Catterall, Chapleau, & Iwanaga (1999)

FIGURE 10.3	Practices That Address the Needs of Underachieving Students Living in Poverty (*continued*)

• Actively engage students in learning experiences for authentic, meaningful purposes.	• Project-based learning • Place-based learning • Authentic assessments	• Smith & Sobel (2010) • Williams (2003)
• Connect physical activity, exercise, and motor development to learning.	• Physical education focused on life-long sports and fitness • Schoolwide fitness goals and progress monitoring • Sensory motor labs	• Sibley & Etnier (2003) • Pellegrini & Bohn (2005) • Newman (2005) • Tremblay, Vitaro, & Brendgen (2000) • Palmer, Giese, & Deboer (2008)
• Provide learning experiences that help students envision their futures and foster hope.	• Service learning • Community-based internships • Mentoring	• Furco & Root (2010)

Assessments and Assessment Literacy

> Things are a lot better now. There's been a culture shift with teachers *and* students using data to make the most of our decisions. We have powerful standards and curriculum maps that really help guide our teaching. We are just beginning to work on developing common assessments.
>
> —*Teacher-leaders, HP/HP high school on the West Coast*

Another important aspect of creating a coherent instructional framework is the use of high-quality assessments. A balanced and effective assessment system includes three levels of assessments: classroom, school, and district. Each assessment serves multiple purposes, including both formative and summative purposes (Stiggins & DuFour, 2009). It is critical that principals and teachers become assessment literate so that assessment can be used to gauge learning and make appropriate instructional and programmatic decisions.

Five elements of sound classroom assessments, the competencies necessary for teachers to develop and use high-quality classroom assessment to measure learning, and recommendations to support students in developing assessment literacy are described in Figure 10.4 (p. 162).

Figure 10.5 (p. 163) lists 10 competencies leaders need to develop to improve the quality of assessment practices schoolwide. Although these competencies were intended to describe "a well-qualified principal," in HP/HP schools these competencies are present in teacher-leaders as well.

FIGURE 10.4	Sound Classroom Assessment Practice

1. Clear purposes Assessment processes and results serve clear and appropriate purposes.	a. Teachers understand who uses classroom assessment information and know their information needs. b. Teachers understand the relationship between assessment and student motivation and craft assessment experiences to maximize motivation. c. Teachers use classroom assessment processes and results formatively (assessment for learning). d. Teachers use classroom assessment results summatively (assessment of learning) to inform someone beyond the classroom about students' achievement at a particular point in time. e. Teachers have a comprehensive plan over time for integrating assessment *for* and *of* learning in the classroom.
2. Clear targets Assessments reflect clear and valued student learning targets.	a. Teachers have clear learning targets for students; they know how to turn broad statements of content standards into classroom-level learning targets. b. Teachers understand the various types of learning targets they hold for students. c. Teachers select learning targets focused on the most important things students need to know and be able to do. d. Teachers have a comprehensive plan over time for assessing learning targets.
3. Sound design Learning targets are translated into assessments that yield accurate results.	a. Teachers understand the various assessment methods. b. Teachers choose assessment methods that match intended learning targets. c. Teachers design assessments that serve intended purposes. d. Teachers sample learning appropriately in their assessments. e. Teachers write assessment questions of all types well. f. Teachers avoid sources of mismeasurement that bias results.
4. Effective communication Assessment results are managed well and communicated effectively.	a. Teachers record assessment information accurately, keep it confidential, and appropriately combine and summarize it for reporting (including grades). Such summary accurately reflects current level of student learning. b. Teachers select the best reporting option (grades, narratives, portfolios, conferences) for each context (learning targets and users). c. Teachers interpret and use standardized test results correctly. d. Teachers effectively communicate assessment results to students. e. Teachers effectively communicate assessment results to a variety of audiences outside the classroom, including parents, colleagues, and other stakeholders.
5. Student involvement Students are involved in their own assessment.	a. Teachers make learning targets clear to students. b. Teachers involve students in assessing, tracking, and setting goals for their own learning. c. Teachers involve students in communicating about their own learning.

Source: From *Classroom Assessment for Student Learning: Doing It Right—Using It Well* by R. Stiggins, J. Arter, J. Chappuis, & S. Chappuis, 2004, Portland, OR: Pearson Assessment Training Institute, 2010. Reprinted with permission.

FIGURE 10.5	Ten Assessment Competencies for School Leaders

1. The leader understands the attributes of a sound and balanced assessment system, and the conditions required to achieve balance in local systems.

2. The leader understands the necessity of clear academic achievement standards, aligned classroom-level achievement targets, and their relationship to the development of accurate assessments.

3. The leader understands the standards of quality for student assessments, helps teachers learn to assess accurately, and ensures that these standards are met in all school/district assessments.

4. The leader knows assessment *for* learning practices and works with staff to integrate them into classroom instruction.

5. The leader creates the conditions necessary for the appropriate use and reporting of student achievement information, and can communicate effectively with all member of the school community about student assessment results, including report card grades, and their relationship to improving curriculum and instruction.

6. The leader understands the issues related to the unethical and inappropriate use of student assessment and protects students and staff from such misuse.

7. The leader can plan, present, and/or secure professional development activities that contribute to the use of sound assessment practices.

8. The leader knows and can evaluate the teacher's classroom assessment competencies, and helps teachers learn to assess accurately and use the results to benefit student learning.

9. The leader analyzes student assessment information accurately, uses the information to improve curriculum and instruction, and assists teachers in doing the same.

10. The leader develops and implements sound assessment and assessment-related policies.

Source: From *Assessment Balance and Quality: An Action Guide for School Leaders* (p. 98), by S. Chappuis, C. Commodore, & R. J. Stiggins, 2009, Portland, OR: Educational Testing Service. Copyright 2009 by ETS. Reprinted with permission.

Early in Lapwai Elementary School's improvement journey, leaders in the district used professional learning time to focus on developing assessment literacy and common, classroom-based assessments. In retrospect they viewed this step as vital to creating coherence in the instructional program and significantly improving student achievement. At Port Chester, teachers and leaders have developed formative and summative common assessments aligned to the content of New York State's redesigned standardized test. Data from these assessments inform decisions related to instruction and program design.

In many HP/HP schools, students actively participate in using assessment to support their learning. Teachers set clear learning targets and engage their students in activities that help them acquire assessment literacy. These include selecting individual learning benchmarks, compiling portfolios, making public presentations of work, completing reflective revisions, and participating in student-led conferences. In these schools, the initiation of student-led conferences not only improved students' understanding of their own learning but also significantly improved parental attendance rates at school conferences.

THE DISTRICT'S "AD-VANTAGE POINT"

Ensuring a Balanced and Effective Assessment System

"To be truly productive, a local district's assessment system must provide different kinds of information to various decision makers in different forms and at different times" (Stiggins & DuFour, 2009, p. 641).

Creating a comprehensive assessment system is a district-level responsibility. At a minimum, district-level leaders can play an important role in supporting high-quality assessments in schools and classrooms by ensuring that components of the leadership infrastructure described in Chapter 6 are in place. This includes access to a comprehensive, user-friendly database and a school calendar that supports time for professional learning.

Rick Stiggins (2007) argues that our current obsession with standardized testing has led to a neglect of classroom assessment. He and others have pointed to the use of classroom assessment as vital to the improvement of teaching and learning, particularly the development and use of common assessments within a professional learning community structure (DuFour & Marzano, 2009; Stiggins & DuFour, 2009). Nearly all the HP/HP schools we studied were engaged in the development and use of common assessments. This high-leverage strategy provides a means for teachers to use their collective wisdom and expertise to (1) address the learning needs of individual students, (2) refine instructional practices, (3) increase the clarity of the learning targets they are attempting to reach, (4) enhance the quality of their assessments, and (5) support the development of a common vision of powerful teaching and learning (Stiggins & DuFour, 2009). High-performing, high-poverty schools connect curriculum and instruction to assessment. The development and use of common assessments in turn contribute to their success with underachieving students.

The Importance of the Teacher

You have to understand when you commit to a job like this, in an area like this where everybody's poor, that you're committing to something that's way different than working in middle- or upper-income neighborhood schools. By necessity, you're a bigger part of the children's lives here. I think the people at this school understand that. The kids know we care about them. If they didn't believe that we cared for them, then I don't think they would do as well as they do.

—Teacher, HP/HP school in the West

Leaders in HP/HP schools know that aligning curriculum, selecting research-based instructional practices, and using high-quality classroom assessments are only part of the picture. The school-related factor that makes the most difference in the lives of students who live in poverty (or all students, for that matter) is the quality of teaching that occurs in the classroom. Moreover, leaders and successful teachers know high-quality teaching includes attributes well beyond technical knowledge and skills. Sara Fry and Kim DeWit (2010) conducted a study of teachers who themselves struggled in school and asked them to identify, based on their experiences in K–12 schooling, what they believed to be the characteristics of effective teachers. Four characteristics emerged. Effective teachers (1) have caring relationships with students, (2) set high standards and help students reach them, (3) connect the curriculum to students' lives, and (4) participate in ongoing professional development. Fry and Dewit state, "These qualities reflect the belief that all children can learn. This disposition comes naturally to the teachers we interviewed because they know exactly what it is like to be the student who can—and did—learn despite facing challenges" (p. 71).

Haberman (1995) identified 15 functions of what he calls "Star Teachers of Children in Poverty." The functions not only encompass characteristics and behaviors demonstrated by effective teachers, but also provide a glimpse into the theories of action that underpin their practice:

- Persistence
- Protecting learners and learning
- Putting ideas into practice
- Approaches to at-risk children
- Professional/personal orientation to students
- Care and feeding of the bureaucracy
- Fallibility
- Emotional and physical stamina
- Organizational ability
- Effort, not ability

- Teaching, not sorting
- Convincing students "I need you here"
- You and me against the material
- Gentle teaching in a violent society
- When teachers face themselves [examine their mental maps]

We explained earlier that a theory of action is both the action chosen and the rationale for action—the *what* and the *why*. These theories are underpinned by mental maps, or mind-sets. Understanding the theories of action and the underlying mind-sets that guide the practice of teachers who are successful with students who live in poverty is equally as important as understanding what teaching techniques they use. In fact, Haberman (1995) warns it is not possible to create "easy steps" for other teachers to follow because the manner in which effective teachers "think about their work cannot be separated from their observable behavior." To do what these successful teachers do requires that others understand the theories that guide their practice "because it is this foundation that guides the countless decisions they make daily" (p. 21).

We consistently found attributes in the teacher-leaders and principals we interviewed that were similar to Haberman's 15 functions. These leaders incorporate into their professional practice a particular ideology related to working with students who live in poverty that is foundational to all that they do. They care about the lives of their students and view them as equally worthy of powerful instruction as their more affluent and, at times, higher-achieving peers.

 SCHOOL CULTURE ALERT

These educators know that their students who live in poverty are capable of learning to high standards; thus they hold high expectations for them, insist they will learn, and provide the support they need to succeed. What was most striking among those with whom we talked was an unwavering professional accountability for learning. Teachers in HP/HP schools are confident in their ability to teach every child and do not make excuses for or blame students and families for their students' performance.

Reflecting on the theories of action underpinning professional practice, fostering a shared vision for what is possible, and developing a common understanding of good teaching are critical for instructional coherence; nevertheless, it can be an overwhelming task for leaders to facilitate. Based on the research on HP/HP schools; our interactions with many educators who work with children and adolescents who live in poverty; and our interviews with school leaders, teachers, and staff in the schools we visited, we have created the mnemonic device shown in Figure 10.6 to help you absorb the information presented thus far in this chapter and to serve as a conversation starter among staff.

FIGURE 10.6   Successful Teachers: A Mnemonic Device

		Teachers Who Succeed with Students Living in Poverty
T	Teach in a thinking way.	Create a thinking-focused, meaning-making classroom in which students develop thinking skills through both explicit instruction and embedded use of problem-centered, inquiry-based learning.
E	Engage students and emphasize effort.	Engage students in learning for authentic, real-life purposes that build understanding of themselves and their world. Emphasize the importance of effort as it relates to targeted outcomes and actual results. Expect persistence, encourage risk taking, and help students view mistakes as opportunities for growth.
A	Accurately assess students and advocate for them.	Accurately assess students' academic, social, emotional, and physical needs. Advocate for students to ensure the school is providing equitable services—and for students' families when needed.
C	Create community.	Create a community in the classroom that provides a learning climate conducive to cooperation, choice, and risk taking.
H	Hold high expectations and are bearers of hope.	Hold high expectations for students, insist they are capable of powerful learning, and provide them the support necessary. Hold in their minds the reality of the students' life circumstances, while steadfastly encouraging students and providing them with challenging learning experiences in the classroom, as well as in the community, that open doors to multiple possible future opportunities.
E	Educate the whole child.	Educate the whole child based on the comprehensive needs that characterize every student. Ensure that music, drama, art, and health/fitness are a part of schooling.
R	Regard relationships as paramount to learning.	Regard relationships of mutual respect as paramount to high-quality teaching and have confidence that through such relationships students will learn.

Targeted Interventions

Question 2: Do we provide targeted interventions for students who need them? In her book *White Teachers/Diverse Classrooms*, Julie Landsman says the following:

> We cannot follow the statement "All children can learn" with conditionals. No matter where we teach, we will rarely have a classroom in which every student is motivated, has a full stomach, lives in a safe neighborhood, and has a relationship with both of his or her parents. We must teach the students we have before us, understanding the complexities of their lives and helping each student deal with these complexities. Teachers must be bearers of hope in places where there are depression and despair. (Landsman & Lewis, 2006, p. 26)

Even with the development of a comprehensive instructional framework that leads to improvement in the quality of teaching and learning in the classroom, underachieving students who live in poverty will need additional support. Catching up often means more time and specific strategies aimed at the unique needs of individual students. Too often, for too many students in poverty, the need for additional support has resulted in referral and placement in special education programs (Howard, Dresser, & Dunklee, 2009). With the advent of Response to Intervention (RTI), many schools are becoming more systematic about the use of interventions. Response to Intervention represents an approach used by many schools to structure the instructional day in such a way that students are systematically provided additional time and support. Based on comprehensive assessments, RTI models provide additional support for students at the Tier 2 level, and for those with exceptional needs, Tier 3 interventions. Our use of the term *targeted intervention* is in some instances synonymous with the RTI Tier 2 support, and in other cases, targeted interventions are offered as extended learning opportunities outside the school day or year.

High-performing, high-poverty schools have long been systematically providing targeted support for students within and outside the traditional school day, week, or year. All HP/HP schools constantly review data to identify students who need before-, during-, and after-school small-group and individual tutoring; self-paced interventions using technology; one-on-one academic advising and coaching; homework support; or additional assessment time.

All the schools we studied provide interventions within the school day. Dayton's Bluff offers preschool and provides full-day kindergarten; Taft Elementary offers reduced-class-size kindergarten, supported in part through

Title I funding; and Lapwai Elementary works in partnership with the Nez Perce tribe to offer preschool.

Molalla High School provides a Learning Strategies Lab, in addition to a regular English course, for students who are English language learners. Molalla teachers work collaboratively to support students enrolled in these labs. When students no longer need to attend, they are able to select another elective immediately. This collaboration often results in a midterm change of schedules, which proves well worth the effort required because it provides an effective incentive for students to work hard to catch up.

All the HP/HP schools we visited also provided interventions outside the school day, week, or year. For example, Port Chester Middle School offers after-school tutoring in language arts and math for students who have not reached state standards.

 UNCOMMON SENSE

Osmond A. Church operates both an after-school program and a Saturday Academy. Students who did not make at least one year's growth in the previous school year are targeted for participation in the after-school program. Additionally, students needing enrichment are encouraged to attend the Saturday Academy, which operates from 8:00 a.m. to 12:00 noon. Approximately 500 students attend the Saturday Academy, which also provides a variety of support courses for the 100 to 300 parents who regularly participate. According to Principal Valarie Lewis of Osmond A. Church, because about 75 percent of the enrolled kindergarten students had no preschool experience, the Core Knowledge preschool program is also offered on Saturdays. As Lewis explains, "You just can't get it done in 6 hours and 20 minutes per day—no way."

Not all interventions are created equal. If an intervention is to be effective, the manner in which it is structured and implemented must be of concern to leaders. Figure 10.7 (pp. 170–172) includes descriptions of four common interventions and tips for design and implementation.

Reading Proficiency

Question 3: Are all students proficient in reading? Second only to safety, ensuring that all students develop literacy skills reflects a core priority in HP/HP schools. As a principal at a middle school in the South put it, "We start

| FIGURE 10.7 | Tips for Design and Implementation of Four Common Interventions |

Before- or After-School Programs

- Document need for before- or after-school program.
- Assess financial capabilities.
- Determine scope of intended program.
- Hire a program director to oversee and coordinate.
- Involve parents, businesspeople, and other community members.
- Provide ongoing evaluation.
- Focus on strengthening academic skills: direct instruction, learning strategies and skills, peer/cross-age tutoring, homework assistance.
- Plan group time focused on building healthy relationships and on opportunities to solve problems and increase self-esteem.
- Provide opportunities to widen students' horizons—recreational and cultural activities, technology-related activities, involvement in community-based youth organizations.
- Establish parent resource centers—parents participate or volunteer in children's activities, offer parenting knowledge/skill development.
- Provide transportation.
- Spend time on project-based, experiential and hands-on learning, challenging students to think.

Related research: Kraft (2001); Schwendiman & Fager (1999)

Tutoring

- Find partner teachers, determine content.
- Determine methodology.
- Determine program length.
- Training and feedback for tutors.
- Prepare the tutees.
- Match tutors and tutees.
- Inform parents.
- Monitor and assess the program.
- Structure lesson plans for tutors to follow.
- Provide frequent tutoring sessions (2–3 per week).
- Identify a framework in order to ensure quality control and participant autonomy.
- Incorporate district administrators, principals, and teachers into the program.
- Provide an avenue to network with other programs.

Related research: Bond (2002); McClure & Vaughn (1997)

Early Childhood/Readiness Programs

- Provide prekindergarten programs, 12 weeks in duration, housed in the school.
- Supply services two or three days per week.
- Staff with teachers with kindergarten experience.

FIGURE 10.7	Tips for Design and Implementation of Four Common Interventions (*continued*)

Early Childhood/Readiness Programs (*continued*)

- Base curriculum on literacy and numeracy.
- Include programs for parents.
- Support 10–15 child-parent dyads (20–30 total).
- Encourage parents to drop in and participate in circle time.
- Extend learning by having teachers spend time in individual or small-group interactions.
- Provide outreach to hard-to-reach families.

Related research: Pelletier & Corter (2005)

Summer School

- Identify potential summer school students early in the year.
- Separate behavior from academics.
- Develop a rubric to determine which students need summer school.
- Make sure class sizes are small and focus on students who have shown a higher level of failure.
- Create a handbook for the summer to include policies and procedures for summer classes.
- Set up courses to fit the compressed schedule.
- Deal with complex topics early in the course.
- Allow students to complete assignments more readily; break larger assignments into frequent short assignments.
- Maintain expectations and standards.
- Assign only one course per teacher.
- Make sure administrators and teachers are available to parents and students beyond class time.
- Ensure teachers aren't teaching the course for the first time in a compressed format.

Related research: Kops (2010); Rischer (2009)

with reading and end with reading. There's a lot of content and important stuff in between, but if our kids can't read at grade level, they'll never do as well as they could or should with the rest." Designing a comprehensive approach to reading improvement entails conducting an analysis of students' unique needs (e.g., those of English language learners), developing an understanding of the influence of poverty on reading achievement (Neuman, 2008), and examining the research base, especially concerning adolescent literacy. (See Slavin, Cheung, Groff, & Lake, 2008.)

Teaching Kids to Read

The goal of many schools is to ensure that all students are reading well by 3rd grade. Taft Elementary focuses on intervention early in students' academic journey. In addition to the district-adopted reading program, Taft Elementary assesses the proficiency of all students and, if necessary, assigns students to one of three targeted reading interventions that provide different approaches to literacy learning.

When students do not learn to read by 3rd grade or develop reading difficulties after 3rd grade, as is disproportionately the case for students living in poverty (Kieffer, 2010), it is critically important that an emphasis on learning to read continue to be an instructional priority in upper-elementary classrooms as well as in middle and high schools. At the secondary level, this often requires supplanting an elective in a student's schedule to provide explicit reading instruction, which can present a dilemma for middle and high school leaders and teachers.

 UNCOMMON SENSE

Increasingly, middle and high schools are finding ways to teach reading as a separate course from English/language arts offerings. A number of school leaders enlist the help of a willing teacher (usually from the English department) to whom they provide support in the form of additional college coursework or professional development in a particular program so that the teacher can gain the knowledge and skills to teach reading to adolescents. In many schools, leaders have gained support from their district office to hire a certificated reading teacher, and in other cases they have turned to entities within the community to access expertise from community volunteers.

The impact this kind of attention can have on a student's self-confidence and progress in school is captured in this story told by a teacher in a K–12 district on the West Coast:

> I can tell you the kind of difference learning to read has made in the lives of these kids. We are a small rural district. Even after we combined funds from general education, special education, and Title I, we could only afford to offer the Read Right program in one location—at the elementary school. But we offer the instruction to kids grade 3 through 12. The other day, a high school student's mother stopped by to tell me how much it meant to her that we were teaching reading to her son. She told me a story about him being sick and refusing to miss his reading class at the elementary school. Apparently he told his mom, "I can read, Mom! I'm not afraid anymore. All the years I've been in school, I've been afraid of people finding out I couldn't read, but not anymore. I'm not missing

that reading class no matter how sick I am. If I puke on the desk, my teacher will understand." When his mother told me this story, we both cried.

Requiring an underachieving student, who is likely to be disillusioned about reading, to take a reading course as an elective might not be the choice of the student. Yet reading is the gateway skill to other knowledge, as well as to self-confidence and self-efficacy. In the end, although still not commonplace, an increasing number of middle and high schools are incorporating needs-driven reading instruction within the school day.

Another approach to teaching reading that serves the needs of underachieving students is incorporating reading instruction into the subjects typically taught in the curriculum at secondary schools. Port Chester Middle School has refined this concept.

UNCOMMON SENSE

All teachers at Port Chester Middle School consider themselves to be English/language arts (ELA) teachers. To sell this idea, school leaders began by helping teachers understand that students' inability to read proficiently was a significant barrier to learning the content the teachers were attempting to teach. Following targeted professional development and collaborative support from the school's ELA faculty, the school studied the interdisciplinary challenges of teaching ELA across the curriculum and created a set of bundled ELA skills to be taught in every class. All teachers now incorporate the 24 bundled key ELA skills in each of their classes.

Motivating Kids to Read

Reading, like any other skill, requires practice to improve. Although it's not an easy undertaking, HP/HP schools find ways to motivate students to read. After students have read 1 million words at Dayton's Bluff, the entire school celebrates with a parade through the school's neighborhood. Principal Andrew Collins explains: "We kick off our Million Word Campaign in the fall. Students pledge to read 1 million words, and when we've reached the goal, all 400 kids with noisemakers, staff, and community partners parade through the streets." Collins, who stands nearly seven feet tall, says, "I get to lead with a big bullhorn. It's pretty powerful when you look at our students stretched about a half a block celebrating reading. There are a lot of parents who come out for it and sit in chairs like at any other parade. It's a good tradition."

High-performing, high-poverty schools keep reading proficiency at the top of their priority list. To ensure all students learn to read well, teachers are willing to gain new knowledge, hone new skills, and in some cases change long-standing school processes. Learning to read changes the lives of students who have struggled. They gain new appreciation for learning, and most important, a sense of self-efficacy that extends to other areas of their lives.

 UNCOMMON SENSE

The principal asked the bus driver to spend the hours between her routes to and from school to help students build fluency in their reading skills. The principal explained: "That particular bus driver was often around the school anyway and one of the teachers needed some extra assistance, so I asked her if she'd be willing to help three days a week. She was delighted to help, and actually had a niece in our school and wanted to feel more connected to the school. Now she is—and most important, she's really helping several kids become better readers!"

Research-Based Models for Professional Learning

Question 4: Are we using research-based models for professional learning and encouraging reflective practice? Leaders in HP/HP schools hold a view similar to this one expressed by a superintendent in a Northwest school district: "There is a bright red thread running from every student-learning problem to a problem of practice for teachers, and finally to a problem of practice for leaders." Professional learning and student learning are two sides of the same coin—they cannot be separated. Many HP/HP schools, including those we studied, are either engaged in the process of developing common assessments or have begun using them within the context of a community of practice. During this work, as students' needs are identified, so too are the learning needs of the adults in the school.

Most of the HP/HP schools were also supporting professional learning through various types of walk-through processes. At Osmond A. Church, principals and teachers are engaged in conducting Instructional Rounds.

Principal Lewis uses a modified version of the model described in *Instructional Rounds in Education: A Networking Approach to Improving Teaching and Learning* (City, Elmore, Fiarman, & Teitel, 2009) to meet the needs of the teachers in the school.

UNCOMMON SENSE

At Taft Elementary, teachers are vertically paired (e.g., a 1st grade teacher with a 2nd grade teacher) as "thinking partners." These two-person teams observe instruction in their school, as well as engage in dialogue and reflection about instructional practice. Each set of thinking partners conducts a 30-minute classroom observation, takes a break to dialogue with each other, and conducts another 30-minute observation. The intervening dialogue is structured using a 3-2-1 model: teachers are asked to list three observed components of the district's instructional framework, two ideas they will take back to their classroom, and one question they are wondering about. After the final classroom observation, teachers engage in reflective journaling.

In addition to the approaches described here, several other structures and processes are effective in supporting professional learning and promoting reflective practices. These include action research, lesson study, case-based learning, networks, journaling, portfolio development, and tuning protocols.

High-performing, high-poverty schools constantly endeavor to enhance professional capacity to better meet the needs of their students. The adults in these schools take their own learning as seriously as their students' learning, understanding they are truly two sides of the same coin. As one teacher explained, "When I learn to do something better, it helps a lot of my kids. We all know this and continually work to find the time it takes."

Continuous Data-Based Inquiry

Question 5: Are we engaging in continuous data-based inquiry as a school?
All HP/HP schools engage in some form of data-based decision making at the school level. This process typically involves identification of a problem, gathering and analysis of data, goal setting, selection and implementation of strategies, and evaluation. Although this form of planning is likely to be used in many schools, what distinguishes HP/HP schools from others is the

manner in which such a cycle of inquiry has become the norm. Second only to the development of caring relationships in the schools we studied, the use of data was credited for much of their success. These schools are places where people tend to be very curious about their practice and are eager to innovate. They continuously seek or create solutions to the challenges posed by poverty and are encouraged to take risks. Principals of these schools play a key role in driving this work.

The Principal's Role

A principal's actions are critical for initiating a school's improvement journey, staying the course when things get tough and sustaining the momentum for the long term. Figure 10.8 describes the actions principals take to ensure the work is focused on improving student, professional, and system-level learning.

In HP/HP schools the gap is small between principals' theories *of* action (espoused theories) and their theories *in* action (the theories that *actually* underpin their professional practice). In other words, their actions are consistent with their message. They are clear about their course of action and

---

FIGURE 10.8 The Principal's Role in Focusing on Learning in HP/HP Schools

The principal—

- Facilitates ongoing conversations about what is possible.
- Continues as chief steward of the school's vision.
- Works with teachers to establish a common understanding of powerful teaching and learning.
- Uses his or her formal authority to ensure school structures and processes are in place to develop communities of practice through which teachers do the following:
  - Align curriculum to state/district standards;
  - Ensure instructional quality;
  - Develop assessment literacy;
  - Use assessments to guide decision making at the classroom and school levels; and
  - Grow as professionals.

- Manages human and material resources to ensure targeted interventions are provided to students who need them.
- Promotes and supports a culture of inquiry as a means for continual improvement in the classroom and schoolwide.

can cogently and concisely articulate the rationale for those actions. Simplifying the message keeps the vision clear and in the forefront of the school's improvement efforts. Leaders in the schools we studied "cut to the chase." Their words reflect the theories that underpin system-level learning in their schools: "We make decisions based on what's best for kids.... We treat them as our own.... It's all about community.... Everyone's a reading/language arts teacher.... We share the big picture with people and give them enough information; then they engage.... We don't throw it at the wall and hope it sticks; we build the wall so we know it will stick.... We control the controllable.... If we think we've arrived, then we need to leave.... We can always get better.... We dare to be different."

 ACTION ADVICE

- Create coherence in the instructional program. Is your curriculum aligned to state and district standards? Have you articulated the curriculum across subjects and grade levels? Have you identified benchmark standards?

- Employ a powerful pedagogy. Are students primarily engaged in meaning making, developing various kinds of understanding, problem solving, reasoning, inquiry, and critical/creative thinking?

- Develop a shared vision of what good teaching looks like. Can all teachers describe a community-held understanding of good teaching? Can they list a core set of things to look for related to what teachers do and what students do when good teaching is happening?

- Use research-based teaching strategies that specifically address the needs of students living in poverty. Do teachers know which instructional strategies have a solid research base? Do teachers have the required expertise to employ research-based strategies?

- Develop assessment literacy. Do teachers understand and employ sound assessment practices? Do principals have the competencies necessary to improve assessment practices schoolwide?

- Involve students in assessing their learning. Are students engaged in activities that help them assess and monitor their own learning?

- Develop and use common formative and summative assessments. Have benchmark standards been identified? Have teachers been provided opportunities to collaborate to both develop assessments and use the information gained to inform instruction?

- Ensure teachers develop and demonstrate the attributes and functions that lead to success with students living in poverty. Do teachers know which teacher attributes and functions lead to success? Do teachers possess these attributes and fulfill such functions?

- Provide targeted interventions when needed. Does your school use data to identify students who need additional support? Has time been scheduled during, before, or after the school day to provide extra help for students?

- Develop reading proficiency in all students. How many students are not proficient in reading by 4th grade? Is reading taught after the elementary years when needed?

- Link professional learning to student learning and employ research-based models. Do students' learning needs drive the content for professional development? Do professional development models support the development of communities of practice and prompt reflection and inquiry?

- Engage in continuous data-based inquiry. Is inquiry embedded in the way the school does business? Are people curious, eager to innovate, and encouraged to take risks?

Action Planning/Next Steps

Use the action planning template in Figure 10.9 to help you and your colleagues reflect on the information and ideas in this chapter. What commitments and actions do you need to develop a focus on learning?

FIGURE 10.9	Action Planning Template for Developing a Focus on Learning

1. What new information, insights, and ideas did we gain from this chapter?

2. Based on our assessment of the school or district, what change needs to occur and what might be our next steps?

3. Are the changes needed in our school or district structural (time, resources), cultural (norms, beliefs, values), or both? What is the evidence?

4. What is the magnitude of change this represents for our school—first order or second order? What is the evidence?

Action Plan		
Next Steps	**Lead Person Responsible**	**Timeline**

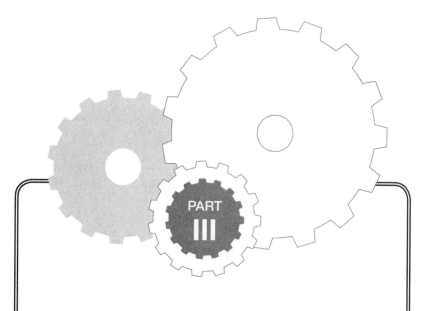

Working Together:

Continuing the Commitment
to Lead Underachieving Students
in Poverty to Success

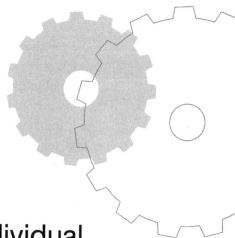

Beyond Improving Individual Schools: Two Critical Questions

High-performing, high-poverty schools sometimes achieve remarkable success in spite of being nested in large systems that are driven by multiple focal points and priorities—a situation sometimes referred to as "mission creep." These systems are often more reactive than proactive and have a tendency to operate as though school-level leaders are to be of service to the district office rather than the other way around. This tendency, at best, inhibits a district's ability to support schools that serve large percentages of underachieving students who live in poverty and, at worst, actively works *against* their improvement.

A growing body of research points to the importance of district-level leadership and seeks to define the nature of the relationship between district- and school-level leaders in cases where entire systems are improving. These studies provide models for transformation of district office functions and examples of system learning that may serve to address two critical questions that must be considered if real strides are to be made in addressing the needs of students who live in poverty. The questions are as follows:

- Can HP/HP schools sustain their success in the long term?
- Can their success be taken to scale?

Without fundamentally rethinking the work of district-level leaders, pockets of excellence will continue to be found within a school district in the form of individual high-performing, high-poverty schools, but the conditions necessary to bring such improvement to scale will simply not exist. And without transformation of the relationship between leaders throughout the system, the success achieved in individual schools will prove difficult to sustain.

In *The Moral Imperative Realized*, Michael Fullan (2011) asserts, "Individual schools cannot get on—or if they do, cannot stay on—the moral track unless the whole district is working on the problem" (p. 39). After studying four such districts, he describes the relationships between district and school leaders as "symbiosis." He says in these districts, leaders at all levels focus "on a small number of goals and corresponding powerful strategies that they employ in concert" (p. 55). When such conditions exist, "Everyone takes pride in whole-system accomplishments and reaches out to help each other whenever it is called for" (p. 55).

Meredith Honig, Mike Copland, and their colleagues (2010) at the University of Washington recently conducted a study titled *Central Office Transformation for District-Wide Teaching and Learning Improvement*. This Wallace Foundation–funded study examined the daily practices and activities of district office personnel as they sought not only to become more efficient, but also to transform the district office into a support system for school-based leaders engaged in endeavors to improve teaching and learning. Leaders in the three urban school districts that demonstrated steady gains in student achievement credit their improvement, in part, to their efforts to fundamentally transform the role of the district office and its relationships with schools. Desiring to radically depart from business as usual, leaders in these districts, according to the study, did the following:

• Focused the work of the central office "centrally and meaningfully" on improvement of teaching and learning. Moving beyond rhetoric about being of service to schools, leaders in these districts could demonstrate how their work supported schools in concrete ways.

• Engaged everyone in the effort, even personnel whose function had not been traditionally defined as connected to "teaching and learning."

• Called upon central office personnel to fundamentally restructure their relationship with schools so that their daily work was in the service of schools' efforts to improve teaching and learning.

• Aimed to transcend programs or initiatives, in contrast to reforming the district office for the purpose of implementing a particular program.

Several other scholars have recently completed additional work on leadership at various levels of the system. In his book *The Case for District-Based Reform: Leading, Building, and Sustaining School Improvement,* Jonathan Supovitz (2006) points to research that "makes the case" for districtwide initiatives focused on the improvement of teaching and learning. Additionally, Robert Marzano and Timothy Waters's (2009) synthesis of studies conducted between 1970 and 2005 demonstrates the importance of district-level leadership in improving academic achievement. Examination of leadership at the state level may also prove relevant to questions related to sustainability and scale (Redding & Walberg, 2009). In *Transforming a Statewide System of Support: The Idaho Story*, author Brett Lane and his colleagues at the Center on Innovation and Improvement, under the leadership of Director Sam Redding, document the efforts of an entire state to support the improvement of teaching and learning in its lowest-performing schools (Lane, 2010).

Efforts of such entities as the Broad Foundation may provide additional insight. The Broad Prize for Urban Education, considered by many to be the nation's top prize in public education, is awarded for significant and sustained progress in student achievement and closing minority achievement gaps. The award carries with it $1 million in postsecondary/college scholarships for low-income students. Gwinnett County, Georgia, winner of the 2010 award, with more than 50 percent of its students eligible for free and reduced-price meals and minority populations of 28 percent African American and 25 percent Hispanic students, outperformed all other Georgia districts with similar economic status. Superintendent J. Alvin Wilbanks, a veteran of more than 15 years in his post, credits the success to collectively believing that every student could succeed and following up on that belief in the district's classrooms every day (Blankinship, 2010).

On a far smaller scale, our own research has documented the success of a small Idaho district in its efforts to comprehensively improve. Located in a rural but increasingly suburbanizing community, 8 of the 10 schools in the Caldwell School District in Caldwell, Idaho, made adequate yearly progress (AYP) after three years of focused effort on the part of district-level leaders to build leadership capacity. In 2007, the district, with a demographic of 62 percent low-income and 70 percent Hispanic students, was the lowest-performing district in the state, with no schools making AYP. The district was placed in corrective action. Recently appointed Superintendent Roger Quarles, together with his leadership team, crafted a focused plan of improvement with the simple goals of raising student achievement and retaining effective leaders, teachers, and staff. Relationship building, leadership and instructional coaching, data-driven interventions, community partnerships, and plain and simple transparency on all district matters and actions prompted the rapid improvement. Student attendance improved, achievement scores shot up, behavioral problems dramatically decreased, community support rallied, and the exodus of teachers and leaders ceased. As of 2010, Caldwell is a desirable school district in which to both work and attend school.

Despite the marked success of districts like Gwinnett County and other Broad awardees, Caldwell and others studied by Honig and colleagues (2010) and Fullan (2011), much work remains to be done to learn from districts that have improved systemwide. However, decades of research demonstrate the significant difference schools can make in the lives of students who live in poverty. As a Molalla High School teacher told us, "Our emphasis changed from a focus on what we couldn't control—the poverty, parents, state policy, all of that—to what we could control." From her perspective, they stopped making excuses, blaming others, and "admiring" their problems. Instead, their energy focused on what they could influence and change.

District leaders must be amenable to learning from the hundreds of high-performing, high-poverty schools in our nation, and much of their function will need to be transformed if they are to support the application of the lessons learned from these schools. It is only through such systemic reform that improvement will be sustained in individual schools and taken to scale at state and national levels.

Concluding Thoughts

Let's presume, as a profession, that we stepped up to the challenge of improving the life chances of all our students who live in poverty. We might begin by drawing on what is known about the problem, together with all that we know about our students, our school and school system, and our neighborhoods and communities. Next, we would relentlessly focus on learning and supporting the specific needs of our students. In fact, high-poverty schools that move from low to high performance work in exactly this fashion. This and other lessons learned from hundreds of HP/HP schools were presented in detail in the preceding chapters. We have developed a framework for all of us to follow, but the framework must be applied to each school's unique context.

The Framework for Action conceptualizes the core elements found in HP/HP schools. These schools have succeeded in their efforts to close achievement gaps and have done so while raising overall student achievement. In these schools, the development of leadership capacity serves as a catalyst for fostering a healthy, safe, and supportive learning environment that enables an intensive focus on student, professional, and system learning. As leaders take action in these domains, a confluence of caring relationships and advocacy, high expectations and support, a commitment to equity, and a sense of professional accountability for student learning, as well as courage and commitment, reshape the school's culture. Moreover, high-performing, high-poverty schools are not insular and do not "go it alone." Beyond taking actions that influence the classroom and the school at large, leaders in these schools develop relationships with district office personnel, families, and community members to further support their mission of high expectations and success for every student. (See Figure 11.1.)

Dedicated leaders in HP/HP schools have helped us link theory and research with the practical ideas we hope will provide guidance for other schools. Throughout the book, we have offered Action Advice, shared creative Uncommon Sense approaches, and identified District "Ad-vantage Points" as ways in which district-level leaders can support school-based

FIGURE 11.1   A Framework for Action

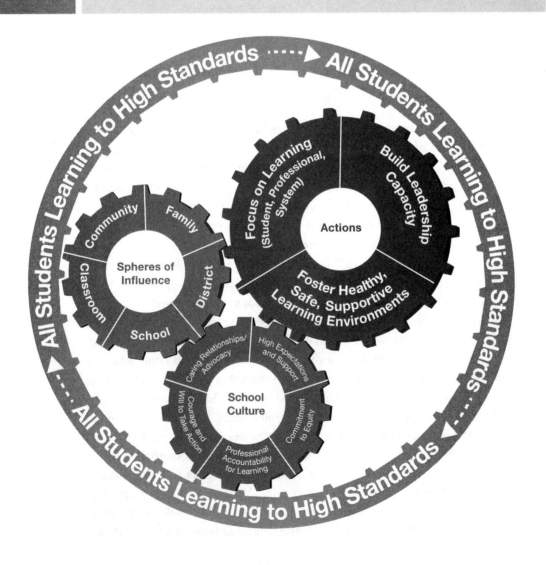

leaders. We have integrated School Culture Alerts that point out key characteristics of school culture as it appears to be shaped in HP/HP schools. We have also included self-assessment rubrics and action planning tools that were field-tested in multiple venues to assist schools leaders in applying the ideas found in this book.

Success at Dayton's Bluff Elementary, Lapwai Elementary, Taft Elementary, Osmond A. Church K–8, Port Chester Middle School, Tekoa High School, and Molalla High School, as well as at the hundreds of other schools that have been studied, is not due to magic or happenstance. These HP/HP schools are places where educators *are* doing their part. In their schools, they are building leadership capacity; fostering a healthy, safe, and supportive learning environment; and focusing on student, professional, and system learning—all of which is improving outcomes for students living in poverty. These schools show us what is possible. Thus the question remains: What is preventing us, as a profession and as a nation, from ensuring all high-poverty schools become high performing?

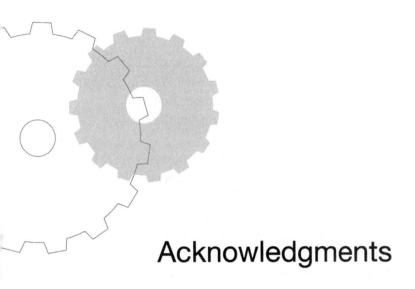

Acknowledgments

Leadership matters...and it matters immensely in high-poverty schools. This book could never have been written without the ingenuity, courage, passion, and persistence of many educators and others whose lives are dedicated to supporting children and adolescents who live in poverty. To all of you, we owe our deepest respect and gratitude.

We wish to acknowledge and thank the many educators, scholars, and individuals who inspired and supported our work over the past three years. Heading this cast of many would be the principals and staffs of the seven remarkable HP/HP schools that opened their doors to our questions and probing inquiries. They include Andrew Collins, former principal (and current associate superintendent, Leadership Development and Turnaround Schools) and the staff of Dayton's Bluff Achievement Plus Elementary in the St. Paul School District in Minnesota; Teri Wagner (principal) and the staff of Lapwai Elementary School in the Lapwai School District in Idaho; Randy Dalton (principal), Kevin Ricker (former principal), and the staff of Molalla High School in the Molalla School District in Oregon; Valarie Lewis (principal) and the staff of Osmond A. Church PS./MS. 124 in the New York City Public Schools in New York; Pat Swift (principal) and the staff of Port Chester Middle School in the Port Chester School District in Westchester County, New York; Wayne Roellich (principal) and the staff of Tekoa High School in the Tekoa School District in Washington; and Susan Williamson (principal) and the staff of William H. Taft Elementary in the Boise Independent School District in Boise, Idaho. To all of you, our heartfelt appreciation for your willingness to work with us but, more important, for what you do on a daily basis for each and every student. We look forward to following your continued efforts and sustained success.

Many scholars came before us, and others are currently at work seeking to better understand how high-poverty schools become high performing. Their collective efforts to disseminate their findings have guided our work, for which we are most appreciative. To many of the true pioneers in this field—Bob Barr, Donna Beegle, Alan Blankstein, Gene Bottoms, Karin Chenoweth, James Comer, Lisa Delpit, Dan Duke, Ron Edmonds, Richard Elmore, Michael Fullan, Martin Haberman, Kati Haycock, Asa Hilliard, Michael Knapp, Henry Levin, Debbie Meier, Doug Reeves, Sam Stringfield, Robert Slavin, and Charles Teddlie—we extend our sincere respect and gratitude.

We also would like to acknowledge and thank other scholars and practitioners who have made invaluable contributions in areas and schools related to our work. They include Greg Alexander, Fally Anderson, Debbie Bailey, Loren Bailey, Robert Balfanz, Marcia Beckman, Molly Bensinger-Lacy, Alan Boyle, Fernanda Brendefur, Anthony Bryk, Samuel Carter, Steve and Jan Chappuis, Jonathan Cline, Mitchell Combs, Jerry Conrath, Joy Dryfoos, Rick and Becky DuFour, Pat Dutweiler, Bob Eaker, Tetsuya Ehara, Fenwick English, Joyce Epstein, Richard Esparza, Carole Evans, Ann Farris, Bill Fetterhoff, Adam Gamoran, Alan Glatthorn, Claude Goldenberg, Paul Gorski, Jerry Hartsock, Susan Hayes, Stan Hill, Gary Howard, Craig and Aimee Howley, George and Clemmye Jackson, Steve Jackstadt, Eric Jensen, Craig Jerald, Michelle Krynicki, Crystal Kuykendall, Gloria Ladsen-Billings, Linda Lambert, Mary Lang, Max McGee, Jay McTighe, G. Manset, Tom Many, Bob Marzano, Diane Massell, Dave and Clara Molden, Ray Morley, Joseph Murphy, Joe Nathan, Susan Neuman, Curt Rathburn, Maryann Raywid, Sam Redding, Tony Richard, Jean Rutherford, Dick Sagor, Frank Schargel, Mike Schmoker, Randy Schrader, Jay Smink, George Theoharis, Abigail and Stephan Thernstrom, Elain Thompson, Wendy Togneri, Steve Underwood, Greg Wallace, Gary Wehlage, Grant Wiggins, Jenny Wilkins, and Katsuhiko Yamashita. We offer our humble appreciation for all you have done, and are doing, to help schools and kids.

Many national and state organizations, as well as individual school districts, provided opportunities for us to share our ideas and garner critique. Over the past three years, we have had the chance to interact with hundreds of educators and to present emerging versions of this book at venues hosted by leading organizations such as ASCD, the Education Trust, the National School Boards Association, High Schools That Work, the Center for Innovation and Improvement, the American Association of Educational Service Agencies, the National Title One Association, the Kentucky School Boards Association, the

Idaho State Department of Education, Boise State University, Castleton State University, Georgia Southern University, Hosei University (Tokyo, Japan), and Louisiana State University, as well as the Minneapolis Principals Network and the following school districts from our fieldwork: Boise, Idaho; Fairfax, Virginia; Godwin Heights, Wyoming, Michigan; Granger, Washington; Lapwai, Idaho; Molalla, Oregon; Port Chester, New York; Queens, New York; St. Paul, Minnesota; and Tekoa, Washington. We also want to thank these additional school districts: Ames, Iowa; Caldwell, Idaho; Columbus, Ohio; Devil's Lake, North Dakota; Hollywood, California; Menasha, Wisconsin; Skinners' Company's School for Girls and Woodbury Down Community Primary School, both in Hackney, England. Our sincere thanks go to the many individuals and groups who welcomed us to their schools and districts and offered their insights. Your contributions have significantly expanded our understanding of, and appreciation for, the complexity of improving high-poverty schools.

We are particularly indebted to the wonderful support of so many at ASCD who have helped us with this and other related projects, beginning with Scott Willis, whose supportive persistence and guidance got us through the proposal, design and early writing process, and Genny Ostertag, whose gracious and frequent encouragement reenergized us. Marge Scherer assisted us in ways she may not really realize, as the article we were invited to author for *Educational Leadership* early in our writing process significantly helped us to crystallize the design for the book. Darcie Russell, our editor extraordinaire, wonderfully managed the complex array of editorial and production details. In truth, Darcie's knowledge, talent, and expertise have made this a far better book, more accessible, and useful. She's the best editor with whom we have ever worked. And finally, working with Debbie Brown and her staff to frequently lead institutes and other ASCD presentations allowed us to pilot ideas and receive important feedback. We also are indebted for the support and encouragement from Ann Cunningham-Morris. She and Scott Willis were some of our first friends and colleagues at ASCD. To all of you, we offer our humble appreciation for your support and friendship.

A special word of gratitude goes to associates, colleagues, students, and mentors who influenced us in ways they may not have known. They begin with Kati Haycock, president, and Karin Chenoweth, senior writer, of the Education Trust, a leading organization in the United States offering research and advocacy for the "cause" of improving the educational circumstances and lives of children and adolescents who live in poverty. Also to Mike Copland, former associate professor and chair of Educational Leadership and Policy Studies, College of Education, University of Washington, now senior program officer with the Bill and Melinda Gates Foundation, who enthusiastically penned the

Foreword for this work. Others include Dana Anderson, Sally Anderson, Sandy Austin, Bob Barr, Jonathan Brendefur, Monte Bridges, Kelly Cross, Steve Fink, Marybeth Flachbart, Tom Hulst, Sharon Jarvis, Mark Johnson, Mark Jones, Rick Kessler, Bill Kiem, Kathy Kimball, Lisa Kinnaman, Mike Knapp, Tim Lowe, Brad Portin, Helene Paroff, Roger Quarles, Sam Redding, Jim Reed, Rosie Santana, Sue Shannon, Bob Smart, Roger Stewart, Ed Taylor, Keith Thiede, Scott Willison, Rob Winslow, and Pat Yockey. Each of these people, at some point in our lives and in their own way, supported and enhanced our work. Some helped to shape us as people, and others pushed our thinking as scholars. All helped us with multiple connections and opportunities throughout this particular endeavor, offering ideas, creative support, endless patience, and encouragement. We are indebted to every one of you.

Several colleagues and friends at Boise State University were always there to support us in this effort. They include the staff of the Center for School Improvement and Policy Studies, particularly Diana Esbensen, our business manager, and Kelli Burnham, our student assistant, who helped us with research and organizational issues too numerous to count. In addition, we are indebted to Margo Healy, our research assistant, whose insights greatly strengthened the manuscript; to Larry Burke, our detail wizard, who provided invaluable suggestions for structure, word choice, and format; and to our graduate assistants Katie Bubak, Glen Croft, and Shelly Wooten for all their help. To others in the Center—Marsha Hale, Kayla Morton, Aimee Tobais, Deborah Weatherspoon, and Briana Yates—thanks for your help as well.

A special thank-you goes to the students in Boise State's Ed.D. and Educational Leadership programs. We have learned much from you, and we admire the courage you have to step into leadership positions at a time when the stakes seem so high and the ability to stay within the comforts of your own classrooms might be the easier route to take.

We are indebted to our families for their love and support.

To my parents, Carey and Jan, who have been there for me though yet another writing project; to my daughter, Mia, the budding writer; and to my son, Jonathan, the aspiring PGA Tour player, thank you both so much for who you are and for all we have as a family. Finally, to Tom and Tess, Patti and Tim, Carey and Danielle, Christina, Jessie my NPN, Jeannie and Holly, and Ahijah, thanks for always being there for me and tolerating all that comes with another book project. I love you all!

—Bill

To my parents, Bud and Carlene, thank you for the unconditional love you gave me to make my own way in the world. To my son, Nathaniel, thank you for your wit and sense of humor that always lighten my load. To my daughter, Katrina, thank you for sharing in my academic journey by engaging in your own! To my new daughter-in-law, Ashley, thank you for what you do every day for the kids we've written about in this book. To my brother, Joel, and my sister-in-law, Anna, thank you for grounding me in what matters when I lose my way. Finally, to my "other" family, thank you to the Happy Campers in the Flathead Valley of Montana—particularly the Ashley Lake Crew of Lisa and Tony Dawson, and Connie and Ivan Lorentzen—who always welcome me home no matter how long I've been away or how far away my professional pursuits, such as this book, take me.

—Kathleen

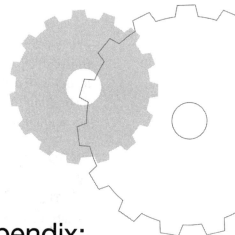

Appendix:
Further Verification
of the Framework

To further verify the accuracy of the framework, we considered the conclusions drawn from eight additional studies of HP/HP schools that were either conducted after Barr and Parrett's (2007) synthesis was developed or not included in their analysis. We provide a brief description of each of the recent studies, together with the conclusions drawn in relationship to the framework.

High-Achieving Middle Schools for Latino Students in Poverty (Jesse, Davis, & Pokorny, 2004)

Researchers Jesse, Davis, and Pokorny identified nine high-performing Texas middle schools serving predominantly Latino students from low-income families (seven of the nine schools had free and reduced-price lunch counts of 90 percent or greater). The students in each school had made consistent improvement on the state's assessments of academic skills. The researchers were "struck by the very strong unity of purpose, cohesive sense of school identity, and joint effort exhibited by educators and students in the nine schools." They suggested that such coherence was accomplished in part through "strong and consistent messages from the principals at the beginning of the year and the echoing of these messages by other leaders throughout the year" (p. 37). They concluded that "having a principal as instructional leader is of prime importance. The principal brings the goals of learning and instruction to the forefront, coordinates the activities of students and teachers, and integrates the other components of effective schools" (p. 33).

Why Some Schools with Latino Children Beat the Odds…and Others Don't (Waits et al., 2006)

This study sought to answer the question "What does it take to get great results in educational achievement in a school with a student enrollment that is mostly poor, and has many students that are still learning English?" (p. 11). Beginning with more than 1,700 Arizona schools, the researchers narrowed the pool by selecting elementary and middle schools where at least 50 percent of the students were Hispanic and 50 percent or more qualified for the free and reduced-price meal program. They then disaggregated eight years of state achievement data for these schools to identify those that were either "steady performers or steady climbers" and without any flagged testing exceptions. This analysis yielded 12 schools—6 elementary, 4 middle and 2 K–8. Following interviews, surveys, and data analysis, the researchers "unearthed six things" at which these schools excelled, which they clustered into three categories borrowed from Jim Collins's (2005) book *Good to Great and the Social Sectors*: (1) disciplined thought, (2) disciplined people, and (3) disciplined action. "Disciplined thought" meant there is a clear bottom line for which professionals take responsibility for student learning and ongoing assessment of student performance. "Disciplined people" referred to strong and steady leadership from the principal and collaboration among teachers and staff who engage in "real teamwork." "Disciplined action" was witnessed in selecting research-based approaches and sticking to them over time and a relentless focus on the instruction, assessment, and intervention cycle, along with building a system tailored to address students' needs.

Profiles of Success: Eight Colorado Schools That Are Closing the Achievement Gap (Anderson & DeCesare, 2007)

This study investigated eight Colorado schools that "had not only closed the achievement gap, but reversed it—students from lower socioeconomic homes were scoring higher than the average Colorado student" (p. 3). These schools included one elementary school, three K–8 schools, three middle schools, and one high school.

The purpose of the study was to identify promising practices. The researchers' conclusions emanated from nine conditions that were established and maintained in each school: (1) a culture of high expectations and accountability for all students, (2) targeted assessments and intensive use of data to guide instruction, (3) individualized support for struggling students, (4) active engagement of teachers in school leadership and decision making, (5) substantial time for collaborative planning and options for professional development, (6) commitment to core academics and standards but not at the expense of other important learning in the arts and humanities, (7) stable and consistent leadership, (8) small learning communities, and (9) flexibility to use resources to support student needs and reinforce school culture.

The most important factor appeared to be the flexibility and authority the leaders of the schools (which in all schools studied included teachers) were afforded to target resources toward the greatest need. Practices common to all of the schools included (1) allowing no excuses for failure, (2) extended-day tutoring, (3) holding Saturday and summer schools, (4) establishing teacher-driven professional development, (5) stabilizing and distributing leadership functions, and (6) showing a high degree of visibility in the classrooms on the part of the school leaders.

It's Being Done—Academic Success in Unexpected Schools (Chenoweth, 2007)

This case study of 14 high-performing, high-poverty schools was conducted by Karin Chenoweth of the Education Trust. The study sought to describe the actions of a carefully selected sample of schools that had consistently beaten the odds by outperforming the majority of their more advantaged peers. The schools included 10 elementary, 1 middle, 2 middle/high, and 1 high school. Chenoweth concluded her two-year study by suggesting that the "it's being done" schools do things differently than other high-poverty, high-minority schools. According to Chenoweth,

> The educators interviewed in this book don't make excuses. They provide clear goals with high expectations and ongoing assessments. They make sure that in every classroom there is a strong teacher who knows the subject and knows how to teach it. They insist on a rigorous curriculum and on giving extra help and extra time to students who are behind. (p. x)

These high-performing, high-poverty schools

- Teach their students.
- Don't teach to the state tests.
- Have high expectations for their students.
- Know what the stakes are.
- Embrace and use all data they can get their hands on.

- Use data to focus on individual students.
- Constantly reexamine what they do.
- Embrace accountability.
- Make decisions based on what is good for kids, not what is good for adults.
- Use school time wisely.
- Leverage as many resources from the community as possible.
- Expand the time students—particularly struggling students—have in school.
- Do not spend a lot of time disciplining students, in the sense of punishing them.
- Establish an atmosphere of respect.
- Like kids.
- Make sure the kids who struggle have the best instruction.
- Ensure principals are a constant presence.
- Ensure principals are important leaders but that they are not the only leaders.
- Pay careful attention to the quality of the teaching staff.
- Provide teachers with the time to meet to plan and work collaboratively.
- Provide teachers time to observe one another.
- Think seriously about professional development.
- Assume that they will have to train new teachers more or less from scratch and carefully acculturate all newly hired teachers.
- Have high-quality, dedicated, and competent office and building staff who feel themselves part of the educational mission of the school.
- Are nice places to work.

School Turnarounds: A Review of the Cross-Sector Evidence on Dramatic Organizational Improvement (Center on Innovation and Improvement, 2007)

Secretary of Education Arne Duncan recently called for "far-reaching reforms that produce turnaround schools," targeting specifically the 5,000 lowest-performing schools in the United States. This challenge implores "all takers" to consider the successes *and* failures of efforts to significantly improve high-poverty, low-performing schools. The concept of "turnaround schools" has focused on the challenge of reversing the historical trend of underachievement by dramatically altering a school's current structures, policies, and practices. Many engaged in leadership preparation, professional development, and school improvement are focusing on better understanding how a high-poverty, low-performing school becomes high performing, as well as how such efforts can be replicated. Leadership actions isolated in studies of "turnaround schools" provide further specificity about how schools have made significant and sustained improvement. These emergent findings are consistent with and most helpful to the growing research base. Attempts to learn from the journey of high-performing, high-poverty schools have the potential to advance local school districts' efforts to improve underperforming schools. A leader in this work, the Center on Innovation and Improvement conducted a study of education literature on school turnarounds in an attempt to determine the specific actions leaders must take to generate increased student performance. The Center published *School Turnarounds: Actions and Results* (Brinson, Kowal, & Hassel, 2008), in which the authors identified 14 specific actions successful leaders implement to turn schools around (see Figure A.1, p. 200).

Case Study of Leadership Practices and School-Community Interrelationships in High-Performing, High-Poverty, Rural California High Schools (Masumoto & Brown-Welty, 2009)

The researchers conducted interviews and observations, as well as analyzed voluminous data, from three schools selected for their case study. All of their conclusions indicated a strong prevalence of distributive, instructional, and transformative leadership. Leaders in these schools facilitate change to support a schoolwide focus on instruction and high expectations, develop multiple support systems for students with varying needs, capitalize on teachers' strengths, use and stretch resources, and establish formal and informal links with the community to accomplish the schools' mission and meet goals.

Roots of Success: Effective Practices in Vermont Schools (Hayes, 2009)

Conducted by the Vermont State Department of Education, the *Roots of Success* study combined data from a survey of 2,000 Vermont teachers, state assessment results, and site visits to three of their highest-performing, high-poverty schools. The study isolated eight specific characteristics of effectiveness found in the high-performing schools (see Figure A.2, p. 202). The report asserts that "these characteristics form the foundation for school effectiveness and are essential to ensuring that all children, regardless of background or socioeconomic status, reach their full potential" (p. 6).

How It's Being Done: Urgent Lessons from Unexpected Schools (Chenoweth, 2009a)

Chenoweth followed her 2007 study with a similar yet deeper analysis of practices that contributed to the sustained success of select HP/HP schools. Building on her original study of 14 schools and adding 8 more in the follow-up

FIGURE A.1	Turnaround Leader Actions Table

Turnaround Leader Action	What It Means
Initial Analysis and Problem Solving	
Collect and Analyze Data	Initially, turnaround leaders personally analyze data about the organization's performance to identify high-priority problems that can be fixed quickly. Later, they establish organization routines that include ongoing data analysis (see section on Measuring, Reporting [and Improving]).
Make Action Plan Based on Data	Turnaround leaders make an action plan so that everyone involved knows specifically what they need to do differently. This allows people to focus on changing what they do, rather than worrying about impending change.
Driving for Results	
Concentrate on Big, Fast Payoffs in Year One	Successful turnaround leaders first concentrate on a very limited number of changes to achieve early, visible wins for the organization. They do this to achieve success in an important area, to motivate staff for further change, and to reduce resistance by those who oppose change.
Implement Practices Even if Require Deviation	Turnaround leaders make changes that deviate from organization norms or rules—not just for change's sake, but to achieve early wins. In a failing organization, existing norms and rules often contribute to failure. Targeted deviations to achieve early wins teach the organization that new practices can lead to success.
Require All Staff to Change	When a turnaround leader implements an action plan, change is mandatory, not optional.
Make Necessary Staff Replacements	Successful turnaround leaders typically do not replace all or most staff. But they often replace some senior staff, particularly those who manage others. After the organization begins to show turnaround success, staff unwilling or unable to make changes that their colleagues have made leave or are removed by the leader.
Focus on Successful Tactics; Halt Others	Successful turnaround leaders are quick to discard tactics that do not work and spend more resources and time on tactics that work. This pruning and growing process focuses limited time and money where they will have the most impact on critical results.
Do Not Tout Progress as Ultimate Success	Turnaround leaders are not satisfied with partial success. They report progress, but keep the organization focused on high goals. When a goal is met, they are likely to raise the bar.
Influencing Inside and Outside the Organization	
Communicate a Positive Vision	Turnaround leaders motivate others inside and outside the organization to contribute their discretionary effort by communicating a clear picture of success and its benefits.

FIGURE A.1	Turnaround Leader Actions Table (*continued*)

Influencing Inside and Outside the Organization (*continued*)	
Help Staff Personally Feel Problems	Turnaround leaders use various tactics to help staff empathize with—or "put themselves in the shoes of"—those whom they serve. This helps staff feel the problems that the status quo is causing and feel motivated to change.
Gain Support of Key Influencers	Turnaround leaders work hard to gain the support of trusted influencers among staff and community. They work through these people to influence those who might oppose change.
Silence Critics with Speedy Success	Early, visible wins are used not just for success in their own right, but to make it harder for others to oppose further change. This reduces leader time spent addressing "politics" and increases time spent managing for results.
Measuring, Reporting (and Improving)	
Measure and Report Progress Frequently	Turnaround leaders set up systems to measure and report interim results often. This enables rapid discard of failed tactics and increase of successful tactics essential for fast results.
Require All Decision Makers to Share Data and Problem Solve	Sharing of results in open-air meetings allows turnaround leaders to hold staff who make key decisions accountable for results, creating discomfort for those who do not make needed changes and providing kudos to those who are achieving success. This shifts the focus of the organization's meetings from power plays, blaming, and excuses to problem solving.

Source: From *School Turnarounds: Actions and Results* (pp. 6–7), by D. Brinson, J. Kowal, & B. Hassel. Chapel Hill, NC: Center on Innovation and Improvement. Copyright 2008 Public Impact, Academic Development Institute. All rights reserved.

study, she sought to further understand how these places, which she refers to as "unexpected schools," could achieve the success they do.

Principal Molly Bensinger-Lacy of Graham Road Elementary, one of the HP/HP schools from the follow-up study, attributes her school's success to five essential domains of action, which she describes as their wheel of school reform: (1) teacher collaboration, (2) laserlike focus on what the school wants students to learn, (3) formative assessments, (4) data-driven instruction, and (5) personal relationship building. Chenoweth suggests that these same elements both exist and drive success in all of the schools she studied.

In a follow-up article published in the September 2009 issue of the *Kappan*, Chenoweth suggests that in their own way and at their own pace, the HP/HP schools she studied "ruthlessly organize themselves around one thing: helping students learn a great deal" (2009b, p. 39). She found that this basic principle resulted in a set of essential practices, including focusing teaching on what students need to know, providing time for teacher learning, insisting on schoolwide adult collaboration, and eliminating teacher isolation.

FIGURE A.2	Eight Characteristics of Effective Schools

1. The belief that all students can succeed;
2. The belief that school staff are ultimately responsible for student success and must therefore continually improve their practice;
3. Effective school leadership that helps translate these beliefs into practice;
4. Ongoing use of data to provide feedback to staff as well as monitor and support students;
5. A professional teaching culture that supports high-quality instruction and is characterized by staff collaboration, trust among staff members, strong staff commitment and dedication, and effective paraprofessionals;
6. A comprehensive and highly functioning support system for students who struggle academically, emotionally, behaviorally, or socially, including early intervention programs;
7. A supportive school climate that makes all students, as well as adults, feel valued and safe; and
8. A commitment to building constructive relationships with families and involving them in their child's learning.

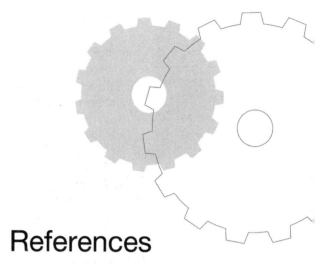

References

Alliance for Excellent Education. (2010). *About the crisis.* From http:/www.all4ed.org/node/13/print

Allington, R., & McGill-Franzen, A. (2008). Got books? *Educational Leadership, 65*(7), 20–23.

Almeida, C., Balfanz, R., & Steinberg, A. (2009, December 16). Dropout factories: New strategies states can use. *Education Week, 29*(15), 20–22.

Anderson, A. B., & DeCesare, D. (2007). *Profiles of success: Eight Colorado schools that are closing the achievement gap.* Denver, CO: Donnell-Kay Foundation.

Anyon, J. (1981). Social class and school knowledge. *Curriculum Inquiry, 11*(1).

Anyon, J. (2005). What "counts" as educational policy? Notes toward a new paradigm. *Harvard Educational Review, 75*(1), 65–88.

Argyris, C., & Schön, D. A. (1974). *Theory in practice: Increasing professional effectiveness* (1st ed.). San Francisco: Jossey-Bass.

Ball, J. (2001, September/October). High poverty, high performing schools. *Leadership,* 8–11.

Bane, M. J., & Ellwood, D. T. (1994). *Welfare realities: From rhetoric to reform.* Cambridge, MA: Harvard University Press.

Barr, R. D., & Parrett, W. (2007). *The kids left behind: Catching up the underachieving children of poverty.* Bloomington, IN: Solution Tree.

Barth, P., Haycock, K., Jackson, H., Mora, K., Ruiz, P., Robinson, S., & Wilkins, A. (Eds.). (1999). *Dispelling the myth: High poverty schools exceeding expectations* [Report]. Washington, DC: Education Trust.

Beegle, D. M. (2006). *See poverty... be the difference! Discover the missing pieces for helping people move out of poverty.* Tigard, OR: Communication Across Barriers.

Benard, B. (1991). *Fostering resiliency in kids: Protective factors in the family, school, and community.* Portland, OR: Northwest Regional Educational Laboratory.

Bernhardt, V. L. (2004). *Data analysis for continuous school improvement* (2nd ed.). Larchmont, NY: Eye on Education.

Bernhardt, V. L. (2005, February). Data tools for school improvement. *Educational Leadership, 62*(5), 66–69.

Berry, B. (2008). Staffing high-needs schools: Insights from the nation's best teachers. *Phi Delta Kappan, 89*(10), 766–771.

Billig, S. (2000a). *Educator's guide to collecting and using data: Conducting surveys.* Denver, CO: RMC Research Corp.

Billig, S. (2000b). *Profiles of success: Engaging young people's hearts and minds through service-learning.* Berkeley, CA: Grantmaker Forum on Community & National Service.

Blankinship, D. G. (2010, October 19). Georgia school district wins $1 million Broad prize. *Associated Press,* Atlanta.

Bond, S. (2002). *Introductory guide for implementing and evaluating volunteer reading tutoring programs.* Greensboro, NC: SERVE (Southeastern Regional Vision for Education).

Borman, G. D., & Dowling, N. M. (2006). The longitudinal achievement effects of multi-year summer school: Evidence from the Teach Baltimore randomized field trial. *Educational Evaluation and Policy Analysis, 28*, 25–48.

Brandt, R. (1998). *Powerful learning.* Alexandria, VA: ASCD.

Bransford, J. D., Brown, A. L., & Cocking, R. R. (Eds.). (2002). *How people learn: Brain, mind, experience, and school.* Washington, DC: National Academy Press.

Brinson, D., Kowal, J., & Hassel, B. (2008). *School turnarounds: Actions and results.* Lincoln, IL: Center of Innovation and Improvement.

Bryk, A. S., Bender Sebring, P., Allensworth, E., Luppescu, S., & Easton, J. Q. (2010). *Organizing schools for improvement: Lessons from Chicago.* Chicago: University of Chicago Press.

Bryk, A., & Schneider, B. (2002). *Trust in schools: A core resource for improvement.* New York: Russell Sage Foundation.

Calkins, A., Guenther, W., Belfiore, G., & Lash, D. (2007). *The turnaround challenge: Why America's best opportunity to dramatically improve student achievement lies in our worst-performing schools: New research, recommendations, and a partnership framework for states and school districts.* Boston: Mass Insight Education & Research Institute.

Campbell, L., & Campbell, B. (1999). *Multiple intelligences and student achievement: Success stories from six schools.* Alexandria, VA: ASCD.

Catterall, J. S., Chapleau, R., & Iwanaga, J. (1999). Involvement in the arts and human development. In E. B. Fiske (Ed.), *Champions of change: The impact of the arts on learning.* Washington, DC: Arts Education Partnership.

Center on Innovation and Improvement. (2007). *School turnarounds: A review of the cross-sector evidence on dramatic organizational improvement.* Chapel Hill, NC: Public Impact, Academic Development Institute.

Chappuis, S., Commodore, C., & Stiggins, R. (2010). *Assessment balance and quality: An action guide for school leaders.* Portland, OR: Assessment Training Institute.

Chau, M., Thampi, K., & Wight, V. (2009). *Basic facts about low-income children, 2009: Children under age 18*. New York: National Center for Children in Poverty.

Chenoweth, K. (2007). *It's being done: Academic success in unexpected schools*. Cambridge, MA: Harvard Education Press.

Chenoweth, K. (2009a). *How it's being done: Urgent lessons from unexpected schools*. Cambridge, MA: Harvard Education Press.

Chenoweth, K. (2009b, September). It can be done, it's being done, and here's how. *Phi Delta Kappan, 91*(1), 38–43.

Ciaccio, J. (2000a). Helping kids excel on state-mandated tests. *Education Digest, 65*(5), 21.

Ciaccio, J. (2000b). A teacher's chance for immortality. *Education Digest, 65*(6), 44–48.

City, E. A., Elmore, R. F., Fiarman, S. E., & Teitel, L. (2009). *Instructional rounds in education: A network approach to improving teaching and learning*. Cambridge, MA: Harvard Education Press.

Clement, M. C. (2009). Hiring highly qualified teachers begins with quality interviews. *Phi Delta Kappan, 91*(2), 22–24.

Coleman, J. C. (1987). *Working with troubled adolescents: A handbook*. London: Academic Press.

Coleman, J. S. (1966). *Equality of educational opportunity*. Washington, DC: U.S. Department of Health, Education, and Welfare.

Collins, J. C. (2001). *Good to great: Why some companies make the leap—and others don't* (1st ed.). New York: Harper Business.

Collins, J. C. (2005). *Good to great and the social sectors: Why business thinking is not the answer*. New York: HarperCollins.

Conrath, J. (1988). *Full-year prevention curriculum: Secondary dropout prevention*. Gig Harbor, WA: Author.

Conrath, J. (2001). Changing the odds for young people: Next steps for alternative education. *Phi Delta Kappan, 82*(8), 585–587.

Corcoran, M. (2008). Childhood poverty, race, and equal opportunity. In S. Neuman (Ed.), *Educating the other America: Top experts tackle poverty, literacy, and achievement in our schools*. Baltimore, MD: Paul H. Brookes.

Correnti, R., & Rowan, B. (2007). Opening up the black box: Literacy instruction in schools participating in three comprehensive school reform programs. *American Educational Research Journal, 44*, 298–338.

Crawford, M. (2008). Think inside the clock. *Phi Delta Kappan, 90*(4), 251–255.

Danielson, C. (1996). *Enhancing professional practice: A framework for teaching*. Alexandria, VA: ASCD.

Dantley, M., & Tillman, L. C. (2006). Social justice and moral transformative leadership. In C. Marshall & M. Oliva (Eds.), *Leadership for social justice: Making revolutions in education*. Boston: Pearson.

Danziger, S. K., & Danziger, S. H. (2008). Childhood poverty in economic and public policy. In S. B. Neuman (Ed.), *Educating the other America: Top experts tackle poverty, literacy, and achievement in our schools*. Baltimore, MD: Paul H. Brookes.

Dryfoos, J. G. (1994). *Full-service schools: A revolution in health and social service for children, youth and families*. San Francisco: Jossey-Bass.

Dryfoos, J. G., & Maguire, S. (2002). *Inside full-service community schools*. Thousand Oaks, CA: Corwin.

DuFour, R., & Marzano, R. J. (2009). High-leverage strategies for principal leadership. *Educational Leadership, 66*(5), 62–68.

Duncan, G. J., & Brooks-Gunn, J. (1997). *Consequences of growing up poor*. New York: Russell Sage Foundation.

Echevarria, J., Vogt, M., & Short, D. (2004). *Making content comprehensible for English learners: The SIOP model* (2nd ed.). Boston: Allyn and Bacon.

Education Trust. (2002). *Dispelling the myth… over time*. Washington, DC: Author.

Education Trust. (2006). *Funding gaps 2006*. Washington, DC: Author.

Eisenman, G., & Payne, B. D. (1997). Effects of the higher-order thinking skills program on at-risk young adolescents' self-concept, reading achievement, and thinking skills. *Research in Middle Level Education Quarterly, 20*(3), 1–25.

Eklund, N. (2009). Sustainable workplaces, retainable teachers. *Phi Delta Kappan, 91*(2), 25–27.

Elmore, R. F. (2000). *Building a new structure for school leadership*. Unpublished paper for Albert Shanker Institute, Washington, DC.

Elmore, R. F. (2006, November/December). Three thousand missing hours: Where does all the instructional time go? *Harvard Educational Newsletter, 22*(6).

Fass, S. (2009). *Measuring poverty in the United States*. New York: National Center for Children in Poverty.

Finn, P. J. (1999). *Literacy with an attitude: Educating working-class children in their own self-interest*. Albany: State University of New York Press.

Fogarty, R. (2009). *Brain-compatible classrooms* (3rd ed.). Thousand Oaks, CA: Corwin Press.

Fry, S., & DeWit, K. (2010). Once a struggling student. *Educational Leadership, 68*(4), 70–73.

Fullan, M. (2011). *The moral imperative realized*. Thousand Oaks, CA: Corwin Press.

Furco, A., & Root, S. (2010). Research demonstrates the value of service learning. *Phi Delta Kappan, 91*(5), 16–20.

Glatthorn, A., & Jailall, J. (2010). *The principal as curriculum leader: Shaping what is taught and tested*. Thousand Oaks, CA: Corwin.

Gorski, P. C. (2007, Spring). The question of class. *Teaching Tolerance, 31*, 26–29.

Gorski, P. (2008). The myth of the culture of poverty. *Educational Leadership, 65*(7), 32–36.

Grubb, W. N. (2009). Correcting the money myth: Re-thinking school resources. *Phi Delta Kappan, 91*(4), 51–55.

Haberman, M. (1991). The pedagogy of poverty versus good teaching. *Phi Delta Kappan, 73*(4), 290–294.

Haberman, M. (1995). *Star teachers of children in poverty*. West Lafayette, IN: Kappa Delta Pi.

Haycock, K. (2007). Foreword. In R. D. Barr & W. Parrett, *The kids left behind*. Bloomington, IN: Solution Tree.

Haycock, K. (2010, November). *Taking charge of change: Effective practices to close achievement gaps and raise achievement* [keynote address]. Taking Charge of Change conference, The Education Trust, Arlington, VA.

Hayes, S. (2009). *Roots of success: Effective practices in Vermont schools.* Montpelier, VT: Vermont Department of Education.

Hirsch, E., & Emerick S. (2006). *Teacher working conditions are student learning conditions: A report on the 2006 North Carolina teacher working conditions survey.* Chapel Hill, NC: Center for Teaching Quality.

Holland, H. (2007). Can educators close the achievement gap? An interview with Richard Rothstein and Kati Haycock. *Journal of Staff Development, 28*(1), 54–58.

Honig, M., Copland, M., Rainey, L., Lorton, J., & Newton, M. (2010). *How district central offices can help lead school improvement.* New York: Wallace Foundation.

Honigsfeld, A., & Dunn, R. (2009). *Differentiating instruction for at-risk students: What to do and how to do it.* Lanham, MD: Rowman & Littlefield Education.

Howard, T., Dresser, S. G., & Dunklee, D. R. (2009). *Poverty is not a learning disability: Equalizing opportunities for low SES students.* Thousand Oaks, CA: Corwin.

Hoy, W., & Miskel, C. (2008). *Educational administration: Theory, research, and practice.* Boston: McGraw-Hill.

Jackson, Y. (2002). Mentoring for delinquent children: An outcome study with young adolescent children. *Journal of Youth and Adolescence, 31*(2), 115–122.

Jensen, E. (1998). *Teaching with the brain in mind.* Alexandria, VA: ASCD.

Jensen, E. (2009). *Teaching with poverty in mind: What being poor does to kids' brains and what schools can do about it.* Alexandria, VA: ASCD.

Jerald, C. D. (2001). *Dispelling the myth revisited: Preliminary findings from a nationwide analysis of "high-flying" schools.* Washington, DC: The Education Trust.

Jesse, D., Davis, A., & Pokorny, N. (2004). High-achieving middle schools for Latino students in poverty. *Journal of Education for Students Placed at Risk, 9*(1), 23–45.

Johannessen, L. R. (2004). Helping "struggling" students achieve success. *Journal of Adolescent & Adult Literacy, 47*(8), 638–647.

Jones, R. (2001). How parents can support learning. *American Board Journal, 188*(9), 18–22.

Kieffer, M. (2010). Socioeconomic status, English proficiency, and late-emerging reading difficulties. *Educational Researcher, 39*(6), 484–486.

Knapp, M. S., & Adelman, N. (1995). *Teaching for meaning in high-poverty classrooms.* New York: Teachers College Press.

Knapp, M. S., Copland, M. A., Ford, B., Markholt, A., McLaughlin, M. W., Milliken, M., et al. (2003). *Leading for learning: Reflective tools for school and district leaders.* Seattle, WA: Center for the Study of Teaching and Policy, University of Washington.

Kops, B. (2010). Best practices for teaching in summer session. *Education Digest, 75*(9), 44–49.

Kovalik, S., & Olsen, K. D. (1998). How emotions run us, our students, and our classrooms. *NASSP Bulletin, 82*(598), 29–37.

Kraft, N. (2001). *Critical characteristics of successful after-school programs: An evaluation of the 21st century initiative.* Paper presented at the annual meeting of the American Educational Research Association, Seattle, WA.

Lalas, J. (2007). Teaching for social justice in multicultural urban schools: Conceptualization and classroom implication. *Multicultural Education, 12*(3), 17–21.

Lambert, A. W. (2005a). *Key elements of comprehensive school reform: A comparative case study between the U.S. Department of Education's whole school reform framework and New Hope Middle School's reform process.* Unpublished doctoral thesis, Peabody College of Vanderbilt University.

Lambert, L. (2005b). Leadership for lasting reform. *Educational Leadership, 62*(5), 62–65.

Lambert, L. (2005c). What does leadership capacity really mean? *Journal of Staff Development, 26*(2), 38–40.

Landsman, J., & Lewis, C. W. (Eds.) (2006). *White teachers, diverse classrooms: A guide to building inclusive schools, promoting high expectations, and eliminating racism* (1st ed.). Sterling, VA: Stylus Publishing.

Lane, B. (2010). *Transforming a statewide system of support: The Idaho story.* Lincoln, IL: Academic Development Institute.

Langer, J. A. (2001). Beating the odds: Teaching middle and high school students to read and write well. *American Education Research Journal, 38*(4), 837–880.

Lareau, A. (1987). Social class differences in family-school relationships: The importance of cultural capital. *Sociology of Education, 60*(2), 73–85.

Leader, G. (2010). *Real leaders, real schools: Stories of success against enormous odds.* Cambridge, MA: Harvard Education Press.

Levin, H. M. (1989). *Accelerated schools: A new strategy for at-risk students.* Bloomington, IN: Indiana Education Policy Center.

Marzano, R. J., & Waters, T., (2009). *District leadership that works: Striking the right balance.* Bloomington, IN: Solution Tree Press.

Marzano, R. J., Waters, T., & McNulty, B. A. (2005). *School leadership that works: From research to results.* Alexandria, VA: ASCD.

Masumoto, M., & Brown-Welty, S. (2009). Case study of leadership practices and school-community interrelationships in high-performing, high-poverty, rural California schools. *Journal of Research in Rural Education, 24*(1), 1–18.

Mayer, M. J., & Cornell, D. G. (2010). *New perspectives on school safety and violence prevention.* Thousand Oaks, CA: Sage.

McClure, J., & Vaughn, L. (1997). *Project Tutor's "how to" guide: For implementing a cross-age tutoring program in your elementary school.* Rohnert Park, CA: California Institute on Human Services.

McCormick, M. K., & Williams, J. H. (1974). Effects of a compensatory program on self-report, achievement, and aspiration level of "disadvantaged" high school students. *Journal of Negro Education, 43*(1), 47–52.

McFadden, L. (2009). District learning tied to student learning. *Phi Delta Kappan, 90*(8), 544–553.

McGee, G. W. (2004). Closing the achievement gap: Lessons from Illinois' gold spike high-poverty, high-performing schools. *Journal of Education for Students Placed at Risk, 9*(2), 97–125.

Merriam, S. B. (1998). *Qualitative research and case study applications in education.* San Francisco: Jossey-Bass.

Middleton, K. (2008, February). Sending teachers on visits to all homes. *The School Administrator, 65*(2). Arlington, VA: American Association of School Administrators.

Murray, C., & Malmgren, K. (2005). Implementing a teacher-student relationship program in a high-poverty urban school: Effects on social, emotional, and academic adjustment and lessons learned. *Journal of School Psychology, 43*(2), 137–152.

Neuman, S. B. (2008). *Educating the other America: Top experts tackle poverty, literacy, and achievement in our schools*. Baltimore, MD: Paul H. Brookes.

Newman, T. (2005). Coaches' roles in the academic success of male student athletes. *The Sport Journal, 8*(2).

Newmann, F. M., & Associates. (1996). *Authentic achievement: Restructuring schools for intellectual quality* (1st ed.). San Francisco: Jossey-Bass.

Ornelles, C. (2007). Providing classroom-based intervention to at-risk students to support their academic engagement and interactions with peers. *Preventing School Failure, 51*(4), 3–12.

Padrón, Y. N., Waxman, H. C., & Rivera, H. H. (2002). *Educating Hispanic students: Obstacles and avenues to improved academic achievement*. Santa Cruz, CA: Center for Research on Education Diversity & Excellence.

Palinscar, A. S., & Brown, A. L. (1985). Reciprocal teaching: Activities to promote "reading with your mind." In T. L. Harris & E. J. Cooper (Eds.), *Reading, thinking, and concept development: Strategies for the classroom*. New York: College Board.

Palmer, L. L., Giese, L., & Deboer B. (2008). *Early literacy champions in North Carolina: Accelerated learning documentation for K–3 SMART (Stimulating Maturity Through Readiness Training)*. Minneapolis, MN: Minnesota Learning Resource Center.

Parker, L., & Shapiro, J. (1993). The context of educational administration and social class. In C. Capper (Ed.), *Educational administration in a pluralistic society*. New York: State University of New York Press.

Pellegrini, A. D., & Bohn, C. M. (2005). The role of recess in children's cognitive performance and school adjustment. *Educational Researcher, 34*(1), 13–19.

Pelletier, J., & Corter, C. (2005). Design, implementation, and outcomes of a school readiness program for diverse families. *The School Community Journal, 15*(1), 89.

Pogrow, S. (2005). HOTS revisited: A thinking development approach to reducing the learning gap after grade 3. *Phi Delta Kappan, 87*(1), 64–75.

Putnam, R. D., & Feldstein, L. M., with Cohen, D. (2003). *Better together: Restoring the American community*. New York: Simon & Schuster.

Redding, S., & Walberg, H. J. (2009). *Handbook on statewide systems of support*. Charlotte, NC: Information Age Publishing.

Rischer, A. D. (2009). Strategies for a successful summer school program. *Education Digest, 74*(9), 34–36.

Rist, M. (2010). 2010 Magna awards. *American School Board Journal*. Alexandria, VA: National School Boards Association.

Rockwell, S. (2007). Working smarter, not harder: Reaching the tough to teach. *Kappa Delta Pi Record, 44*(1), 8–12.

Rodriguez, G. M., & Fabionar, J. (2010). The impact of poverty on students and schools: Exploring the social justice leadership implications. In C. Marshall & M. Oliva (Eds.), *Leadership for social justice* (pp. 55–73). Upper Saddle River, NJ: Pearson.

Rothstein, R. (2008, April). Whose problem is poverty? *Educational Leadership, 65*(7), 8–13.

Sadowski, M. (Ed.). (2004). *Teaching immigrant and second-language students.* Cambridge, MA: Harvard University Press.

San Antonio, D. (2008). Understanding students' strengths and struggles. *Educational Leadership, 65*(7), 74–79.

Sapp, J. (2009, Spring). How school taught me I was poor. *Teaching Tolerance, 35.*

Scheurich, J. J., & Skrla, L. (2003). *Leadership for equity and excellence: Creating high-achievement classrooms, schools, and districts.* Thousand Oaks, CA: Corwin Press.

Schlichter, C. L., Hobbs, D., & Crump, W. D. (1988, April). Extending Talents Unlimited to secondary schools. *Educational Leadership, 45*(7), 36–40.

Schorr, L. B., & Schorr, D. (1989). *Within our reach: Breaking the cycle of disadvantage.* New York: Anchor Books Doubleday.

Schwendiman, J., & Fager, J., (1999). *After-school programs: Good for kids, good for communities.* Portland, OR: Northwest Regional Educational Laboratory.

Sibley, B. A., & Etnier, J. L. (2003). The relationship between physical activity and cognition in children: A meta-analysis. *Pediatric Exercise Science, 15*, 243–256.

Skrla, L., McKenzie, K. B., & Scheurich, J. J. (2009). *Using equity audits to create equitable and excellent schools.* Thousand Oaks, CA: Corwin.

Slavin, R. E., Cheung, A., Groff, C., & Lake, C. (2008). *Effective reading programs for middle and high schools: A best-evidence synthesis.* Newark, DE: International Reading Association.

Smerdon, B. A. (2002). Students' perceptions of membership in their high schools. *Sociology of Education, 75*(4), 287–305.

Smith, G. A., & Sobel, D. (2010). *Place- and community-based education in schools.* New York: Routledge.

Stiggins, R. (2007, October 17). Five assessment myths and their consequences. *Education Week.*

Stiggins, R., & DuFour, R. (2009). Maximizing the power of formative assessments. *Phi Delta Kappan, 90*(9), 640–644.

Supovitz, J. (2006). *The case for district-based reform.* Cambridge, MA: Harvard Education Press.

Teddlie, C., & Stringfield, S. (1993). *Schools make a difference: Lessons learned from a 10-year study of school effects.* New York: Teachers College Press.

Theoharis, G. (2009). *The school leaders our children deserve: Seven keys to equity, social justice, and school reform.* New York: Teachers College Press.

Tomlinson, C. A., Brighton, C., Hertberg, H., Callahan, C. H., Moon, T. R., Brimijoin, K., Conover, L. A., & Reynolds, T. (2003, Winter). Differentiating instruction in response to student readiness, interest, and learning profile in academically diverse classrooms: A review of the literature. *Journal for the Education of the Gifted, 27*(2/3), 119–145.

Tremblay, R. E., Vitaro, F., & Brendgen, M. (2000). Influence of deviant friends on delinquency: Searching for moderator variables. *Journal of Abnormal Child Psychology, 28*(4), 313–325.

U.S. Census Bureau. (2009). POV14: Families by householder's work experience and family structure: 2009. *Current Population Survey.* Available: http://www.census.gov/hhes/www/cpstables/032010/pov/new14_150_08.htm

U.S. Census Bureau. (2010). Income, poverty and health insurance in the United States: 2009—Highlights. From http://census.gov/hhes/www/poverty/data/incpovhlth/009/highlights.html

Valencia, R. R. (1997). *The evolution of deficit thinking: Educational thought and practice.* London: Falmer Press.

Waits, M. J., Campbell, H. E., Gau, R., Jacobs, E., Rex, T., & Hess R. K. (2006). *Why some schools with Latino children beat the odds...and others don't.* Tempe, AZ: Morrison Institute for Public Policy.

Weinstein, R. (2002). *Reaching higher: The power of expectations in schooling.* Cambridge, MA: Harvard University Press.

Wenger, E. (1998). *Communities of practice: Learning, meaning, and identity.* New York: Cambridge University Press.

West Coast Poverty Center. (2010). *Demographics and poverty: Poverty basics.* Seattle, WA: University of Washington. Available: http://depts.washington.edu/wcpc/Poverty/Basics

Wiggins, G. P., & McTighe, J. (2005). *Understanding by design* (Expanded 2nd ed.). Alexandria, VA: ASCD.

Williams, D. T. (2003). Rural routes to success. *Educational Leadership, 61*(3), 66–70.

Wiltz, S. (2008, January/February). Neither art nor accident. *Harvard Education Letter, 24*(1).

Winters, V. E., & Cowie, B. (2009). Cross-cultural communications: Implications for social work practice and a departure from Payne. *Journal of Educational Controversy.* Available: http://www.wce.wwu.edu/resources/cep/ejournal/v004n001/a003.shtml

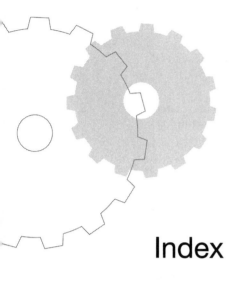

Index

Note: The letter *f* following a page number indicates reference to a figure.

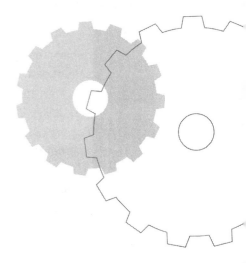

About the Authors

William H. Parrett is the director of the Center for School Improvement & Policy Studies (CSI&PS) and a professor of Education at Boise State University. He has received international recognition for his work in school improvement, small schools, and alternative education and for his efforts to help youth at risk. His professional experiences include public school and university teaching, curriculum design, principalships, and college leadership.

Parrett holds a Ph.D. in secondary education from Indiana University. He has served on the faculties of Indiana University, the University of Alaska, and Boise State University. As director of the CSI&PS (1996 to present), Parrett coordinates funded projects and school improvement initiatives that have exceeded $32 million. His research on reducing achievement gaps, effective schooling practices for youth at risk, and low-performing schools has gained widespread national recognition.

Parrett has also served as visiting faculty at Indiana University, the University of Manitoba, Oregon State University, Hokkaido University of Education (Japan), Nagoya Gakiun (Japan), Gifu University (Japan), and Heilongjiang University (People's Republic of China). His consultancies include state departments, boards of education, state and regional service providers, and school districts in 41 states and 10 nations.

Parrett is the coauthor of *Saving Our Students, Saving Our Schools* (2003 and 2008); *The Kids Left Behind: Catching Up the Underachieving Children of Poverty* (2007); *Hope Fulfilled for At-Risk & Violent Youth* (2001); *How to Create Alternative, Magnet, and Charter Schools That Work* (1997); *Hope at Last for At-Risk Youth* (1995); *Inventive Teaching: Heart of the Small School* (1993); *The Inventive Mind: Portraits of Effective Teaching* (1991); and numerous contributions to national journals and international and national conferences.

Parrett's media production, *Heart of the Country* (1998), is an award-winning documentary about an extraordinary principal of a village elementary school in Hokkaido, Japan, and the collective passion of the community to educate the heart as well as the mind. It has received critical acclaim for its insight into the universal correlates of effective teaching and learning and the power of community participation in public schools.

Throughout his career, Parrett has worked to improve the educational achievement of all children and youth, particularly those less advantaged. These efforts have positively impacted the lives of thousands of young people.

Kathleen M. Budge is the coordinator of the Leadership Development Program at Boise State University. She has led the development of this innovative, nontraditional preparation program, the purpose of which is to develop leaders who have the commitment and capabilities to lead schools where all students succeed.

Budge also serves as an associate professor in the Curriculum, Instruction, and Foundational Studies Department, where her research and scholarly activity focuses on educational leadership, leadership development, rural education, school improvement, and poverty. She has conducted numerous presentations at national and state conferences and has provided frequent contributions to educational journals and other publications on these topics.

Budge earned her doctorate from the University of Washington in educational leadership and policy studies in 2005. She was selected to participate in Leadership for Learning, an innovative, cohort-based program that emphasized the link between leadership and learning, as well as the development of leaders willing and able to address and redress issues of equity and social justice.

Before joining the faculty at Boise State, Budge served as the Assistant Superintendent for Teaching and Learning at Educational Service District 113 in Olympia, Washington. She provided leadership to 45 predominately rural school districts. She led the development of a highly successful regional, job-embedded professional development model and facilitated data-based improvement planning with more than 150 schools. Her leadership was recognized through awards from the Washington Association of School Administrator's (WASA) Regional President's Award, the WASA Award of Merit, and the Washington Association of Educational Service Districts President's Award for significant contribution to the state's educational service agencies.

Budge served as a Washington State Distinguished Educator/School Improvement Specialist, providing training and consultation to superintendents, central office administrators, building principals, and teacher-leaders. She also served on the Statewide School Improvement Technical Assistance Council and the Office of Superintendent of Public Instruction's Curriculum Advisory and Review Committee. Additionally, she was a contributing author to the *School System Improvement Guide* and the *Washington State School Improvement Planning Guide*.

Budge has worked as a district curriculum director, an elementary principal, and an elementary and special education teacher. She continues to maintain that her most important work has been teaching 1st graders to read.

Related ASCD Resources: Improving Student Motivation, Raising Student Achievement, Community Involvement in Schools

ASCD Study Guides are available free for many ASCD books. For a list of available study guides, including one for this book, go to www.ascd.org/publications/books/study-guides.aspx.

At the time of publication, the following ASCD resources were available (ASCD stock numbers appear in parentheses). For up-to-date information about ASCD resources, go to www.ascd.org. You can search the complete archives of *Educational Leadership* at www.ascd.org/el.

ASCD EDge Groups

Exchange ideas and connect with other educators interested in The Whole Child, Inspiring Student Motivation, Closing the Achievement Gap and other great topics on the social networking site ASCD EDge™ at http://ascdedge.ascd.org/

Print

Becoming a Great High School: 6 Strategies and 1 Attitude That Make a Difference Tim R. Westerberg (#109052)

Closing the Achievement Gap: A Vision for Changing Beliefs and Practices 2nd ed. Belinda Williams (#102010)

Create Success: Unlocking the Potential of Urban Students Kadhir Rajagopal (#111022)

Creating the Opportunity to Learn: Moving from Research to Practice to Close the Achievement Gap A. Wade Boykin and Pedro Noguera (#107016)

Educating the Whole Child: An ASCD Action Tool (#709036)

Enhancing Student Achievement: A Framework for School Improvement Charlotte Danielson (#102109)

Meeting Students Where They Live: Motivation in Urban Schools Richard L. Curwin (#109110)

Mobilizing the Community to Help Students Succeed Hugh B. Price (#107055)

Motivating Black Males to Achieve in School and in Life Baruti K. Kafele (#109013)

Raising Black Students' Achievement Through Culturally Responsive Teaching Johnnie McKinley (#110004)

Reaching Out to Latino Families of English Language Learners David Campos, Rocio Delgado, and Mary Esther Soto Huerta (#110005)

Simply Better: Doing What Matters Most to Change the Odds for Student Success Bryan Goodwin (#111038)

Teaching with Poverty in Mind: What Being Poor Does to Kids' Brains and What Schools Can Do About It Eric Jensen (#109074)

Video

Motivating Black Males to Achieve in School and in Life Baruti K. Kafele (#611087)

The Sights and Sounds of Equitable Practices (#610013)

Teaching with Poverty in Mind: Elementary and Secondary (#610135)

THE WHOLE CHILD The Whole Child Initiative helps schools and communities create learning environments that allow students to be healthy, safe, engaged, supported, and challenged. To learn more about other books and resources that relate to the whole child, visit www.wholechildeducation.org.

For more information: send e-mail to member@ascd.org; call 1-800-933-2723 or 703-578-9600, press 2; send a fax to 703-575-5400; or write to Information Services, ASCD, 1703 N. Beauregard St., Alexandria, VA 22311-1714 USA.